May. 2014

S0-AIG-248

3 1488 00001 4251

ROCKY & BULLWINKLE ™
CLASSICS

WITHDRAWN

Algonquin Area Public Library
2600 Harnish Dr.
Algonquin, IL 60102
www.aapld.org

Through credited to **Al Kilgore**, research has shown that artists **Fred Fredericks**, **Jerry Robinson**, and **Mel Crawford**, likely contributed artwork to stories written by **Jack Mendelsohn**, **Dave Berg**, and others.

Cover by **Roger Langridge** • Collection Edits by **Justin Eisinger** & **Alonzo Simon** • Collection Design by **Tom B. Long**

ISBN: 978-1-61377-914-9

www.IDWPUBLISHING.com
IDW founded by Ted Adams, Alex Garner, Kris Oprisko, and Robbie Robbins

Ted Adams, CEO & Publisher
Greg Goldstein, President & COO
Robbie Robbins, EVP/Sr. Graphic Artist
Chris Ryall, Chief Creative Officer/Editor-in-Chief
Matthew Ruzicka, CPA, Chief Financial Officer
Alan Payne, VP of Sales
Dirk Wood, VP of Marketing
Lorelei Bunjes, VP of Digital Services
Jeff Webber, VP of Digital Publishing & Business Development

17 16 15 14   1 2 3 4

Facebook: **facebook.com/idwpublishing**
Twitter: **@idwpublishing**
YouTube: **youtube.com/idwpublishing**
Instagram: **instagram.com/idwpublishing**
deviantART: **idwpublishing.deviantart.com**
Pinterest: **pinterest.com/idwpublishing/idw-staff-faves**

ROCKY & BULLWINKLE CLASSICS, VOLUME 1: STAR BILLING. MARCH 2014. FIRST PRINTING. ROCKY AND BULLWINKLE AND FRIENDS™ © 2014 Ward Productions, Inc. Licensed by Bullwinkle Studios, LLC. All rights reserved. © 2014 Idea and Design Works, LLC. The IDW logo is registered in the U.S. Patent and Trademark Office. IDW Publishing, a division of Idea and Design Works, LLC. Editorial offices: 5080 Santa Fe St., San Diego, CA 92109. Any similarities to persons living or dead are purely coincidental. With the exception of artwork used for review purposes, none of the contents of this publication may be reprinted without the permission of Idea and Design Works, LLC. IDW Publishing does not read or accept unsolicited submissions of ideas, stories, or artwork. Printed in Korea.

Originally published by Gold Key as BULLWINKLE issues #1–4.

BULLWINKLE

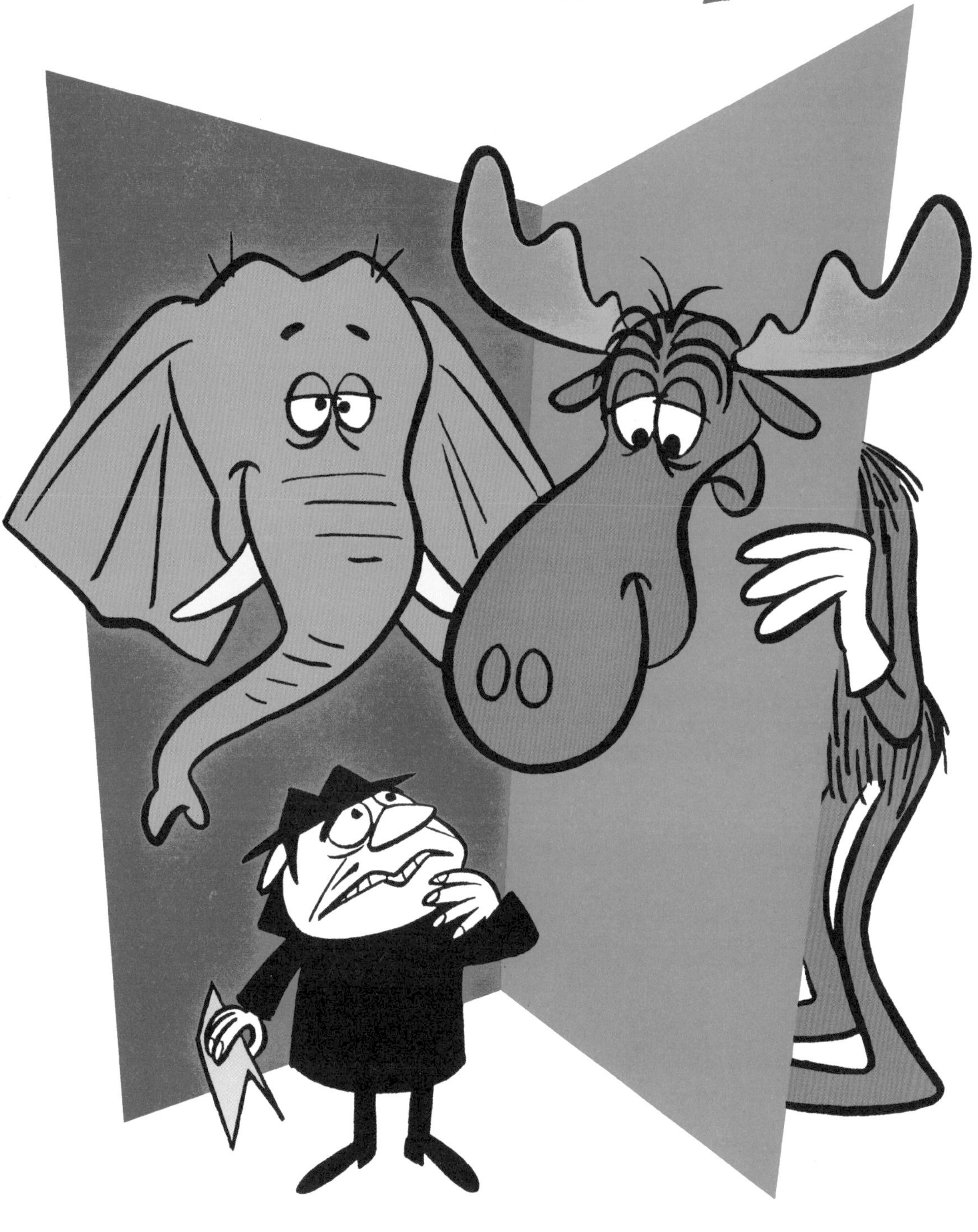

ISSUE #1 · GOLD KEY · NOVEMBER 1962

BULLWINKLE

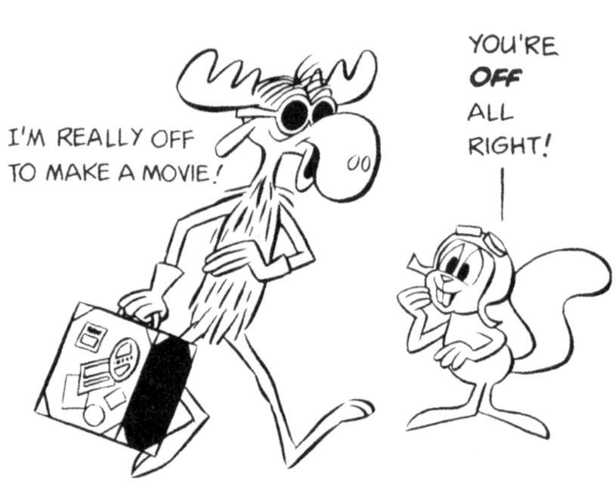

I'M REALLY OFF TO MAKE A MOVIE!
YOU'RE *OFF* ALL RIGHT!

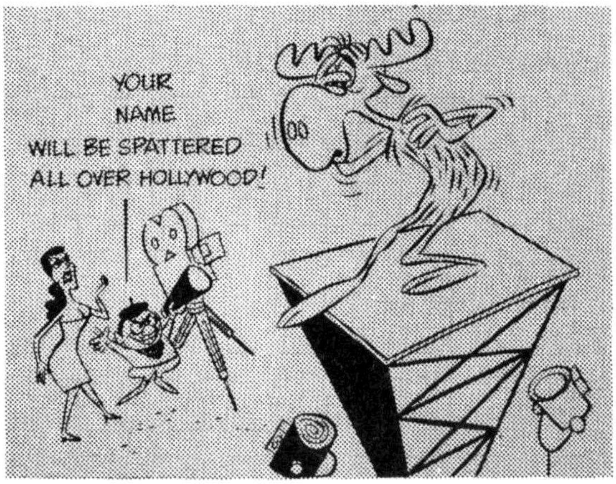

YOUR NAME WILL BE SPATTERED ALL OVER HOLLYWOOD!

STAR BILLING . . . . . . **Bullwinkle is invited to Hollywood to star in an epic production.**

But Boris Badenov has made special plans for Bullwinkle's finale!

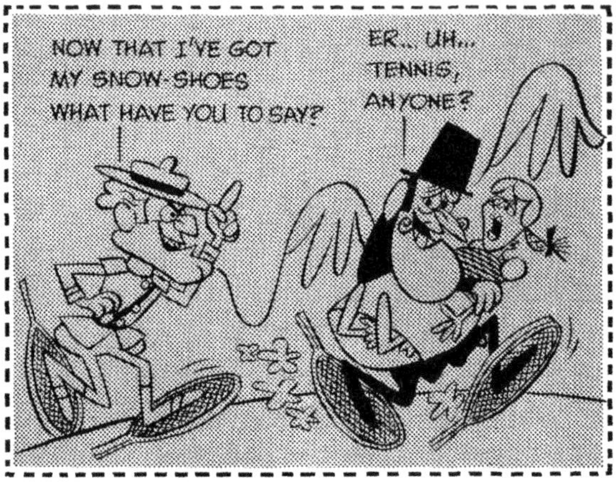

NOW THAT I'VE GOT MY SNOW-SHOES WHAT HAVE YOU TO SAY?
ER... UH... TENNIS, ANYONE?

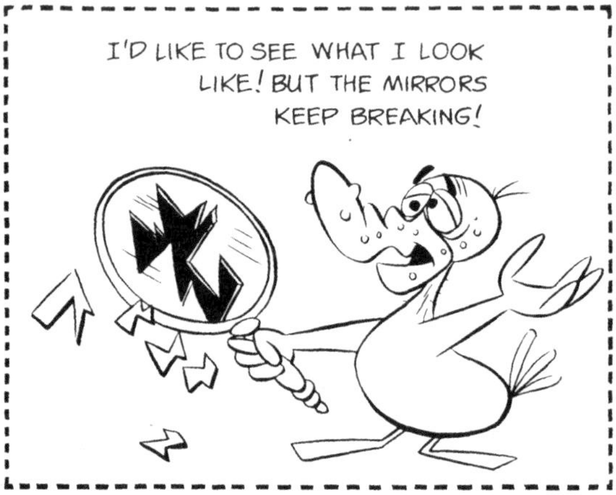

I'D LIKE TO SEE WHAT I LOOK LIKE! BUT THE MIRRORS KEEP BREAKING!

DUDLEY DO-RIGHT **Dudley battles with Snidely Whiplash high in the snow-capped Rockies!**

FRACTURED FAIRY TALE **About the duckling who was an outcast because he was so ugly.**

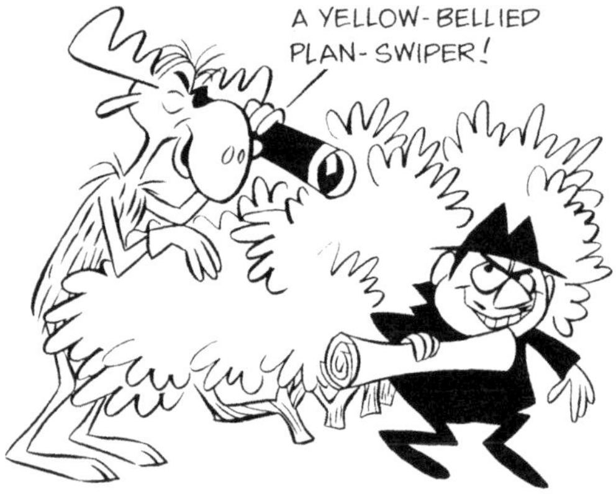

A YELLOW-BELLIED PLAN-SWIPER!

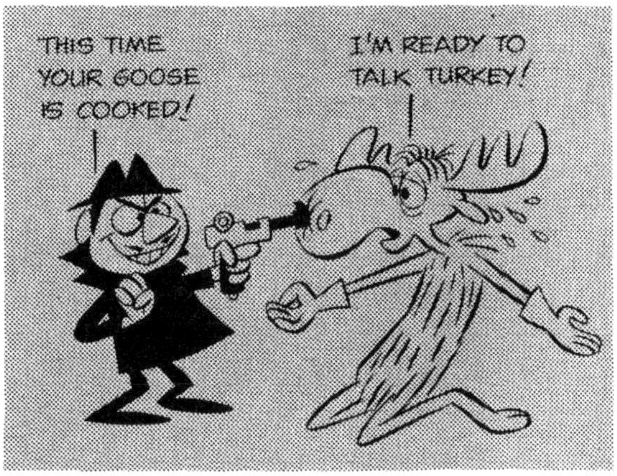

THIS TIME YOUR GOOSE IS COOKED!
I'M READY TO TALK TURKEY!

STRICTLY FOR THE BIRDS . . . **Bullwinkle looks for rare birds . . . and nearly winds up a dead duck!**

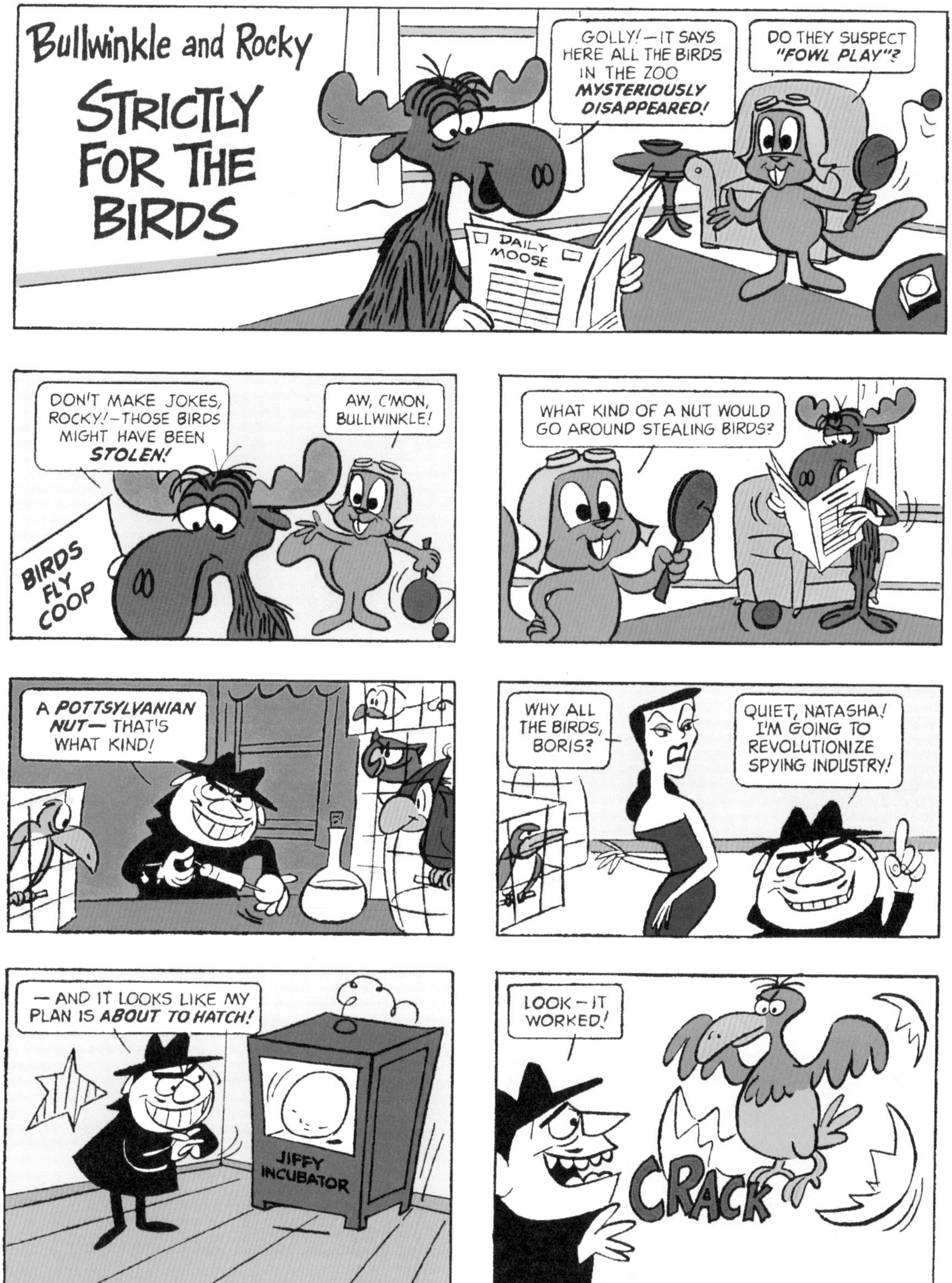
Bullwinkle and Rocky
STRICTLY FOR THE BIRDS
GOLLY! — IT SAYS HERE ALL THE BIRDS IN THE ZOO MYSTERIOUSLY DISAPPEARED!
DAILY MOOSE
DO THEY SUSPECT "FOWL PLAY"?
DON'T MAKE JOKES, ROCKY! — THOSE BIRDS MIGHT HAVE BEEN STOLEN!
AW, C'MON, BULLWINKLE!
BIRDS FLY COOP
WHAT KIND OF A NUT WOULD GO AROUND STEALING BIRDS?
A POTTSYLVANIAN NUT — THAT'S WHAT KIND!
WHY ALL THE BIRDS, BORIS?
QUIET, NATASHA! I'M GOING TO REVOLUTIONIZE SPYING INDUSTRY!
— AND IT LOOKS LIKE MY PLAN IS ABOUT TO HATCH!
JIFFY INCUBATOR
LOOK — IT WORKED!
CRACK

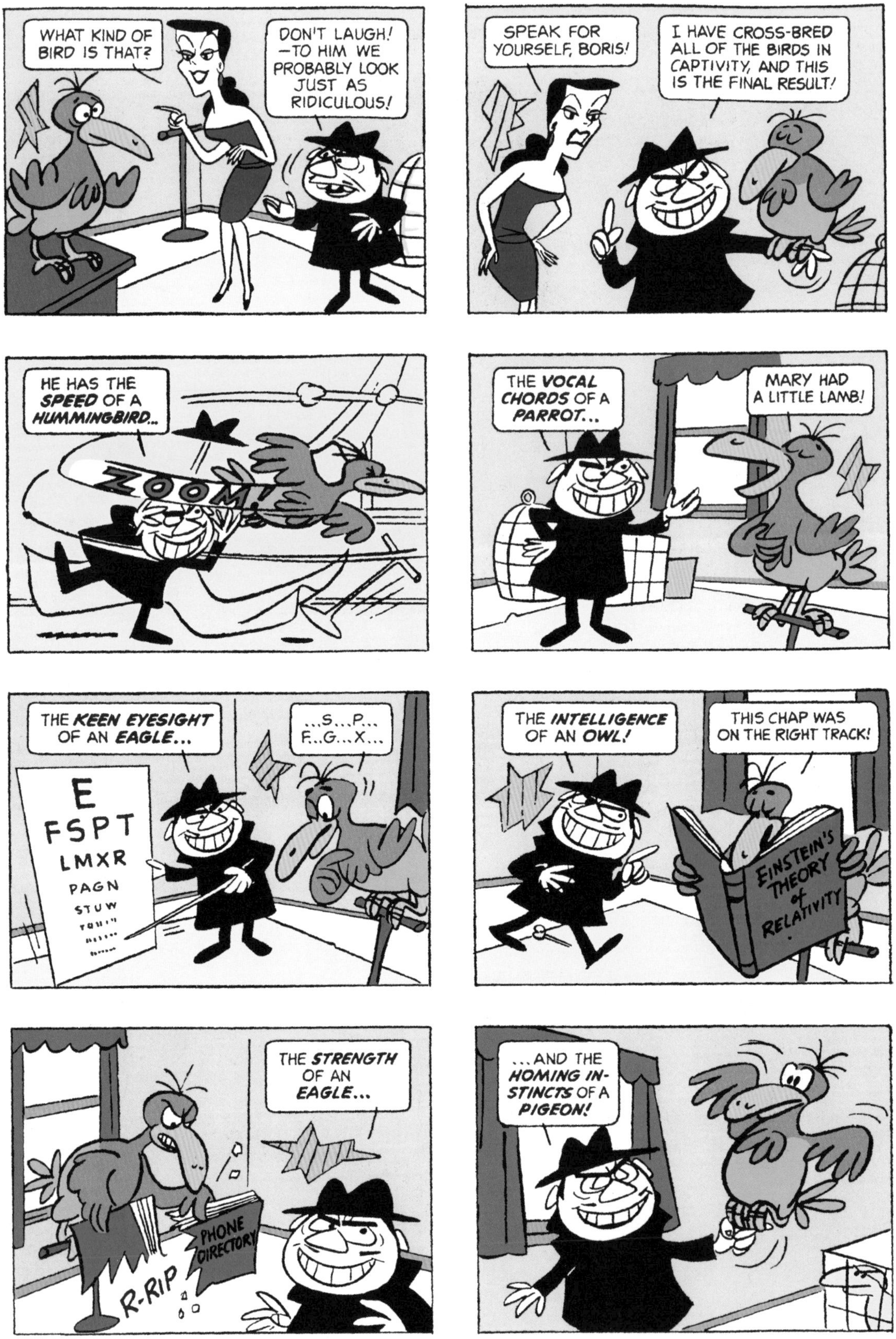

WHAT KIND OF BIRD IS THAT?
DON'T LAUGH! —TO HIM WE PROBABLY LOOK JUST AS RIDICULOUS!
SPEAK FOR YOURSELF, BORIS!
I HAVE CROSS-BRED ALL OF THE BIRDS IN CAPTIVITY, AND THIS IS THE FINAL RESULT!
HE HAS THE SPEED OF A HUMMINGBIRD...
ZOOM!
THE VOCAL CHORDS OF A PARROT...
MARY HAD A LITTLE LAMB!
THE KEEN EYESIGHT OF AN EAGLE...
...S...P... F...G...X...
E
FSPT
LMXR
PAGN
STUW
THE INTELLIGENCE OF AN OWL!
THIS CHAP WAS ON THE RIGHT TRACK!
EINSTEIN'S THEORY of RELATIVITY
THE STRENGTH OF AN EAGLE...
PHONE DIRECTORY
R-RIP
...AND THE HOMING INSTINCTS OF A PIGEON!

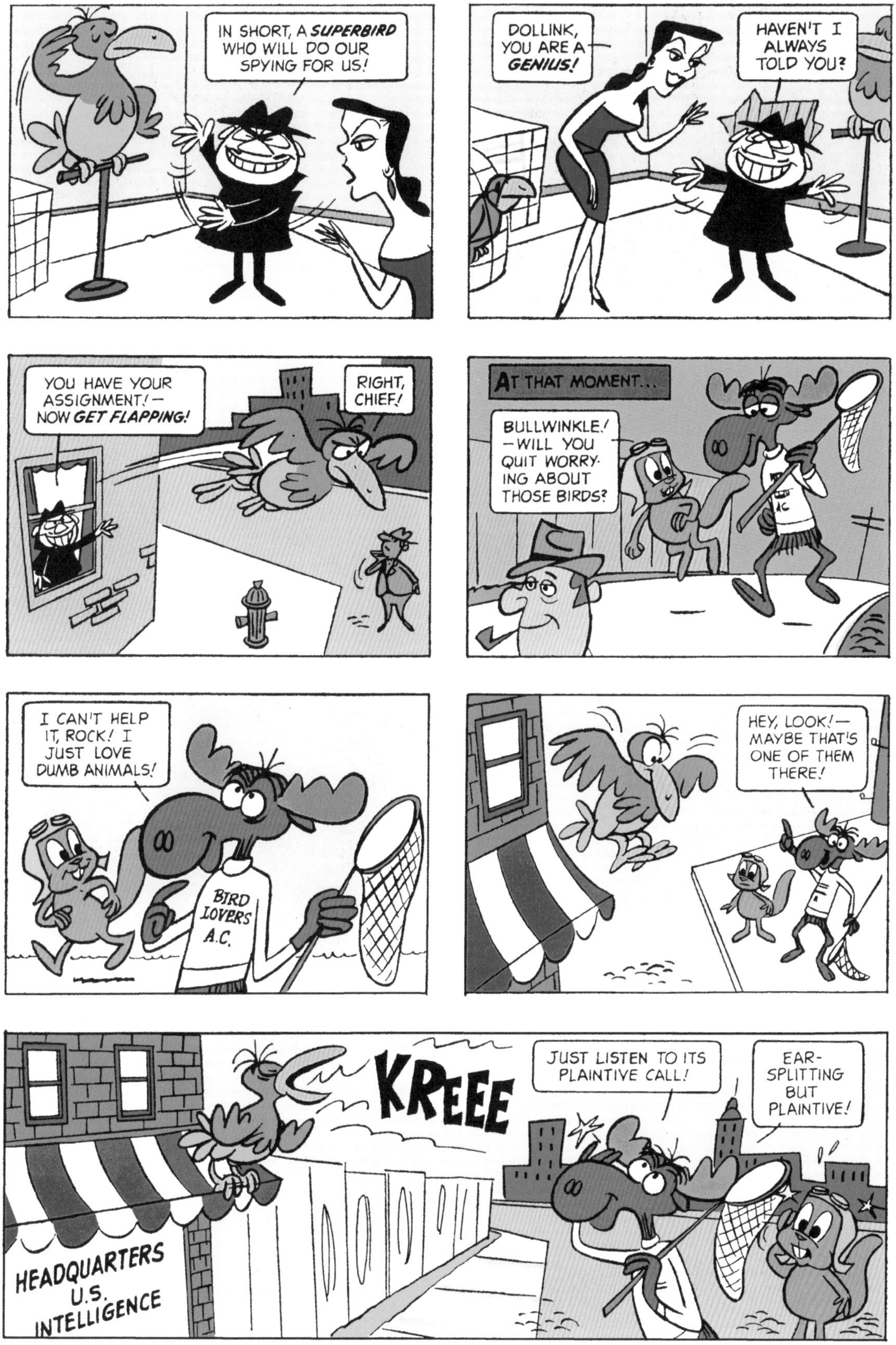
IN SHORT, A SUPERBIRD WHO WILL DO OUR SPYING FOR US!
DOLLINK, YOU ARE A GENIUS!
HAVEN'T I ALWAYS TOLD YOU?
YOU HAVE YOUR ASSIGNMENT! — NOW GET FLAPPING!
RIGHT, CHIEF!
AT THAT MOMENT...
BULLWINKLE! — WILL YOU QUIT WORRYING ABOUT THOSE BIRDS?
I CAN'T HELP IT, ROCK! I JUST LOVE DUMB ANIMALS!
BIRD LOVERS A.C.
HEY, LOOK! — MAYBE THAT'S ONE OF THEM THERE!
KREEE
JUST LISTEN TO ITS PLAINTIVE CALL!
EAR-SPLITTING BUT PLAINTIVE!
HEADQUARTERS U.S. INTELLIGENCE

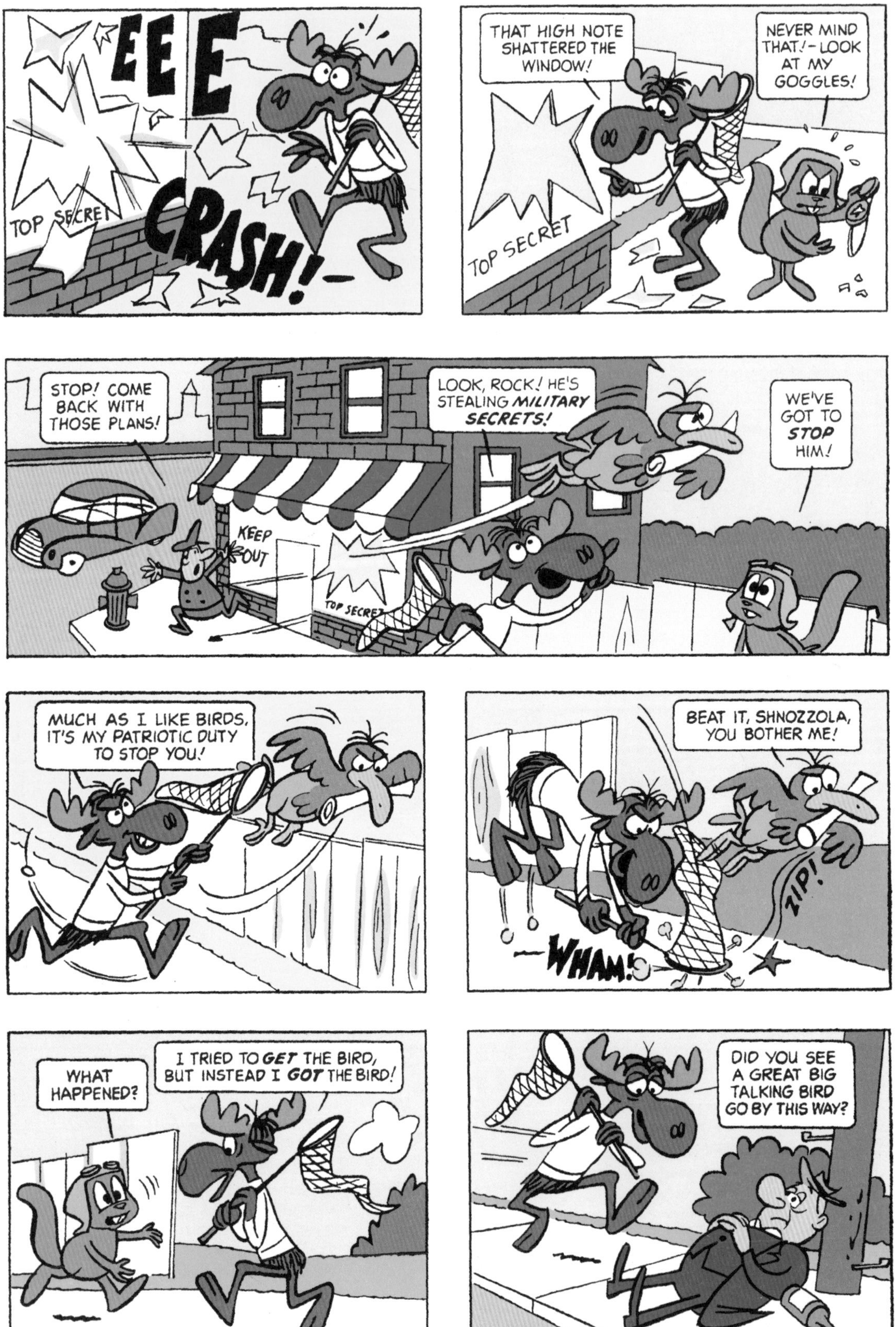
EEE
CRASH!
TOP SECRET
THAT HIGH NOTE SHATTERED THE WINDOW!
NEVER MIND THAT!–LOOK AT MY GOGGLES!
TOP SECRET
STOP! COME BACK WITH THOSE PLANS!
LOOK, ROCK! HE'S STEALING MILITARY SECRETS!
WE'VE GOT TO STOP HIM!
KEEP OUT
TOP SECRET
MUCH AS I LIKE BIRDS, IT'S MY PATRIOTIC DUTY TO STOP YOU!
BEAT IT, SHNOZZOLA, YOU BOTHER ME!
ZIP!
WHAM!
WHAT HAPPENED?
I TRIED TO GET THE BIRD, BUT INSTEAD I GOT THE BIRD!
DID YOU SEE A GREAT BIG TALKING BIRD GO BY THIS WAY?

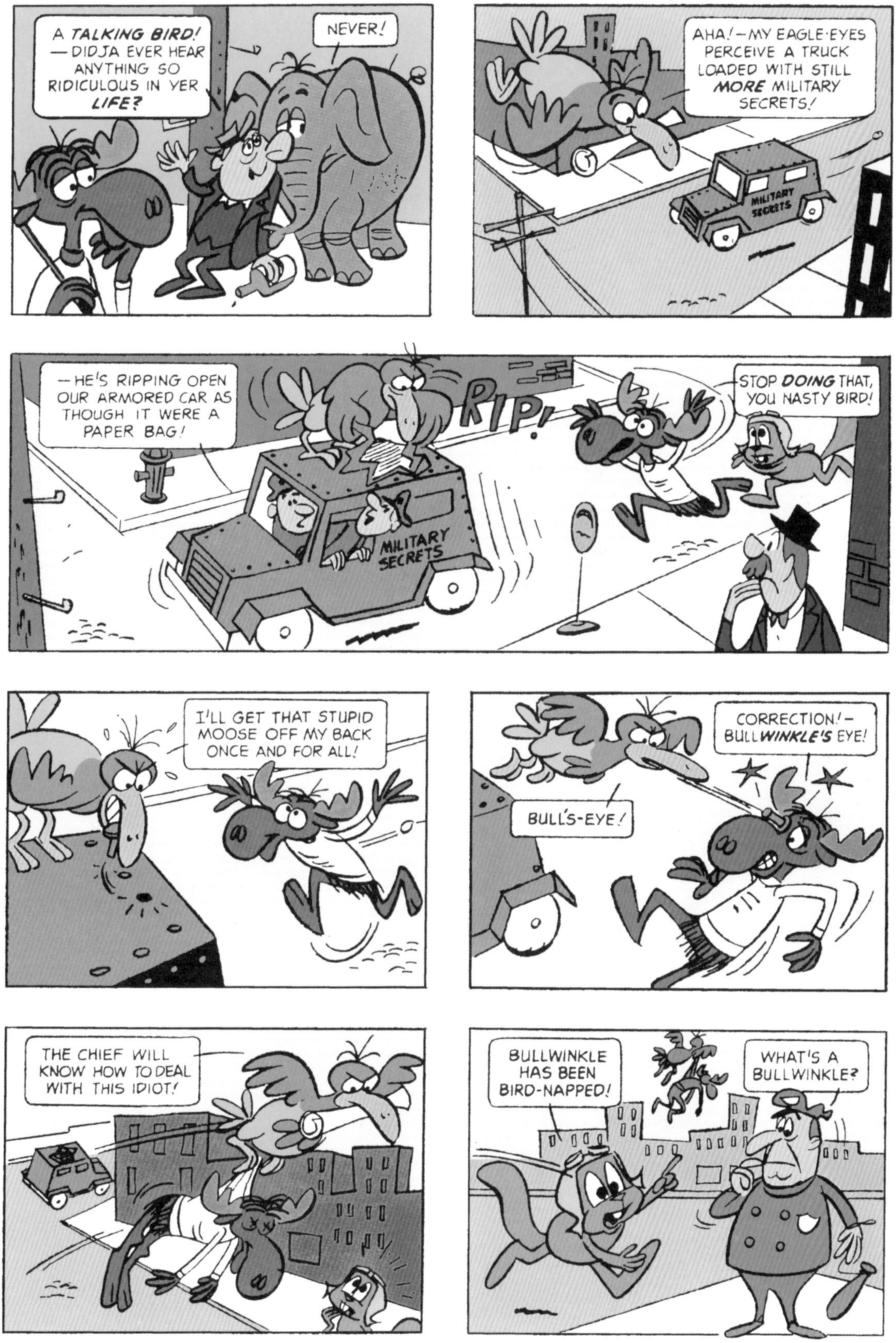
A TALKING BIRD! —DIDJA EVER HEAR ANYTHING SO RIDICULOUS IN YER LIFE?
NEVER!
AHA!—MY EAGLE-EYES PERCEIVE A TRUCK LOADED WITH STILL MORE MILITARY SECRETS!
MILITARY SECRETS
—HE'S RIPPING OPEN OUR ARMORED CAR AS THOUGH IT WERE A PAPER BAG!
RIP!
STOP DOING THAT, YOU NASTY BIRD!
MILITARY SECRETS
I'LL GET THAT STUPID MOOSE OFF MY BACK ONCE AND FOR ALL!
CORRECTION!—BULLWINKLE'S EYE!
BULL'S-EYE!
THE CHIEF WILL KNOW HOW TO DEAL WITH THIS IDIOT!
BULLWINKLE HAS BEEN BIRD-NAPPED!
WHAT'S A BULLWINKLE?

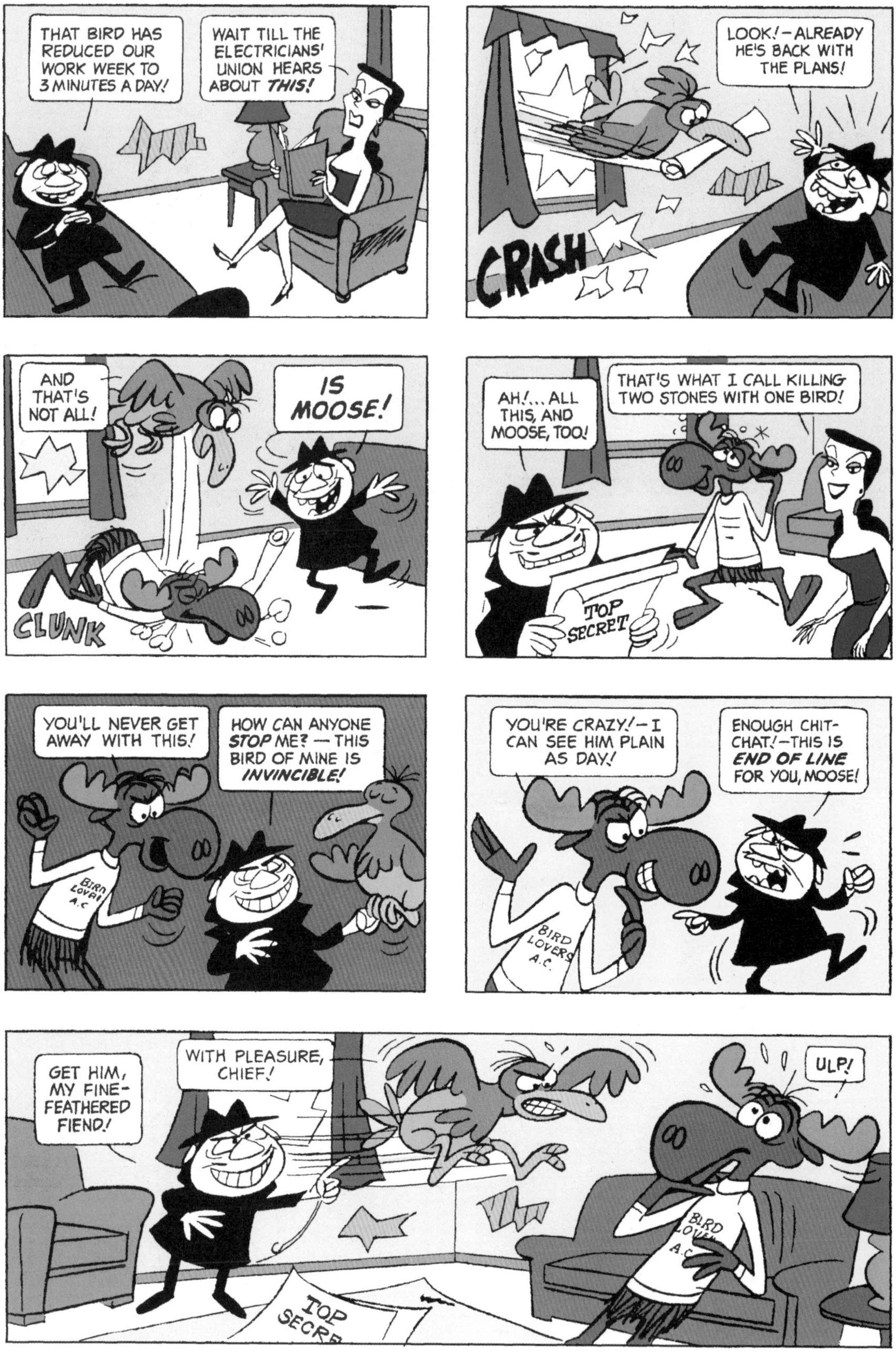
THAT BIRD HAS REDUCED OUR WORK WEEK TO 3 MINUTES A DAY!
WAIT TILL THE ELECTRICIANS' UNION HEARS ABOUT *THIS!*
LOOK!—ALREADY HE'S BACK WITH THE PLANS!
CRASH
AND THAT'S NOT ALL!
IS MOOSE!
CLUNK
AH!... ALL THIS, AND MOOSE, TOO!
THAT'S WHAT I CALL KILLING TWO STONES WITH ONE BIRD!
TOP SECRET
YOU'LL NEVER GET AWAY WITH THIS!
HOW CAN ANYONE *STOP* ME? —THIS BIRD OF MINE IS *INVINCIBLE!*
YOU'RE CRAZY!—I CAN SEE HIM PLAIN AS DAY!
ENOUGH CHIT-CHAT!—THIS IS *END OF LINE* FOR YOU, MOOSE!
GET HIM, MY FINE-FEATHERED FIEND!
WITH PLEASURE, CHIEF!
ULP!

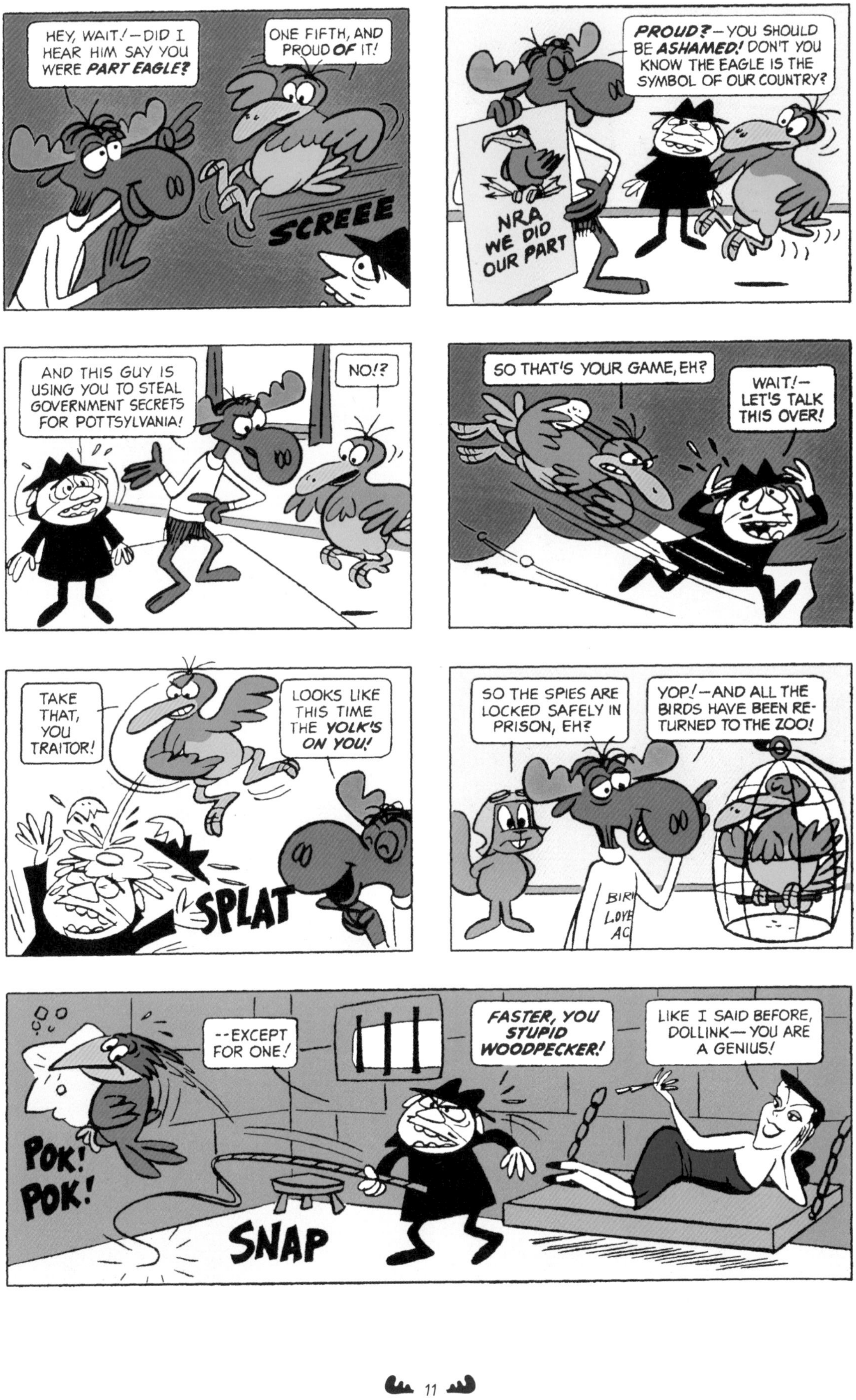
HEY, WAIT!—DID I HEAR HIM SAY YOU WERE PART EAGLE?
ONE FIFTH, AND PROUD OF IT!
SCREEE
PROUD?—YOU SHOULD BE ASHAMED! DON'T YOU KNOW THE EAGLE IS THE SYMBOL OF OUR COUNTRY?
NRA WE DID OUR PART
AND THIS GUY IS USING YOU TO STEAL GOVERNMENT SECRETS FOR POTTSYLVANIA!
NO!?
SO THAT'S YOUR GAME, EH?
WAIT!— LET'S TALK THIS OVER!
TAKE THAT, YOU TRAITOR!
LOOKS LIKE THIS TIME THE YOLK'S ON YOU!
SPLAT
SO THE SPIES ARE LOCKED SAFELY IN PRISON, EH?
YOP!—AND ALL THE BIRDS HAVE BEEN RE-TURNED TO THE ZOO!
--EXCEPT FOR ONE!
FASTER, YOU STUPID WOODPECKER!
LIKE I SAID BEFORE, DOLLINK— YOU ARE A GENIUS!
POK! POK!
SNAP

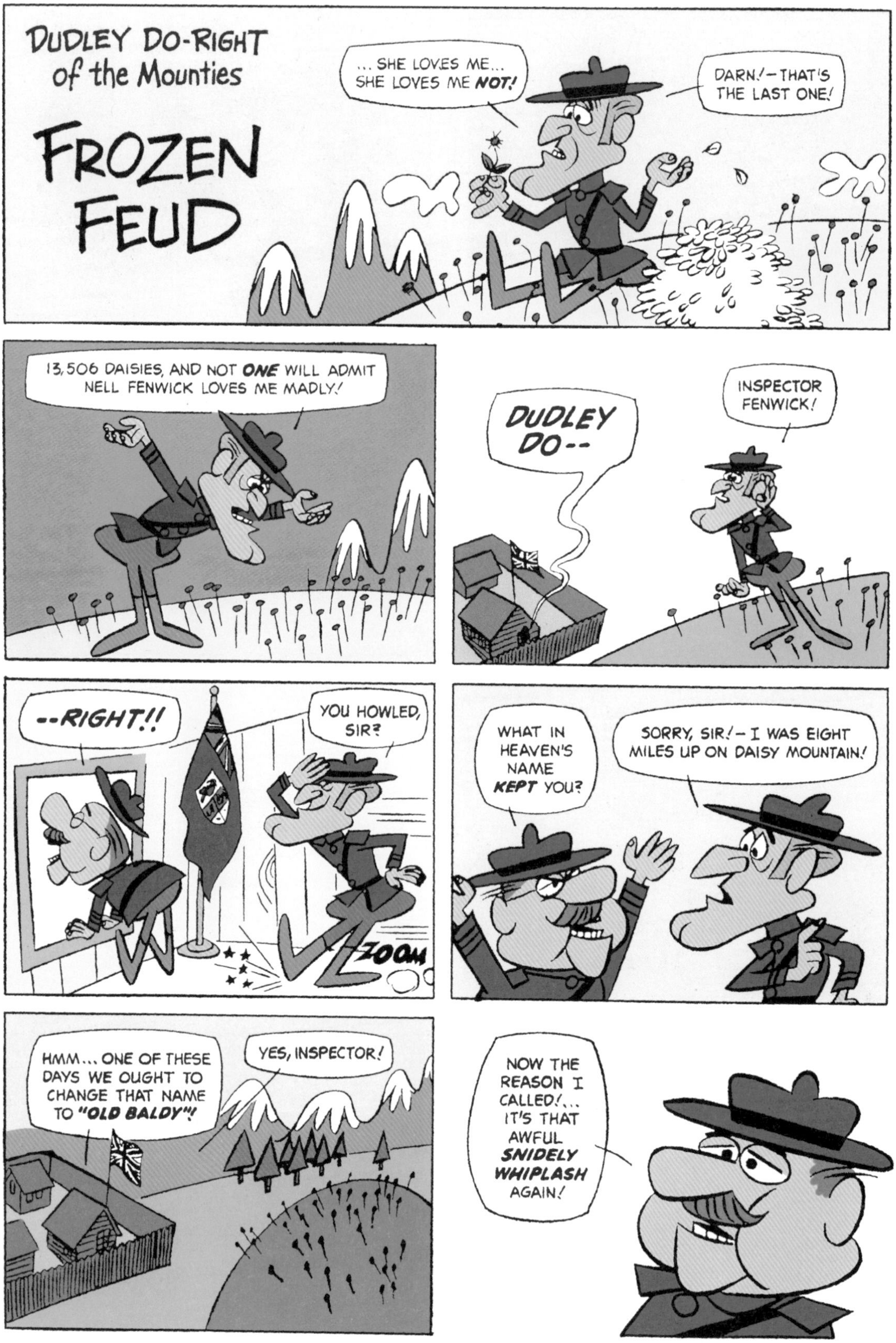
DUDLEY DO-RIGHT of the Mounties
FROZEN FEUD
... SHE LOVES ME... SHE LOVES ME NOT!
DARN!—THAT'S THE LAST ONE!
13,506 DAISIES, AND NOT ONE WILL ADMIT NELL FENWICK LOVES ME MADLY!
DUDLEY DO--
INSPECTOR FENWICK!
--RIGHT!!
YOU HOWLED, SIR?
ZOOM
WHAT IN HEAVEN'S NAME KEPT YOU?
SORRY, SIR!—I WAS EIGHT MILES UP ON DAISY MOUNTAIN!
HMM... ONE OF THESE DAYS WE OUGHT TO CHANGE THAT NAME TO "OLD BALDY"!
YES, INSPECTOR!
NOW THE REASON I CALLED!... IT'S THAT AWFUL SNIDELY WHIPLASH AGAIN!

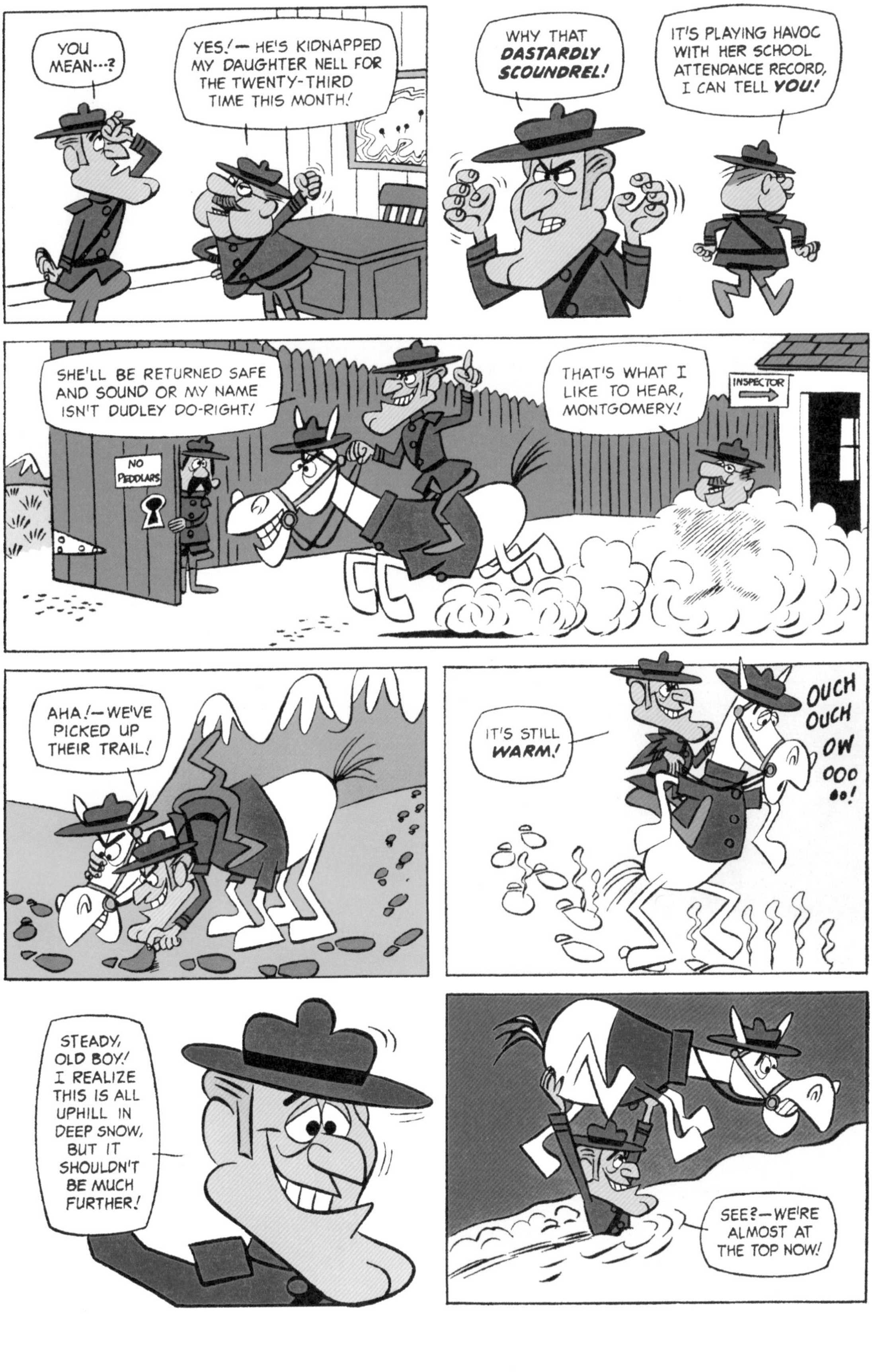
YOU MEAN...?
YES!— HE'S KIDNAPPED MY DAUGHTER NELL FOR THE TWENTY-THIRD TIME THIS MONTH!
WHY THAT DASTARDLY SCOUNDREL!
IT'S PLAYING HAVOC WITH HER SCHOOL ATTENDANCE RECORD, I CAN TELL YOU!
SHE'LL BE RETURNED SAFE AND SOUND OR MY NAME ISN'T DUDLEY DO-RIGHT!
NO PEDDLARS
THAT'S WHAT I LIKE TO HEAR, MONTGOMERY!
INSPECTOR
AHA!—WE'VE PICKED UP THEIR TRAIL!
IT'S STILL WARM!
OUCH OUCH OW OOO OO!
STEADY, OLD BOY! I REALIZE THIS IS ALL UPHILL IN DEEP SNOW, BUT IT SHOULDN'T BE MUCH FURTHER!
SEE?—WE'RE ALMOST AT THE TOP NOW!

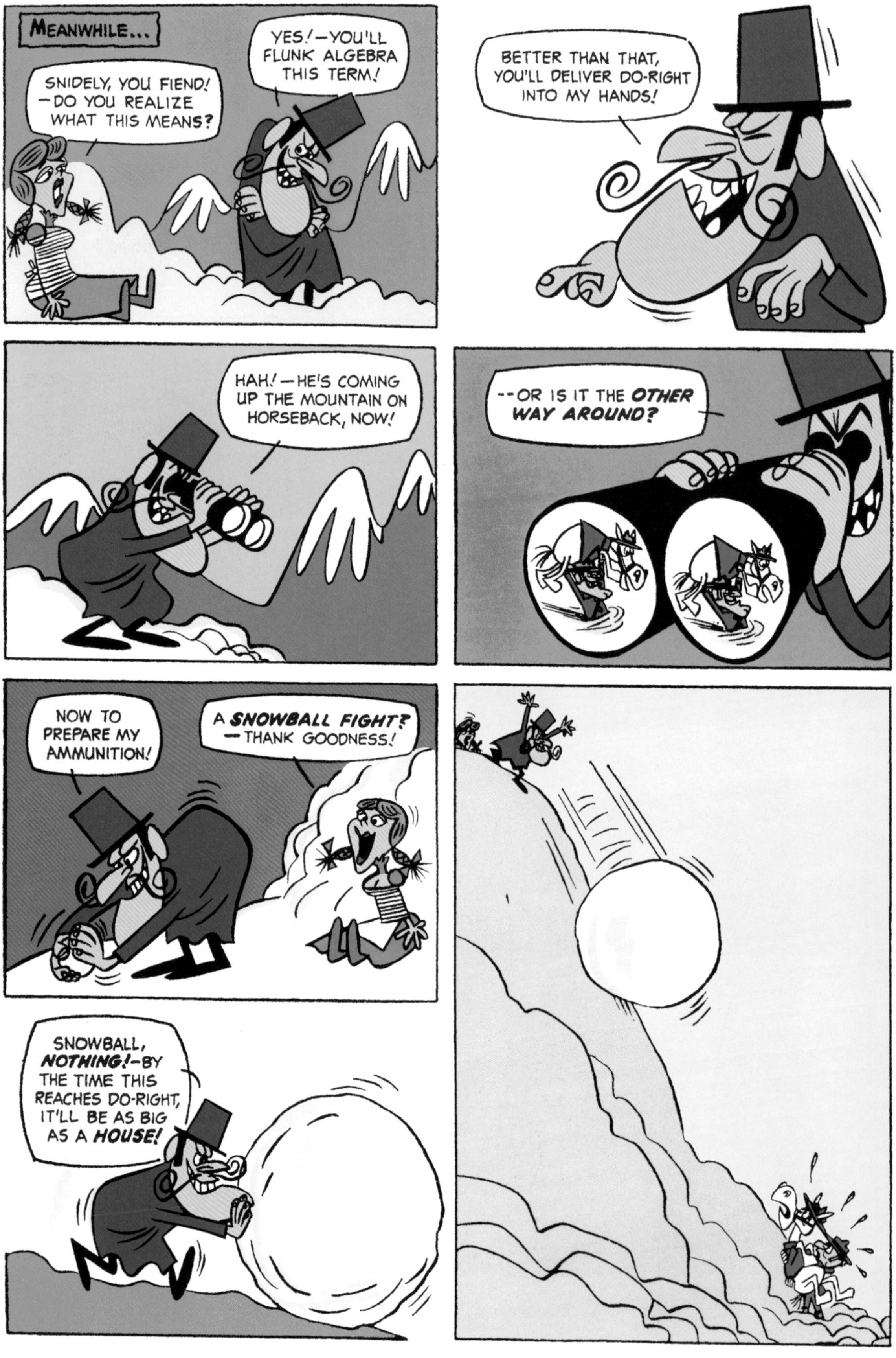
MEANWHILE...
SNIDELY, YOU FIEND! —DO YOU REALIZE WHAT THIS MEANS?
YES!—YOU'LL FLUNK ALGEBRA THIS TERM!
BETTER THAN THAT, YOU'LL DELIVER DO-RIGHT INTO MY HANDS!
HAH!—HE'S COMING UP THE MOUNTAIN ON HORSEBACK, NOW!
--OR IS IT THE OTHER WAY AROUND?
NOW TO PREPARE MY AMMUNITION!
A SNOWBALL FIGHT? —THANK GOODNESS!
SNOWBALL, NOTHING!—BY THE TIME THIS REACHES DO-RIGHT, IT'LL BE AS BIG AS A HOUSE!

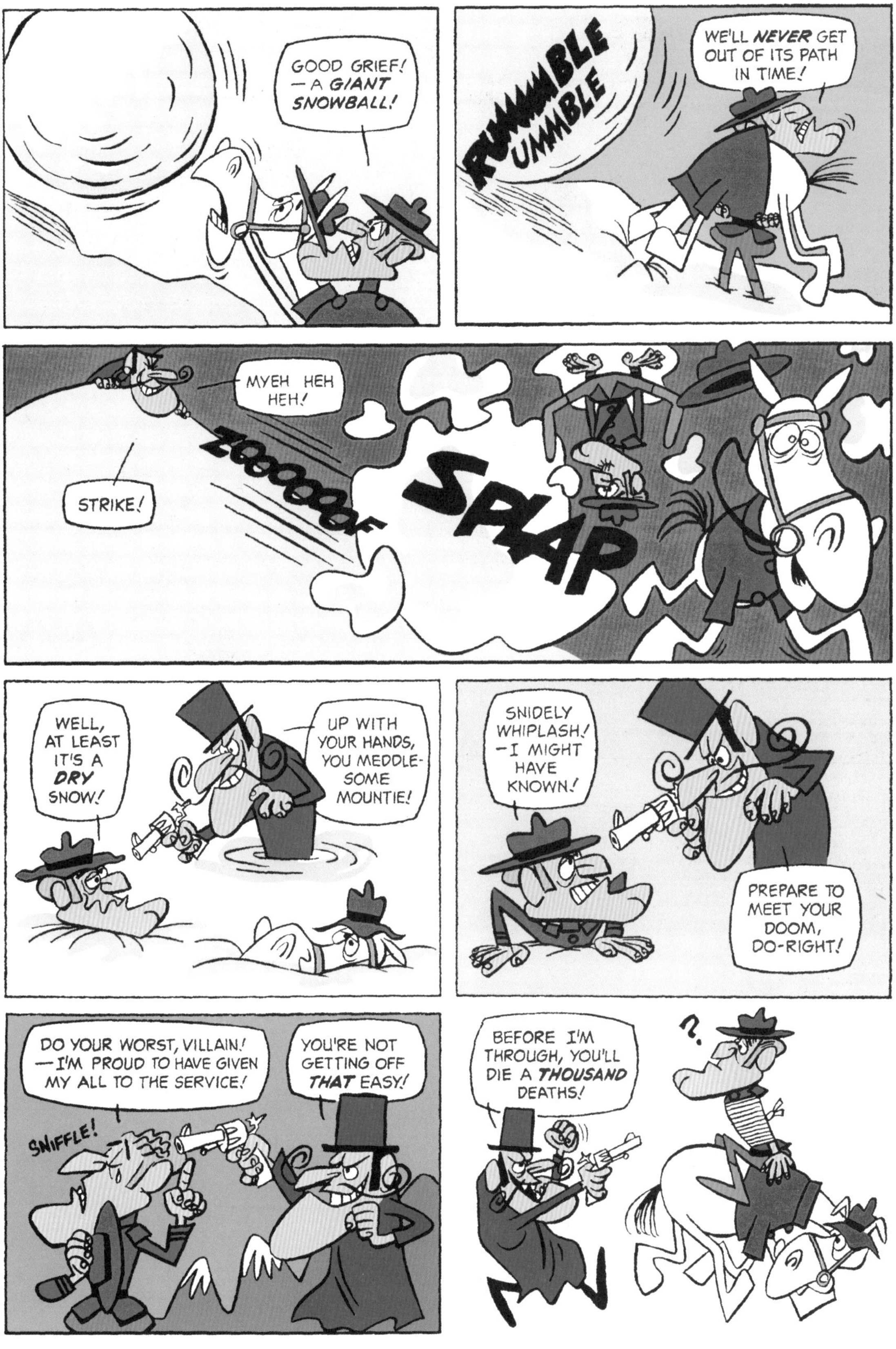
GOOD GRIEF! —A GIANT SNOWBALL!
RUMMMBLE UMMBLE
WE'LL NEVER GET OUT OF ITS PATH IN TIME!
MYEH HEH HEH!
STRIKE!
ZOOOOOOF
SPLAP
WELL, AT LEAST IT'S A DRY SNOW!
UP WITH YOUR HANDS, YOU MEDDLE-SOME MOUNTIE!
SNIDELY WHIPLASH! —I MIGHT HAVE KNOWN!
PREPARE TO MEET YOUR DOOM, DO-RIGHT!
DO YOUR WORST, VILLAIN! —I'M PROUD TO HAVE GIVEN MY ALL TO THE SERVICE!
YOU'RE NOT GETTING OFF THAT EASY!
SNIFFLE!
BEFORE I'M THROUGH, YOU'LL DIE A THOUSAND DEATHS!
?

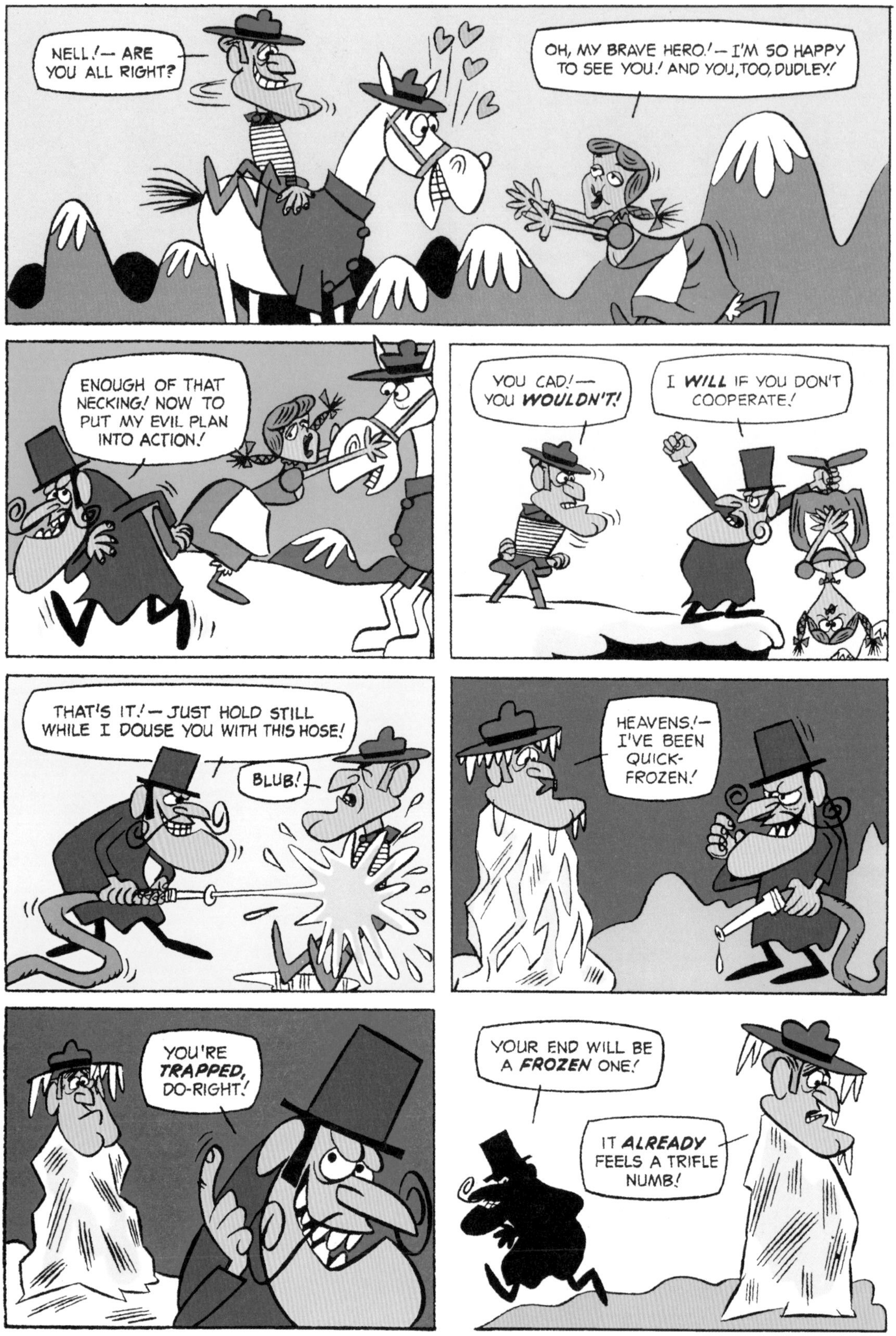
NELL!— ARE YOU ALL RIGHT?
OH, MY BRAVE HERO!— I'M SO HAPPY TO SEE YOU! AND YOU, TOO, DUDLEY!
ENOUGH OF THAT NECKING! NOW TO PUT MY EVIL PLAN INTO ACTION!
YOU CAD!— YOU ***WOULDN'T!***
I ***WILL*** IF YOU DON'T COOPERATE!
THAT'S IT!— JUST HOLD STILL WHILE I DOUSE YOU WITH THIS HOSE!
BLUB!
HEAVENS!— I'VE BEEN QUICK-FROZEN!
YOU'RE ***TRAPPED,*** DO-RIGHT!
YOUR END WILL BE A ***FROZEN*** ONE!
IT ***ALREADY*** FEELS A TRIFLE NUMB!

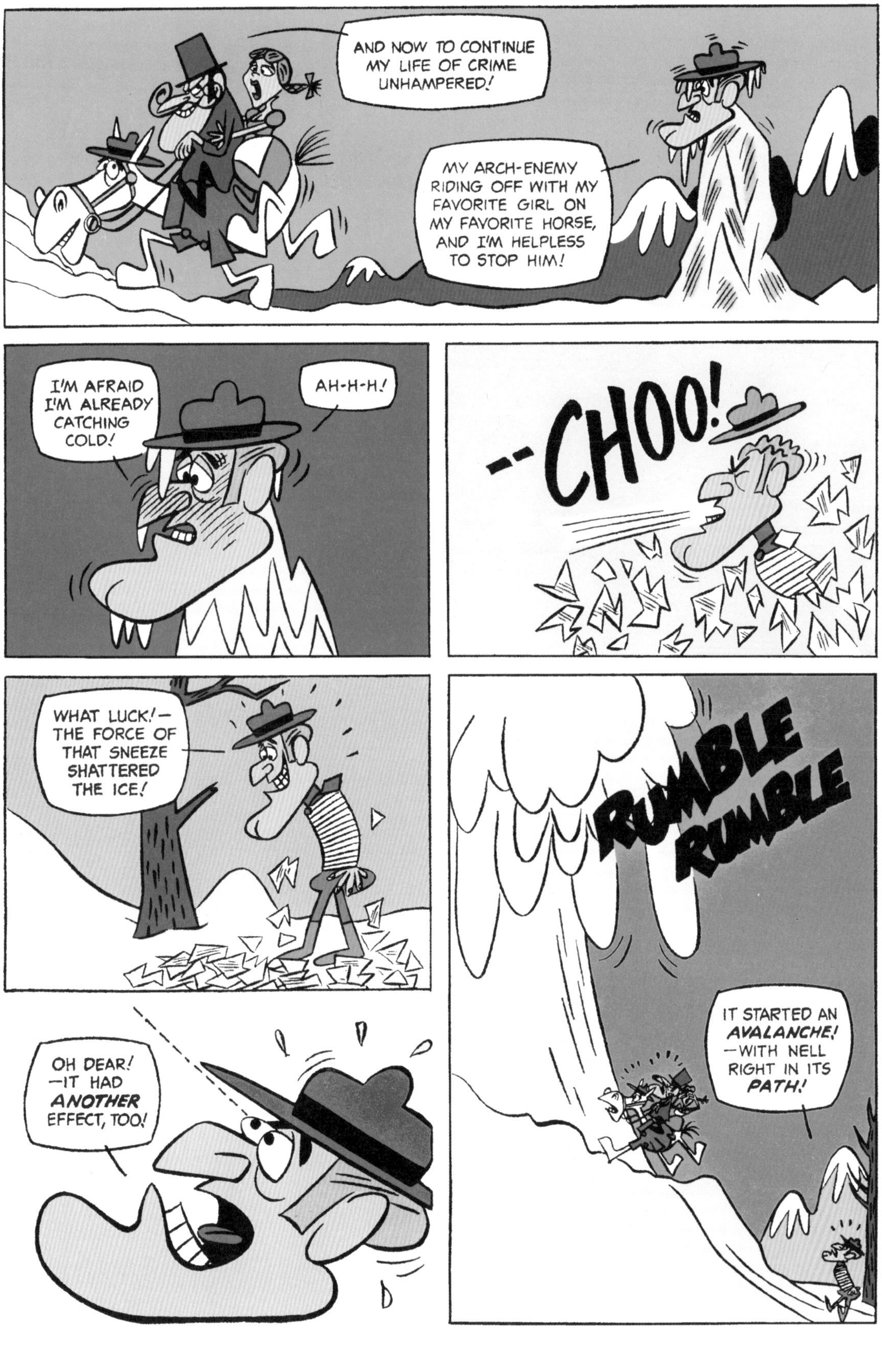
AND NOW TO CONTINUE MY LIFE OF CRIME UNHAMPERED!
MY ARCH-ENEMY RIDING OFF WITH MY FAVORITE GIRL ON MY FAVORITE HORSE, AND I'M HELPLESS TO STOP HIM!
I'M AFRAID I'M ALREADY CATCHING COLD!
AH-H-H!
--CHOO!
WHAT LUCK!—THE FORCE OF THAT SNEEZE SHATTERED THE ICE!
RUMBLE RUMBLE
OH DEAR! —IT HAD ANOTHER EFFECT, TOO!
IT STARTED AN AVALANCHE! —WITH NELL RIGHT IN ITS PATH!

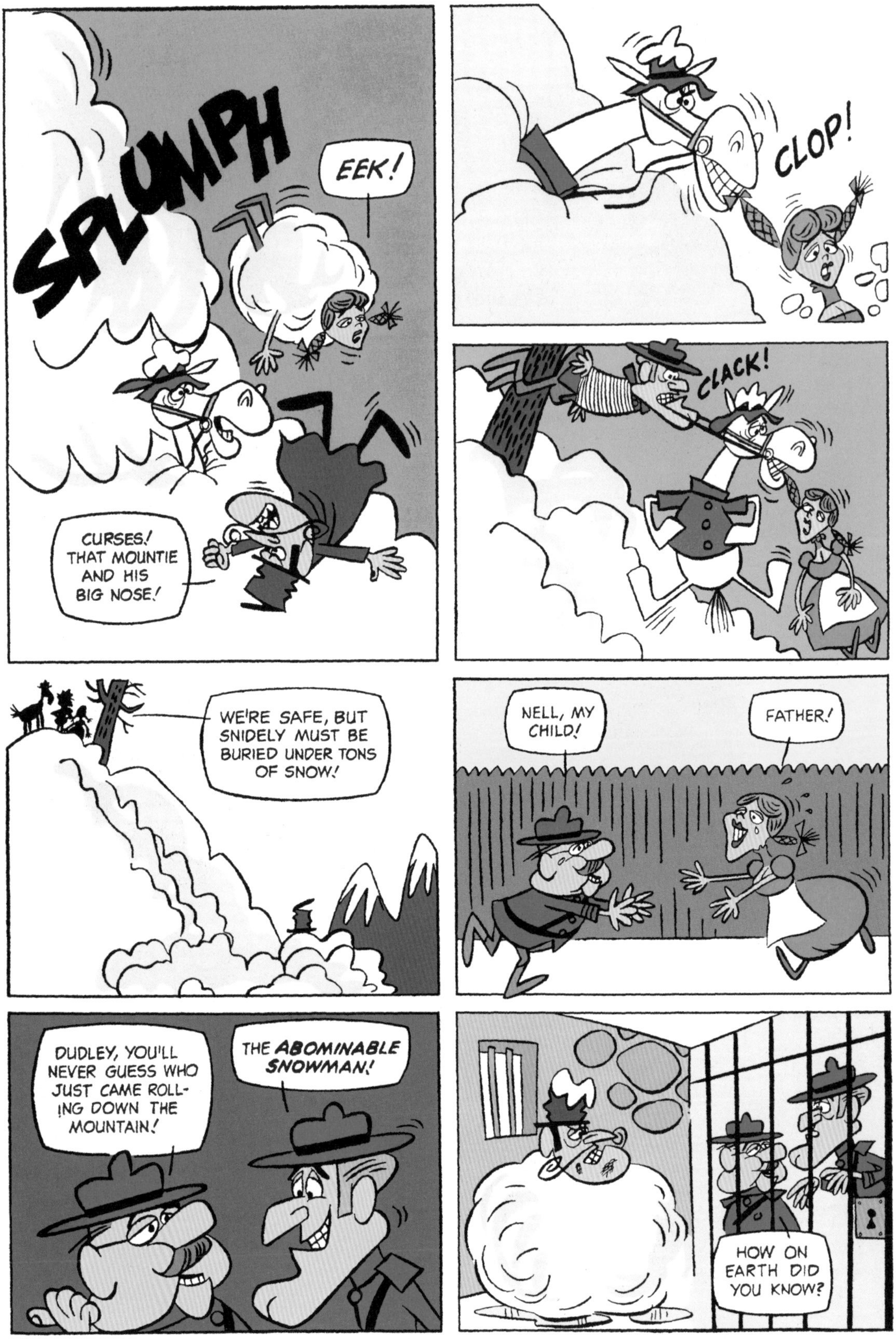
SPLUMPH
EEK!
CURSES! THAT MOUNTIE AND HIS BIG NOSE!
CLOP!
CLACK!
WE'RE SAFE, BUT SNIDELY MUST BE BURIED UNDER TONS OF SNOW!
NELL, MY CHILD!
FATHER!
DUDLEY, YOU'LL NEVER GUESS WHO JUST CAME ROLL-ING DOWN THE MOUNTAIN!
THE ABOMINABLE SNOWMAN!
HOW ON EARTH DID YOU KNOW?

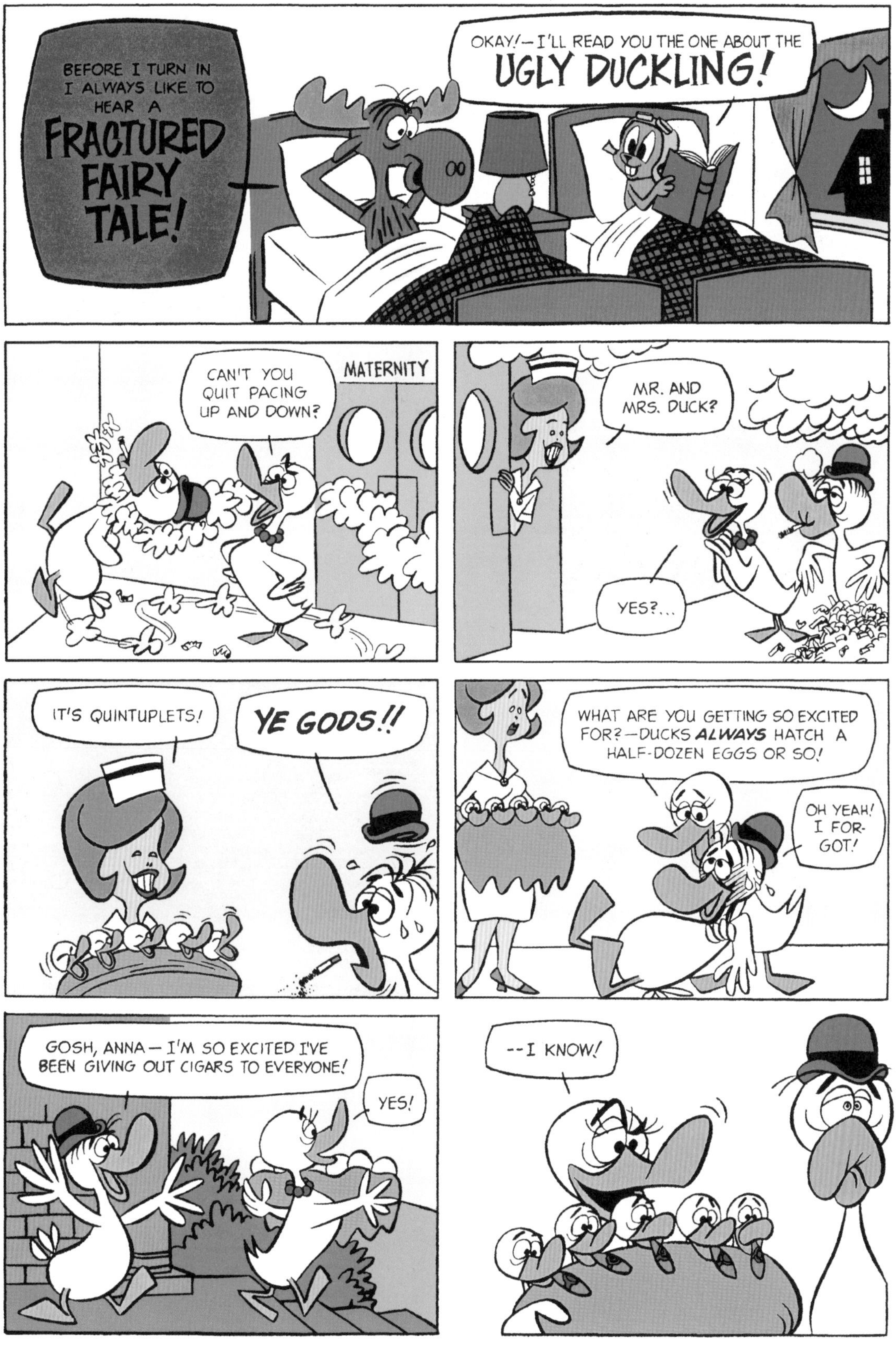
BEFORE I TURN IN I ALWAYS LIKE TO HEAR A FRACTURED FAIRY TALE!
OKAY!—I'LL READ YOU THE ONE ABOUT THE UGLY DUCKLING!
CAN'T YOU QUIT PACING UP AND DOWN?
MATERNITY
MR. AND MRS. DUCK?
YES?...
IT'S QUINTUPLETS!
YE GODS!!
WHAT ARE YOU GETTING SO EXCITED FOR?—DUCKS ALWAYS HATCH A HALF-DOZEN EGGS OR SO!
OH YEAH! I FOR-GOT!
GOSH, ANNA—I'M SO EXCITED I'VE BEEN GIVING OUT CIGARS TO EVERYONE!
YES!
--I KNOW!

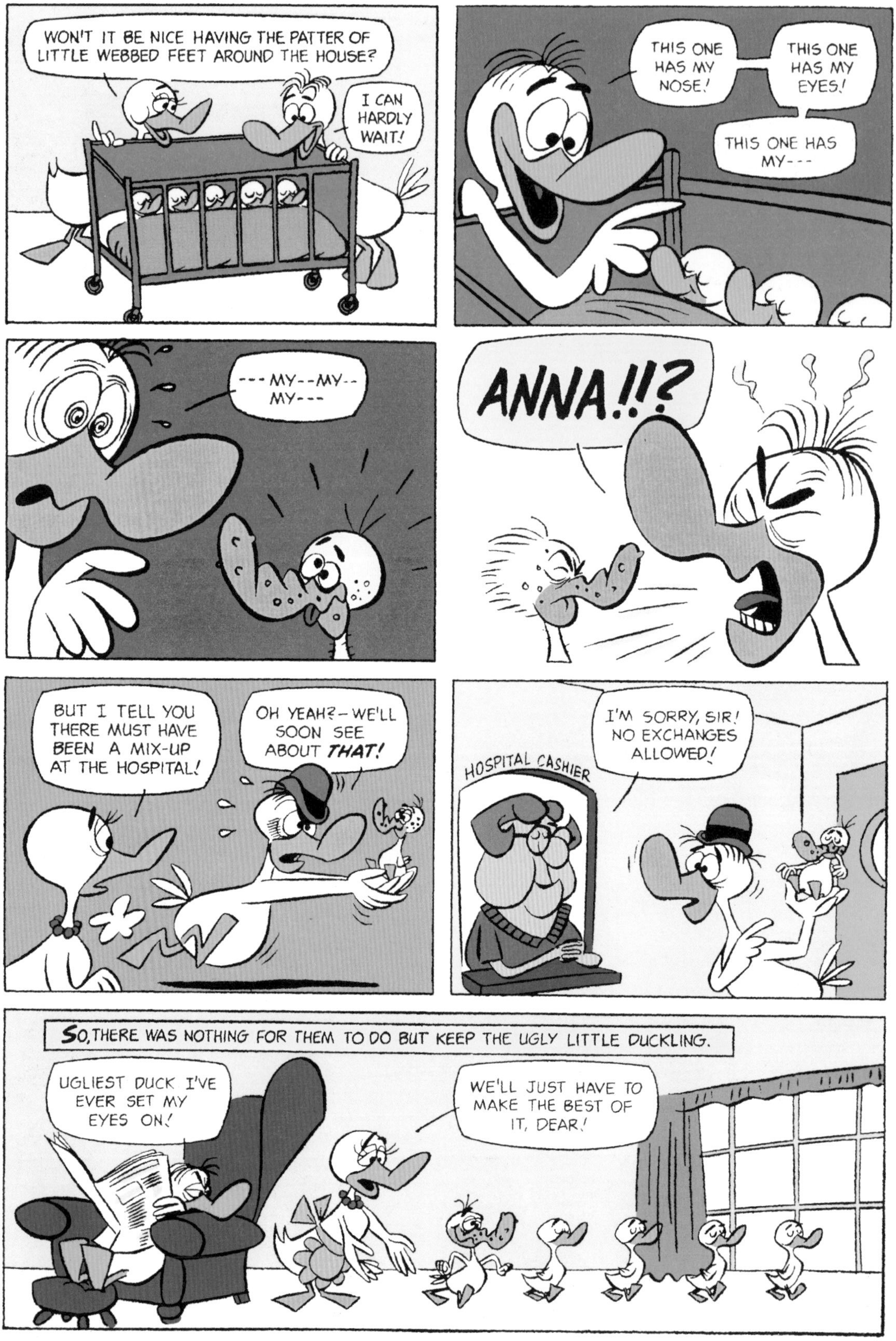

WON'T IT BE NICE HAVING THE PATTER OF LITTLE WEBBED FEET AROUND THE HOUSE?
I CAN HARDLY WAIT!
THIS ONE HAS MY NOSE!
THIS ONE HAS MY EYES!
THIS ONE HAS MY---
---MY--MY-- MY---
ANNA!!?
BUT I TELL YOU THERE MUST HAVE BEEN A MIX-UP AT THE HOSPITAL!
OH YEAH?—WE'LL SOON SEE ABOUT THAT!
HOSPITAL CASHIER
I'M SORRY, SIR! NO EXCHANGES ALLOWED!
SO, THERE WAS NOTHING FOR THEM TO DO BUT KEEP THE UGLY LITTLE DUCKLING.
UGLIEST DUCK I'VE EVER SET MY EYES ON!
WE'LL JUST HAVE TO MAKE THE BEST OF IT, DEAR!

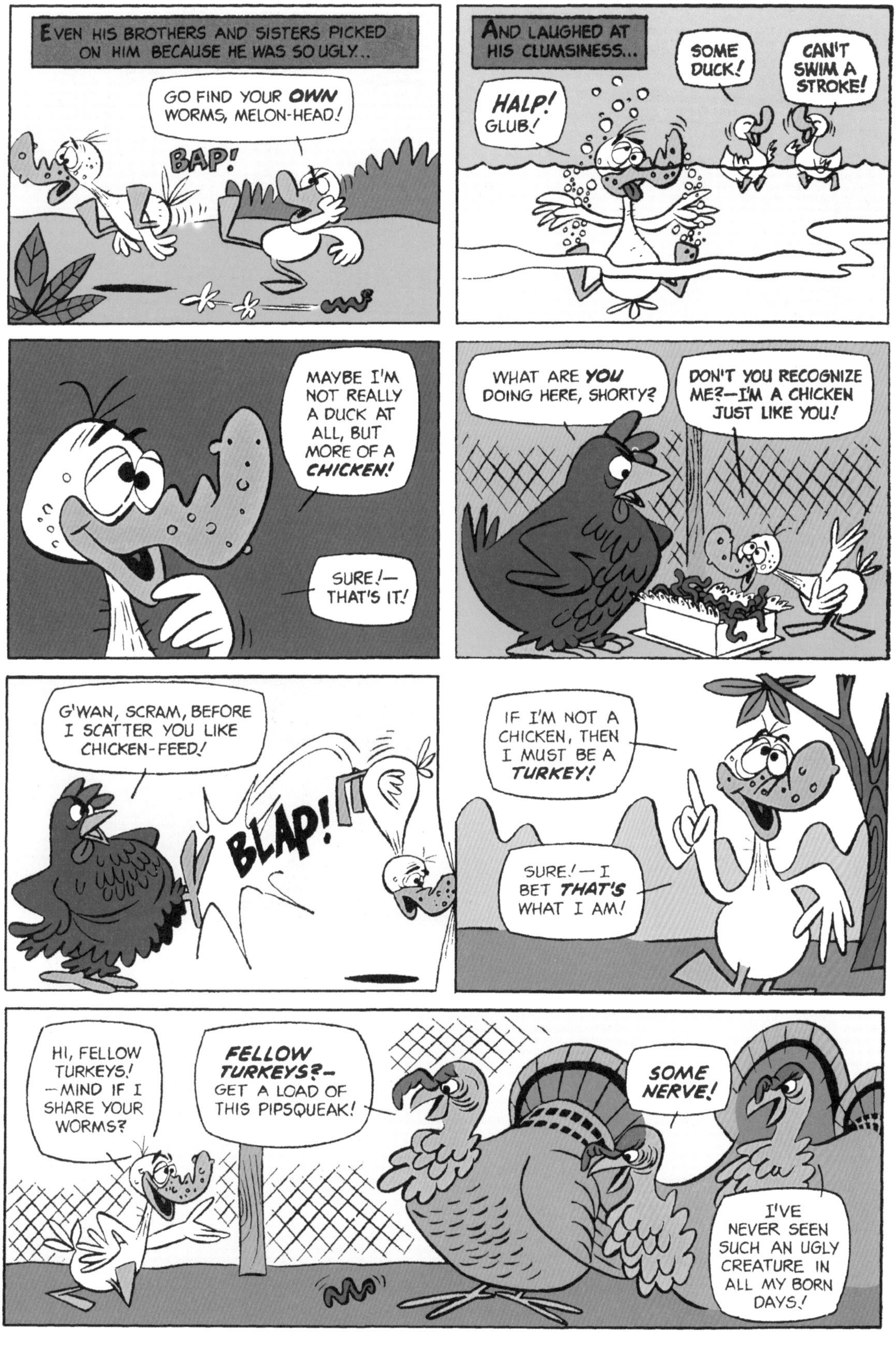
EVEN HIS BROTHERS AND SISTERS PICKED ON HIM BECAUSE HE WAS SO UGLY...
GO FIND YOUR OWN WORMS, MELON-HEAD!
BAP!
AND LAUGHED AT HIS CLUMSINESS...
HALP! GLUB!
SOME DUCK!
CAN'T SWIM A STROKE!
MAYBE I'M NOT REALLY A DUCK AT ALL, BUT MORE OF A CHICKEN!
SURE!—THAT'S IT!
WHAT ARE YOU DOING HERE, SHORTY?
DON'T YOU RECOGNIZE ME?—I'M A CHICKEN JUST LIKE YOU!
G'WAN, SCRAM, BEFORE I SCATTER YOU LIKE CHICKEN-FEED!
BLAP!
IF I'M NOT A CHICKEN, THEN I MUST BE A TURKEY!
SURE!—I BET THAT'S WHAT I AM!
HI, FELLOW TURKEYS! —MIND IF I SHARE YOUR WORMS?
FELLOW TURKEYS?—GET A LOAD OF THIS PIPSQUEAK!
SOME NERVE!
I'VE NEVER SEEN SUCH AN UGLY CREATURE IN ALL MY BORN DAYS!

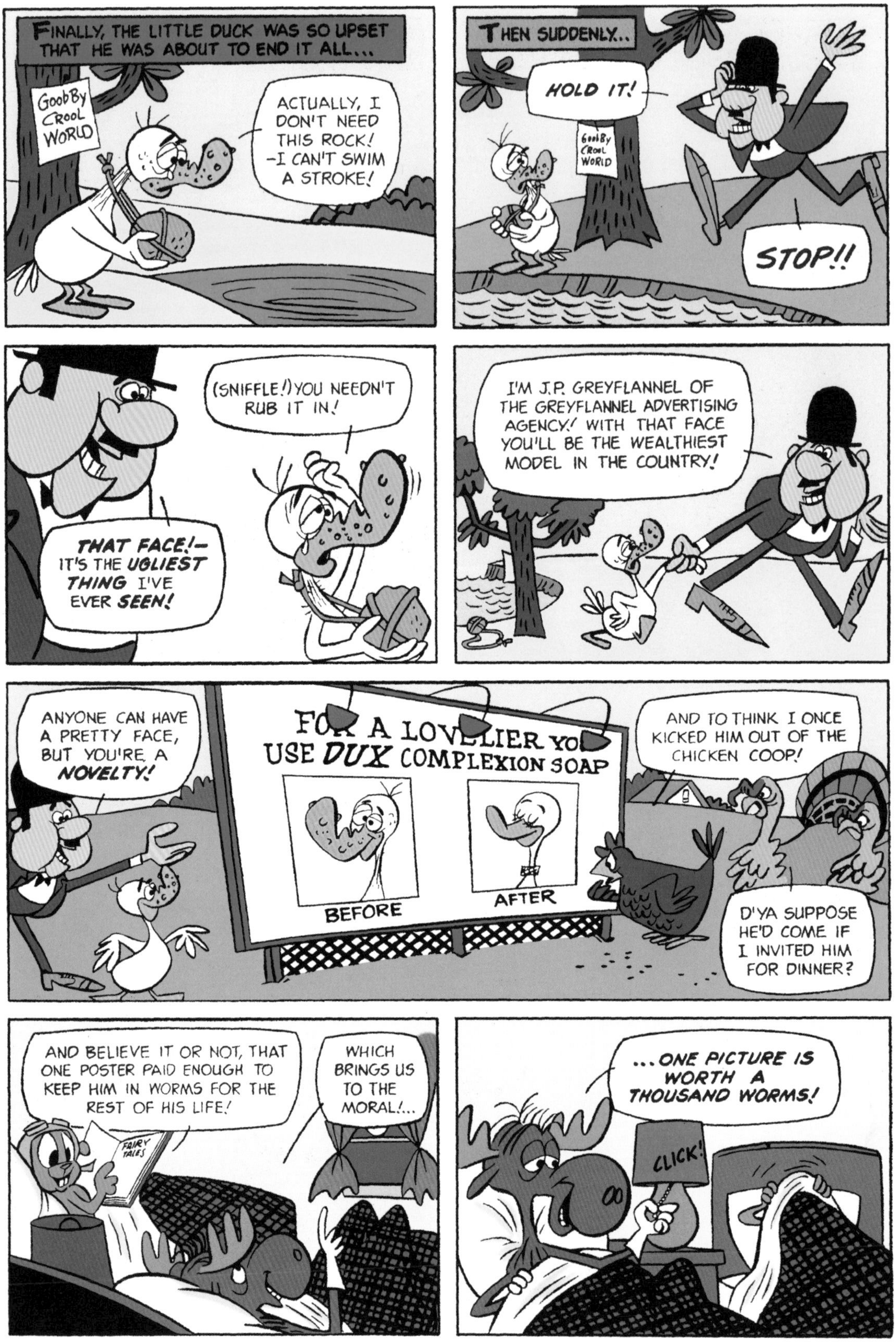
FINALLY, THE LITTLE DUCK WAS SO UPSET THAT HE WAS ABOUT TO END IT ALL...
GoobBy CrooL WORLD
ACTUALLY, I DON'T NEED THIS ROCK! -I CAN'T SWIM A STROKE!
THEN SUDDENLY...
HOLD IT!
GoobBy CrooL WorLD
STOP!!
(SNIFFLE!) YOU NEEDN'T RUB IT IN!
THAT FACE!— IT'S THE UGLIEST THING I'VE EVER SEEN!
I'M J.P. GREYFLANNEL OF THE GREYFLANNEL ADVERTISING AGENCY! WITH THAT FACE YOU'LL BE THE WEALTHIEST MODEL IN THE COUNTRY!
ANYONE CAN HAVE A PRETTY FACE, BUT YOU'RE A NOVELTY!
FOR A LOVELIER YO USE DUX COMPLEXION SOAP
BEFORE
AFTER
AND TO THINK I ONCE KICKED HIM OUT OF THE CHICKEN COOP!
D'YA SUPPOSE HE'D COME IF I INVITED HIM FOR DINNER?
AND BELIEVE IT OR NOT, THAT ONE POSTER PAID ENOUGH TO KEEP HIM IN WORMS FOR THE REST OF HIS LIFE!
WHICH BRINGS US TO THE MORAL!...
FAIRY TALES
...ONE PICTURE IS WORTH A THOUSAND WORMS!
CLICK!

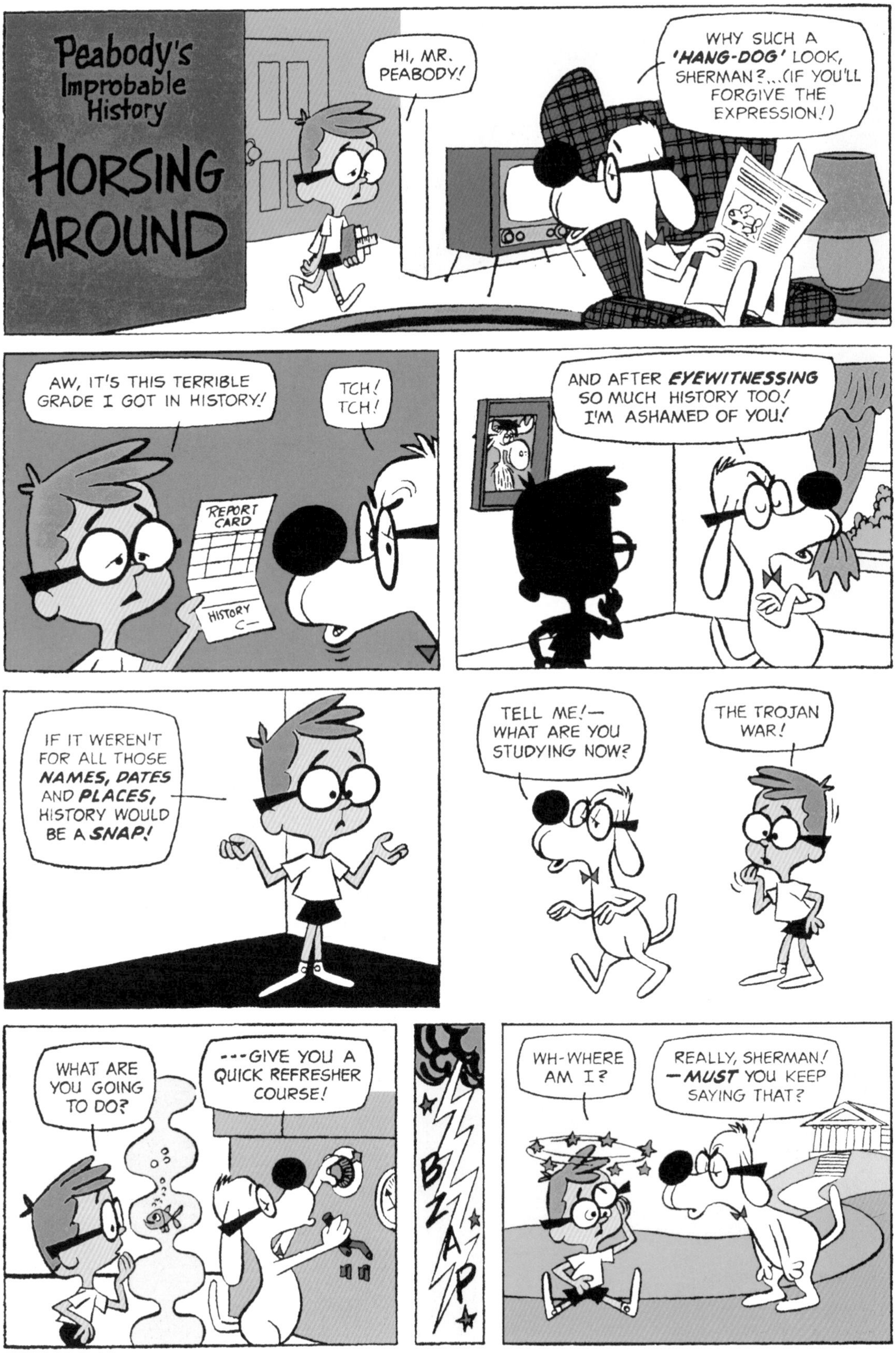
Peabody's Improbable History
HORSING AROUND
HI, MR. PEABODY!
WHY SUCH A 'HANG-DOG' LOOK, SHERMAN?...(IF YOU'LL FORGIVE THE EXPRESSION!)
AW, IT'S THIS TERRIBLE GRADE I GOT IN HISTORY!
REPORT CARD
HISTORY C—
TCH! TCH!
AND AFTER EYEWITNESSING SO MUCH HISTORY TOO! I'M ASHAMED OF YOU!
IF IT WEREN'T FOR ALL THOSE NAMES, DATES AND PLACES, HISTORY WOULD BE A SNAP!
TELL ME!— WHAT ARE YOU STUDYING NOW?
THE TROJAN WAR!
WHAT ARE YOU GOING TO DO?
---GIVE YOU A QUICK REFRESHER COURSE!
BZAP
WH-WHERE AM I?
REALLY, SHERMAN! —MUST YOU KEEP SAYING THAT?

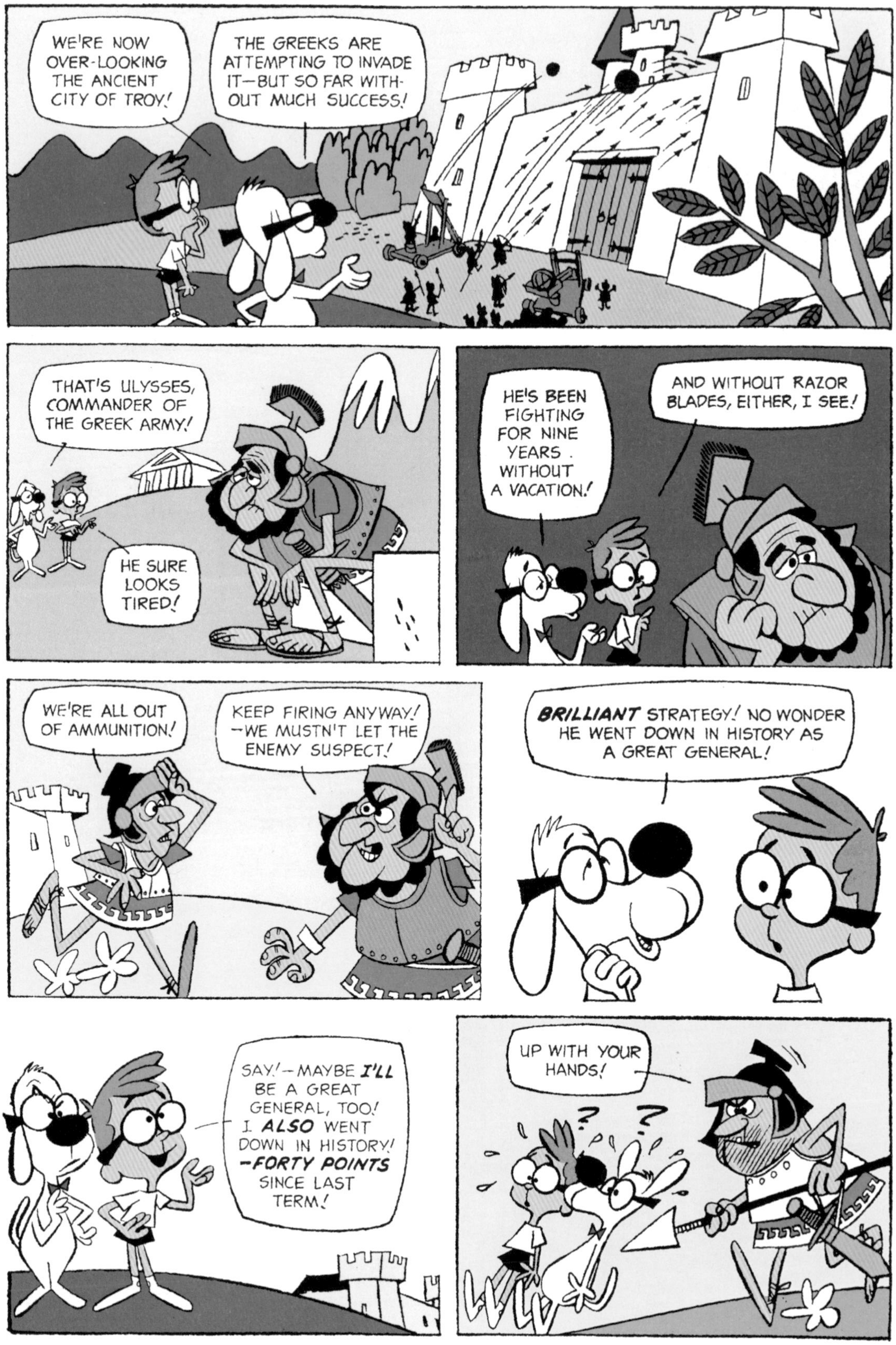
WE'RE NOW OVER-LOOKING THE ANCIENT CITY OF TROY!
THE GREEKS ARE ATTEMPTING TO INVADE IT—BUT SO FAR WITH-OUT MUCH SUCCESS!
THAT'S ULYSSES, COMMANDER OF THE GREEK ARMY!
HE SURE LOOKS TIRED!
HE'S BEEN FIGHTING FOR NINE YEARS . WITHOUT A VACATION!
AND WITHOUT RAZOR BLADES, EITHER, I SEE!
WE'RE ALL OUT OF AMMUNITION!
KEEP FIRING ANYWAY! —WE MUSTN'T LET THE ENEMY SUSPECT!
BRILLIANT STRATEGY! NO WONDER HE WENT DOWN IN HISTORY AS A GREAT GENERAL!
SAY!—MAYBE **I'LL** BE A GREAT GENERAL, TOO! I **ALSO** WENT DOWN IN HISTORY! **—FORTY POINTS** SINCE LAST TERM!
UP WITH YOUR HANDS!
? ?

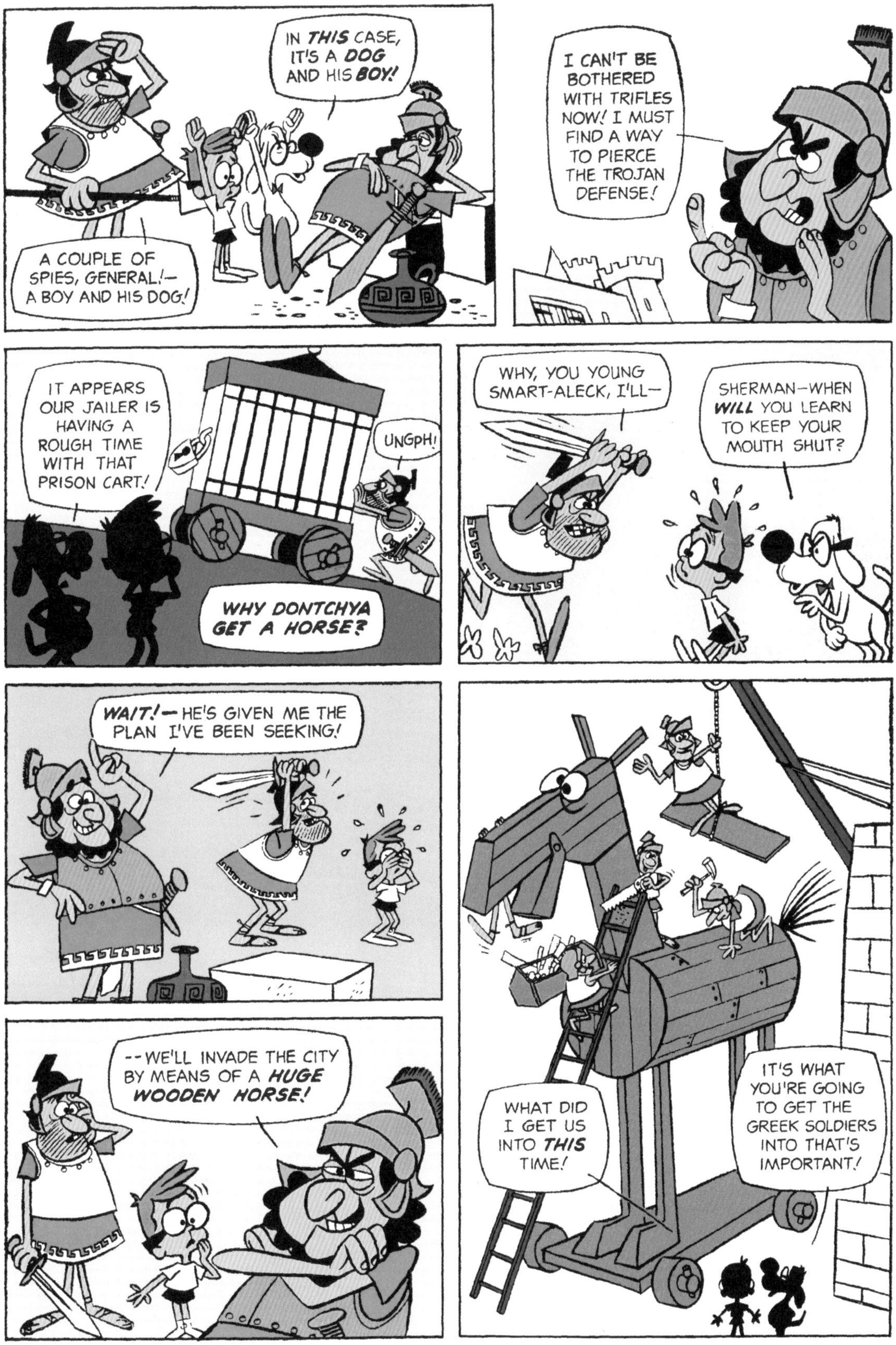

A COUPLE OF SPIES, GENERAL!— A BOY AND HIS DOG!
IN THIS CASE, IT'S A DOG AND HIS BOY!
I CAN'T BE BOTHERED WITH TRIFLES NOW! I MUST FIND A WAY TO PIERCE THE TROJAN DEFENSE!
IT APPEARS OUR JAILER IS HAVING A ROUGH TIME WITH THAT PRISON CART!
UNGPH!
WHY DONTCHYA GET A HORSE?
WHY, YOU YOUNG SMART-ALECK, I'LL—
SHERMAN—WHEN WILL YOU LEARN TO KEEP YOUR MOUTH SHUT?
WAIT!—HE'S GIVEN ME THE PLAN I'VE BEEN SEEKING!
--WE'LL INVADE THE CITY BY MEANS OF A HUGE WOODEN HORSE!
WHAT DID I GET US INTO THIS TIME!
IT'S WHAT YOU'RE GOING TO GET THE GREEK SOLDIERS INTO THAT'S IMPORTANT!

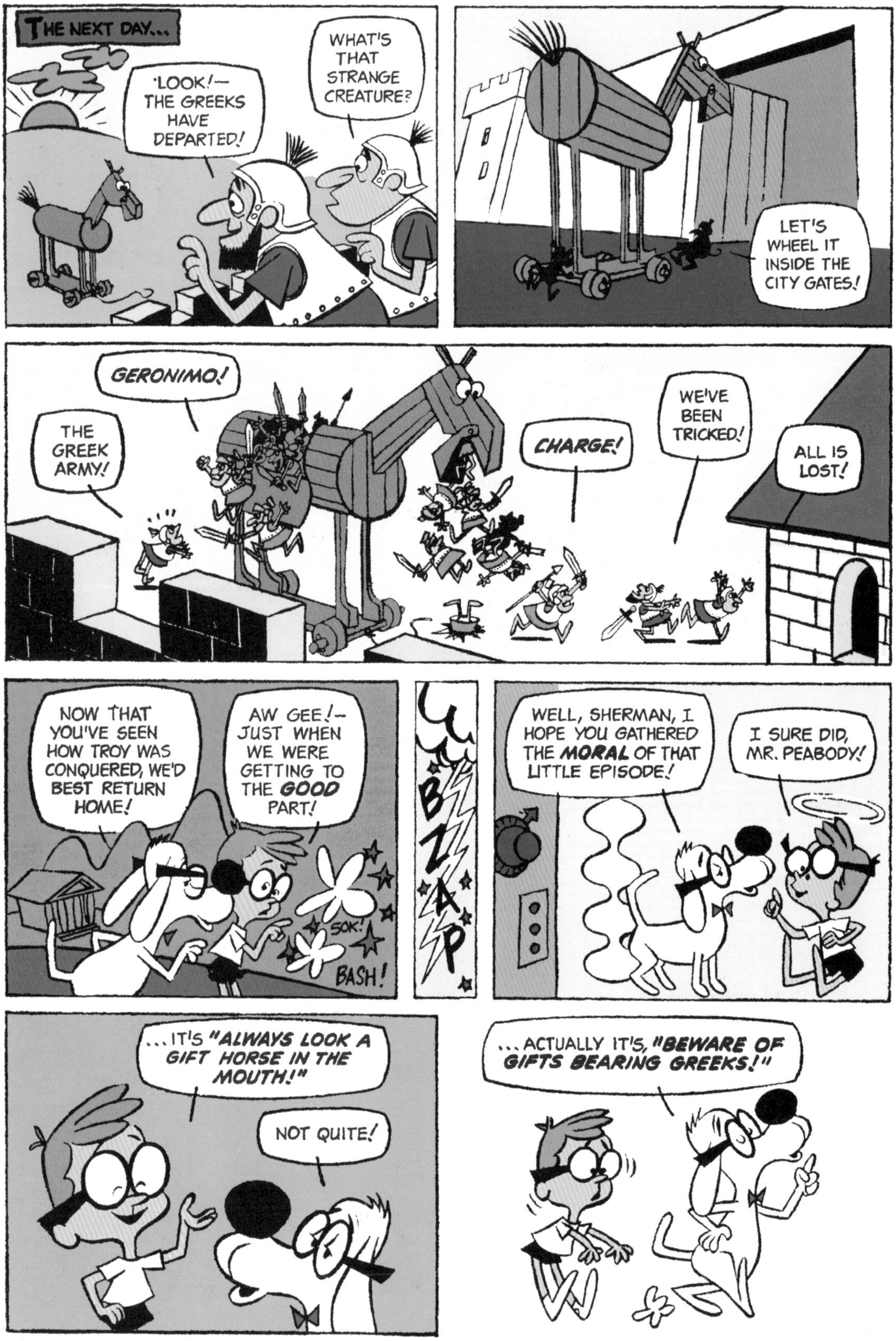
THE NEXT DAY...
'LOOK!— THE GREEKS HAVE DEPARTED!
WHAT'S THAT STRANGE CREATURE?
LET'S WHEEL IT INSIDE THE CITY GATES!
GERONIMO!
THE GREEK ARMY!
CHARGE!
WE'VE BEEN TRICKED!
ALL IS LOST!
NOW THAT YOU'VE SEEN HOW TROY WAS CONQUERED, WE'D BEST RETURN HOME!
AW GEE!— JUST WHEN WE WERE GETTING TO THE GOOD PART!
SOK!
BASH!
BZAP
WELL, SHERMAN, I HOPE YOU GATHERED THE MORAL OF THAT LITTLE EPISODE!
I SURE DID, MR. PEABODY!
...IT'S "ALWAYS LOOK A GIFT HORSE IN THE MOUTH!"
NOT QUITE!
...ACTUALLY IT'S, "BEWARE OF GIFTS BEARING GREEKS!"

Ridiculous isn't it?

Tourists will be happy to know that the first round trips to the moon will cost a mere $15,000,000. But within a few years the price is expected to drop to the bargain rate of $2,000,000.

Talk about beauty queens! Out in Chicago one lucky miss was chosen as "Queen of National Frankfurter and Sauerkraut Week." The only thing they left out was the mustard.

The Agriculture Department reports that whirling a fruit fly at 240 revolutions per minute will reduce its egg production by 60 per cent! But for real results, stick to the old-fashioned fly swatter!

In California there's a firm that exports Pizza pies. To Italy of all places!

A famous Chicago restaurant is planning a special dining room for dieters who want to cheat without being seen.

In case anybody cares, a fellow down in New Zealand claims a new world's record for dancing the twist, non-stop—55 hours and fifty minutes!

Anything for a buck department: Out in California there's a fellow who earns his living by picking up stuff thrown or blown from cars traveling the high-speed desert highways. Choice items include deposit bottles, hub-caps, shirts, hats, blankets and even wrist watches.

Here's something to remember the next time they serve you a glass of milk. Cow juice is also used to manufacture paints, glue, textiles, dyes and even as a non-chipping surface for ice-skating rinks.

An astronaut who zoomed through space at thousands of miles per hour was stopped in Florida for speeding! his car was doing 45 miles per hour in a 40 mile per hour zone.

There's a sign in a Philadelphia restaurant which reads: "HELP STAMP OUT HOME-COOKING!"

In England, Nottingham jail is reported to be building a 9-hole golf course for its guests.

A car thief arrested in Chicago told the police that he kept a list of the hundreds of cars he'd stolen, to prevent stealing the same car twice. It's thoughtfulness and consideration like that that makes the world pleasant for the rest of us.

A special flash for the social set! You can hire a beatnik as entertainment for your party! Bearded poets and bongo players make dandy conversation pieces at swank affairs.

When two African soccer teams met for a match, the affair ended in a squabble! It seems that one team brought along a witch doctor to put the whammy on the opposition.

Honest, fellahs! It really happened! Back in 1896 two men actually rowed across the Atlantic for a $10,000 prize! They paddled 3250 miles in 55 days to reach England. And then followed it up with a 250-mile pleasure jaunt to France.

Bothered by the King-sized phone bills piled up by his guests, a millionaire has installed pay telephones in his mansion.

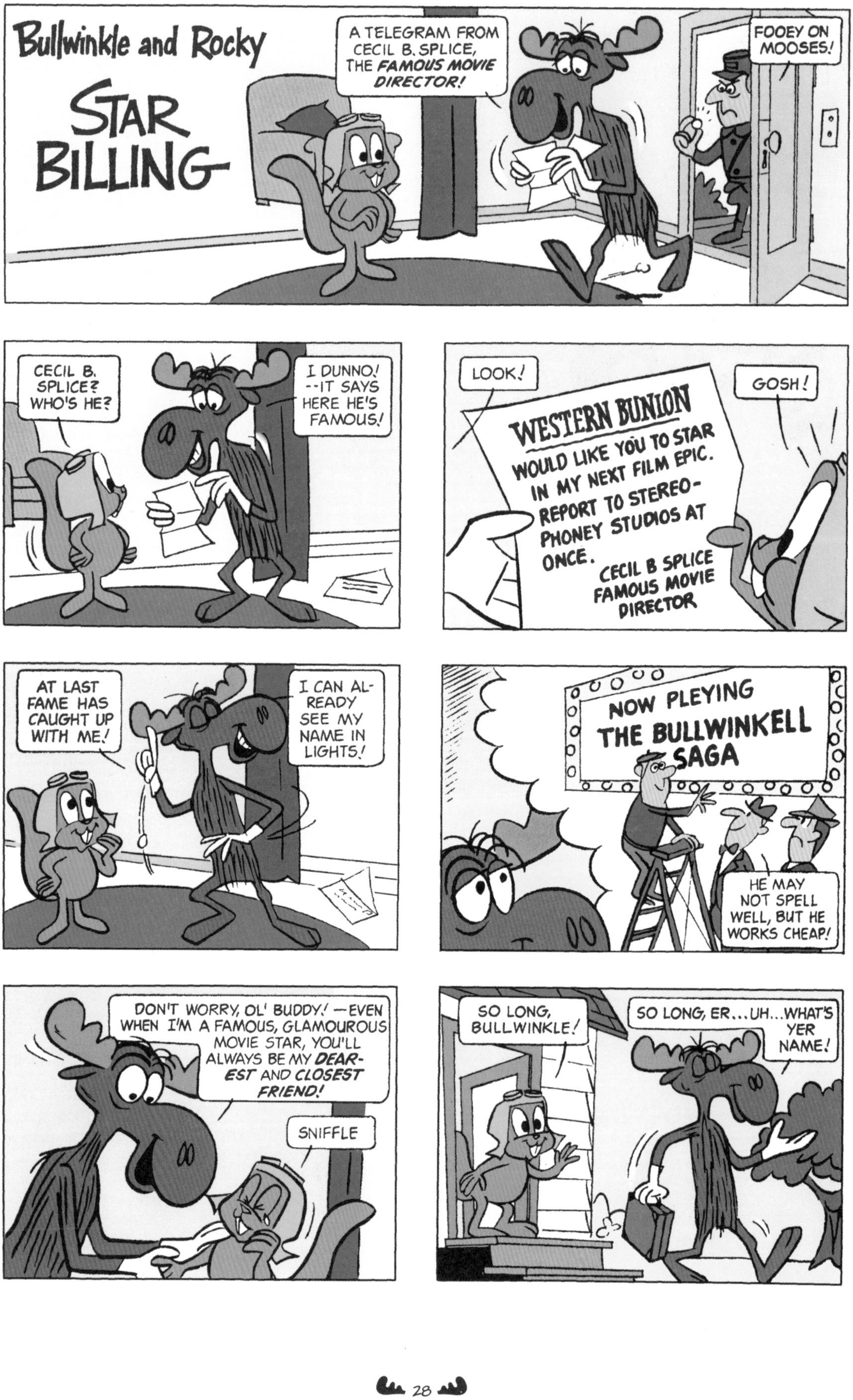

Bullwinkle and Rocky
STAR BILLING
A TELEGRAM FROM CECIL B. SPLICE, THE FAMOUS MOVIE DIRECTOR!
FOOEY ON MOOSES!
CECIL B. SPLICE? WHO'S HE?
I DUNNO! --IT SAYS HERE HE'S FAMOUS!
LOOK!
WESTERN BUNION
WOULD LIKE YOU TO STAR IN MY NEXT FILM EPIC. REPORT TO STEREO-PHONEY STUDIOS AT ONCE.
CECIL B SPLICE FAMOUS MOVIE DIRECTOR
GOSH!
AT LAST FAME HAS CAUGHT UP WITH ME!
I CAN AL-READY SEE MY NAME IN LIGHTS!
NOW PLEYING THE BULLWINKELL SAGA
HE MAY NOT SPELL WELL, BUT HE WORKS CHEAP!
DON'T WORRY, OL' BUDDY! —EVEN WHEN I'M A FAMOUS, GLAMOUROUS MOVIE STAR, YOU'LL ALWAYS BE MY DEAR-EST AND CLOSEST FRIEND!
SNIFFLE
SO LONG, BULLWINKLE!
SO LONG, ER...UH...WHAT'S YER NAME!

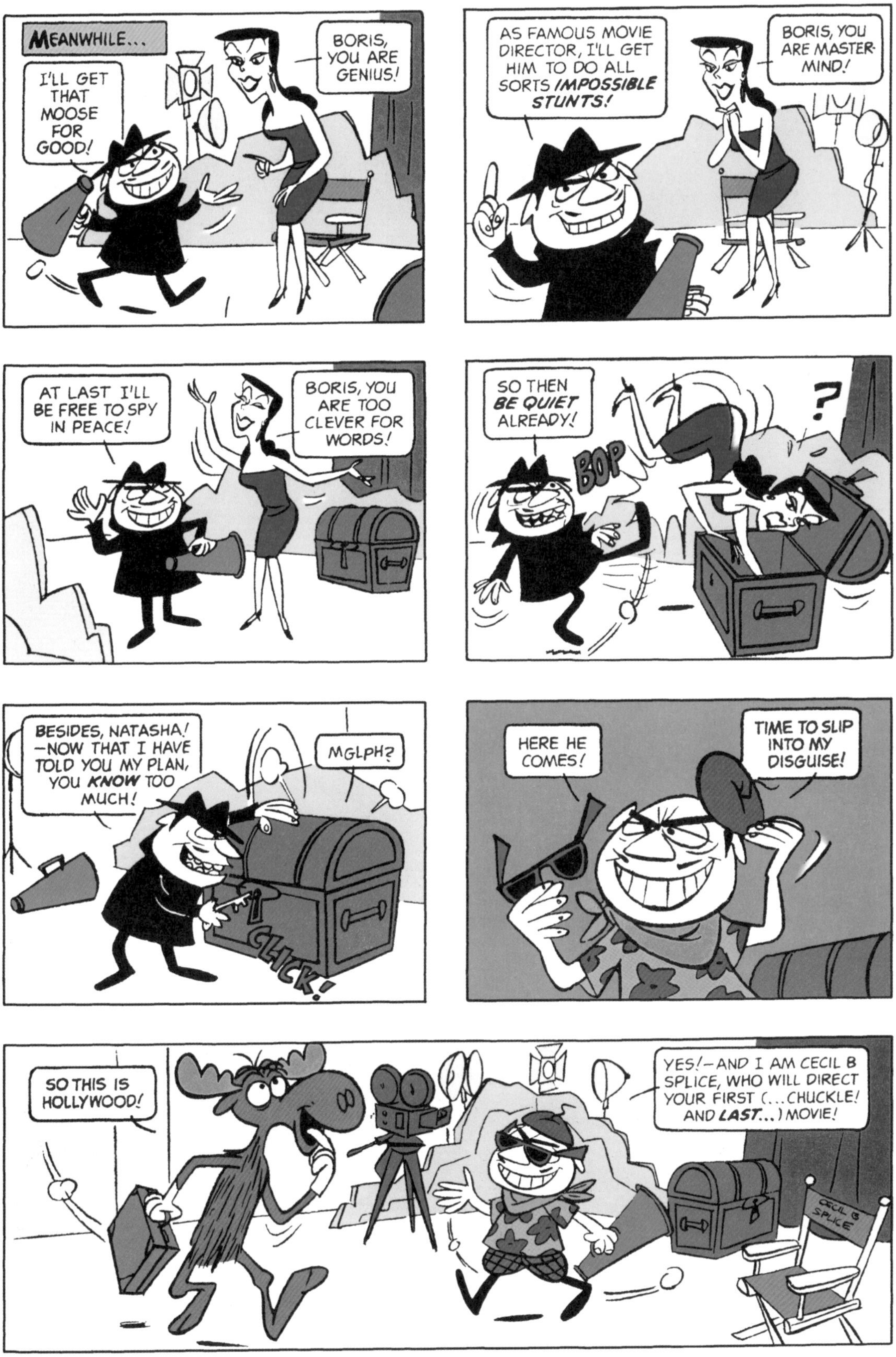
MEANWHILE...
I'LL GET THAT MOOSE FOR GOOD!
BORIS, YOU ARE GENIUS!
AS FAMOUS MOVIE DIRECTOR, I'LL GET HIM TO DO ALL SORTS IMPOSSIBLE STUNTS!
BORIS, YOU ARE MASTER-MIND!
AT LAST I'LL BE FREE TO SPY IN PEACE!
BORIS, YOU ARE TOO CLEVER FOR WORDS!
SO THEN BE QUIET ALREADY!
BOP
?
BESIDES, NATASHA! —NOW THAT I HAVE TOLD YOU MY PLAN, YOU KNOW TOO MUCH!
MGLPH?
CLICK!
HERE HE COMES!
TIME TO SLIP INTO MY DISGUISE!
SO THIS IS HOLLYWOOD!
YES!—AND I AM CECIL B SPLICE, WHO WILL DIRECT YOUR FIRST (...CHUCKLE! AND LAST...) MOVIE!
CECIL B SPLICE

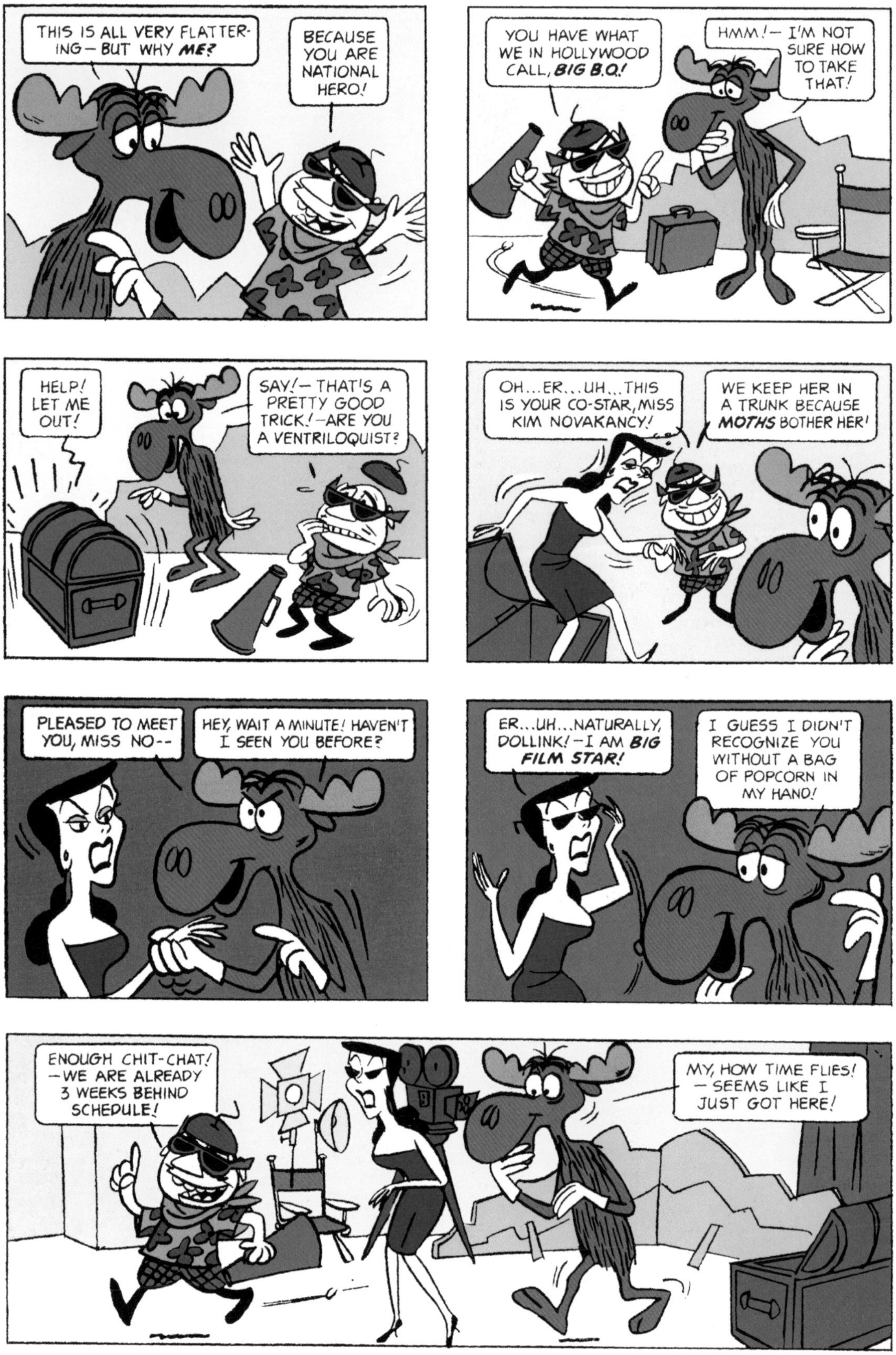
THIS IS ALL VERY FLATTERING— BUT WHY ME?
BECAUSE YOU ARE NATIONAL HERO!
YOU HAVE WHAT WE IN HOLLYWOOD CALL, BIG B.O.!
HMM!— I'M NOT SURE HOW TO TAKE THAT!
HELP! LET ME OUT!
SAY!— THAT'S A PRETTY GOOD TRICK!—ARE YOU A VENTRILOQUIST?
OH...ER...UH...THIS IS YOUR CO-STAR, MISS KIM NOVAKANCY!
WE KEEP HER IN A TRUNK BECAUSE MOTHS BOTHER HER!
PLEASED TO MEET YOU, MISS NO--
HEY, WAIT A MINUTE! HAVEN'T I SEEN YOU BEFORE?
ER...UH...NATURALLY, DOLLINK!—I AM BIG FILM STAR!
I GUESS I DIDN'T RECOGNIZE YOU WITHOUT A BAG OF POPCORN IN MY HAND!
ENOUGH CHIT-CHAT! —WE ARE ALREADY 3 WEEKS BEHIND SCHEDULE!
MY, HOW TIME FLIES! — SEEMS LIKE I JUST GOT HERE!

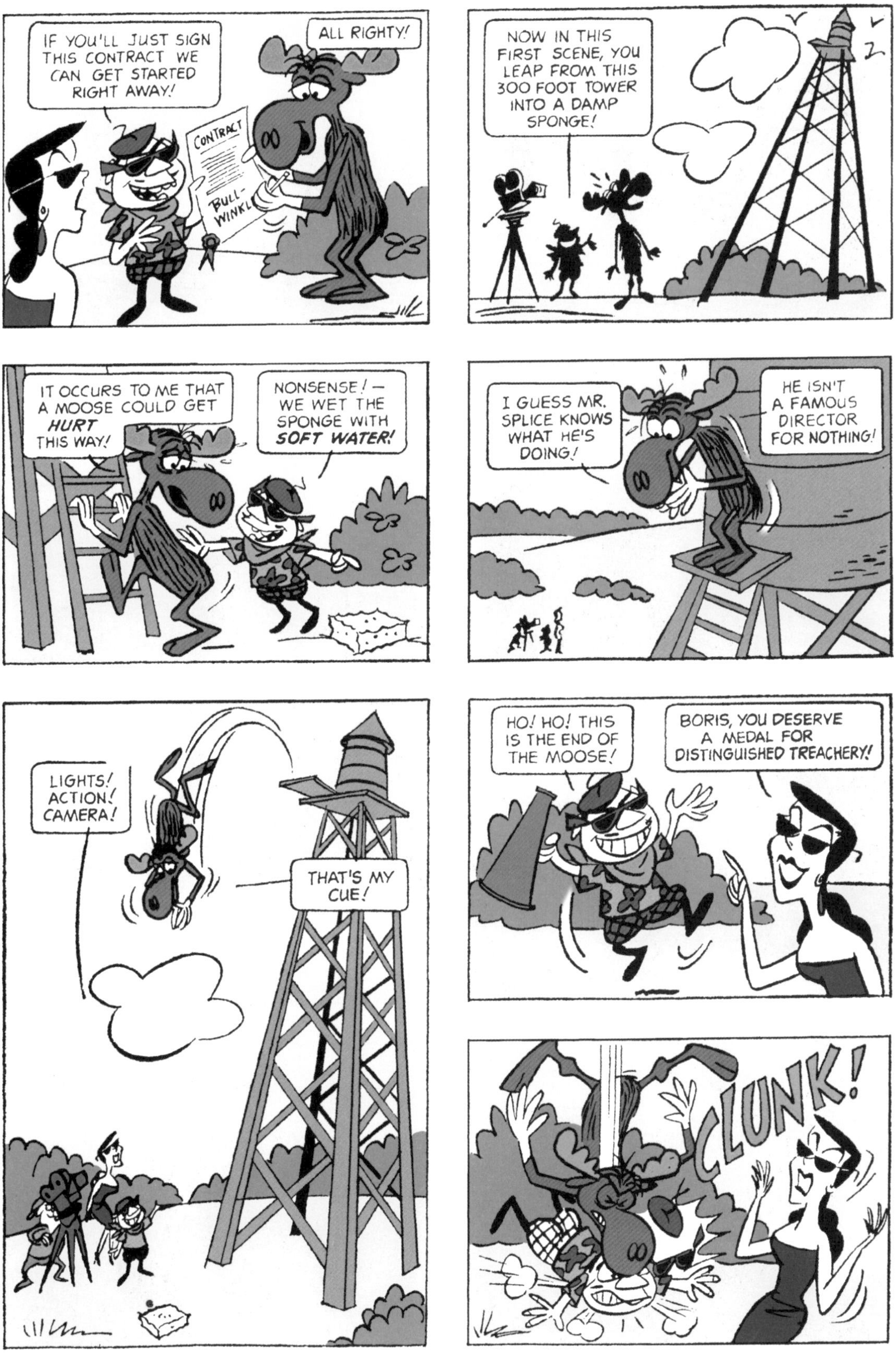
IF YOU'LL JUST SIGN THIS CONTRACT WE CAN GET STARTED RIGHT AWAY!
ALL RIGHTY!
CONTRACT
BULL-WINKLE
NOW IN THIS FIRST SCENE, YOU LEAP FROM THIS 300 FOOT TOWER INTO A DAMP SPONGE!
IT OCCURS TO ME THAT A MOOSE COULD GET HURT THIS WAY!
NONSENSE! — WE WET THE SPONGE WITH SOFT WATER!
I GUESS MR. SPLICE KNOWS WHAT HE'S DOING!
HE ISN'T A FAMOUS DIRECTOR FOR NOTHING!
LIGHTS! ACTION! CAMERA!
THAT'S MY CUE!
HO! HO! THIS IS THE END OF THE MOOSE!
BORIS, YOU DESERVE A MEDAL FOR DISTINGUISHED TREACHERY!
CLUNK!

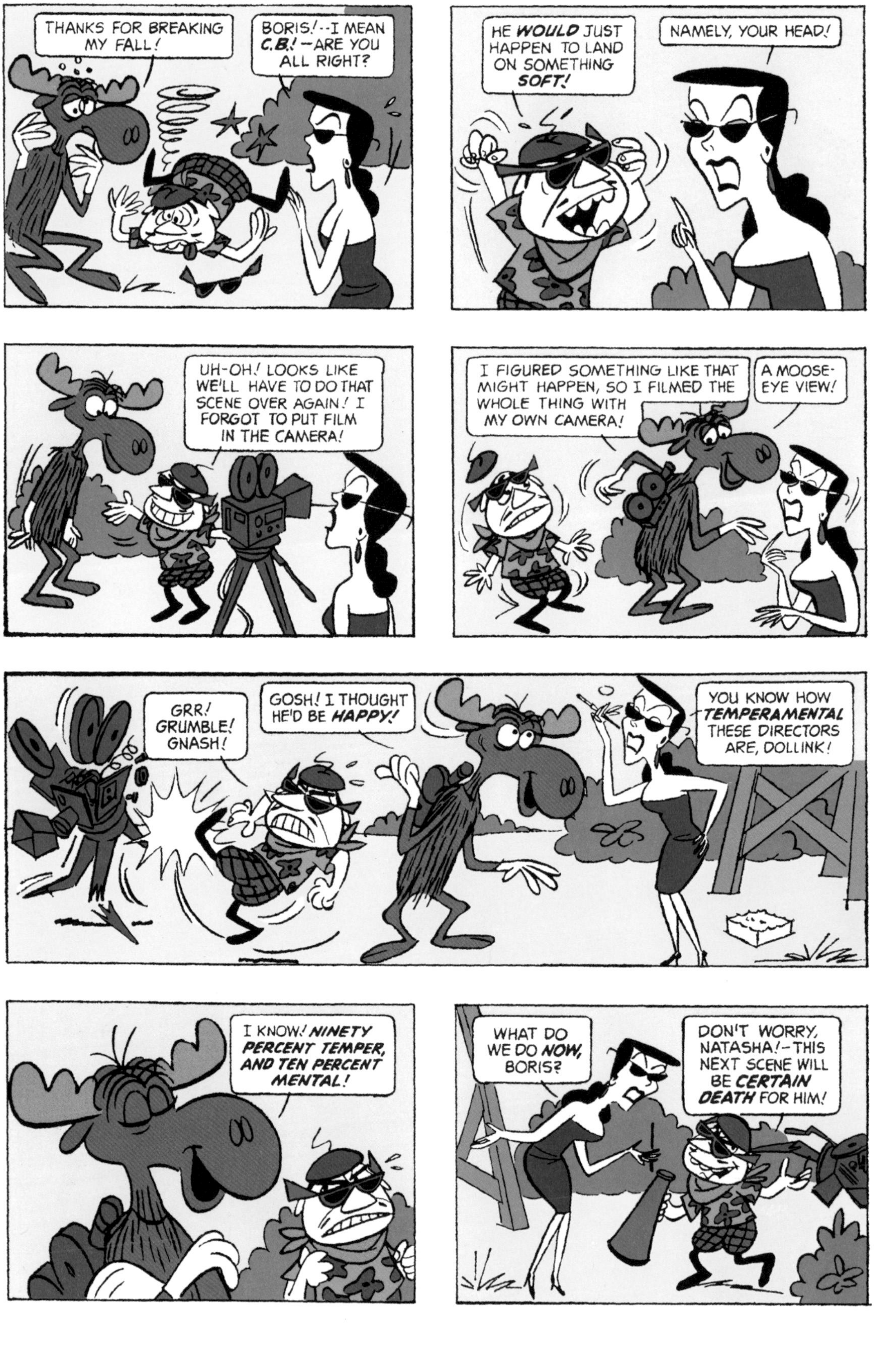
THANKS FOR BREAKING MY FALL!
BORIS!--I MEAN C.B.!—ARE YOU ALL RIGHT?
HE WOULD JUST HAPPEN TO LAND ON SOMETHING SOFT!
NAMELY, YOUR HEAD!
UH-OH! LOOKS LIKE WE'LL HAVE TO DO THAT SCENE OVER AGAIN! I FORGOT TO PUT FILM IN THE CAMERA!
I FIGURED SOMETHING LIKE THAT MIGHT HAPPEN, SO I FILMED THE WHOLE THING WITH MY OWN CAMERA!
A MOOSE-EYE VIEW!
GRR! GRUMBLE! GNASH!
GOSH! I THOUGHT HE'D BE HAPPY!
YOU KNOW HOW TEMPERAMENTAL THESE DIRECTORS ARE, DOLLINK!
I KNOW! NINETY PERCENT TEMPER, AND TEN PERCENT MENTAL!
WHAT DO WE DO NOW, BORIS?
DON'T WORRY, NATASHA!—THIS NEXT SCENE WILL BE CERTAIN DEATH FOR HIM!

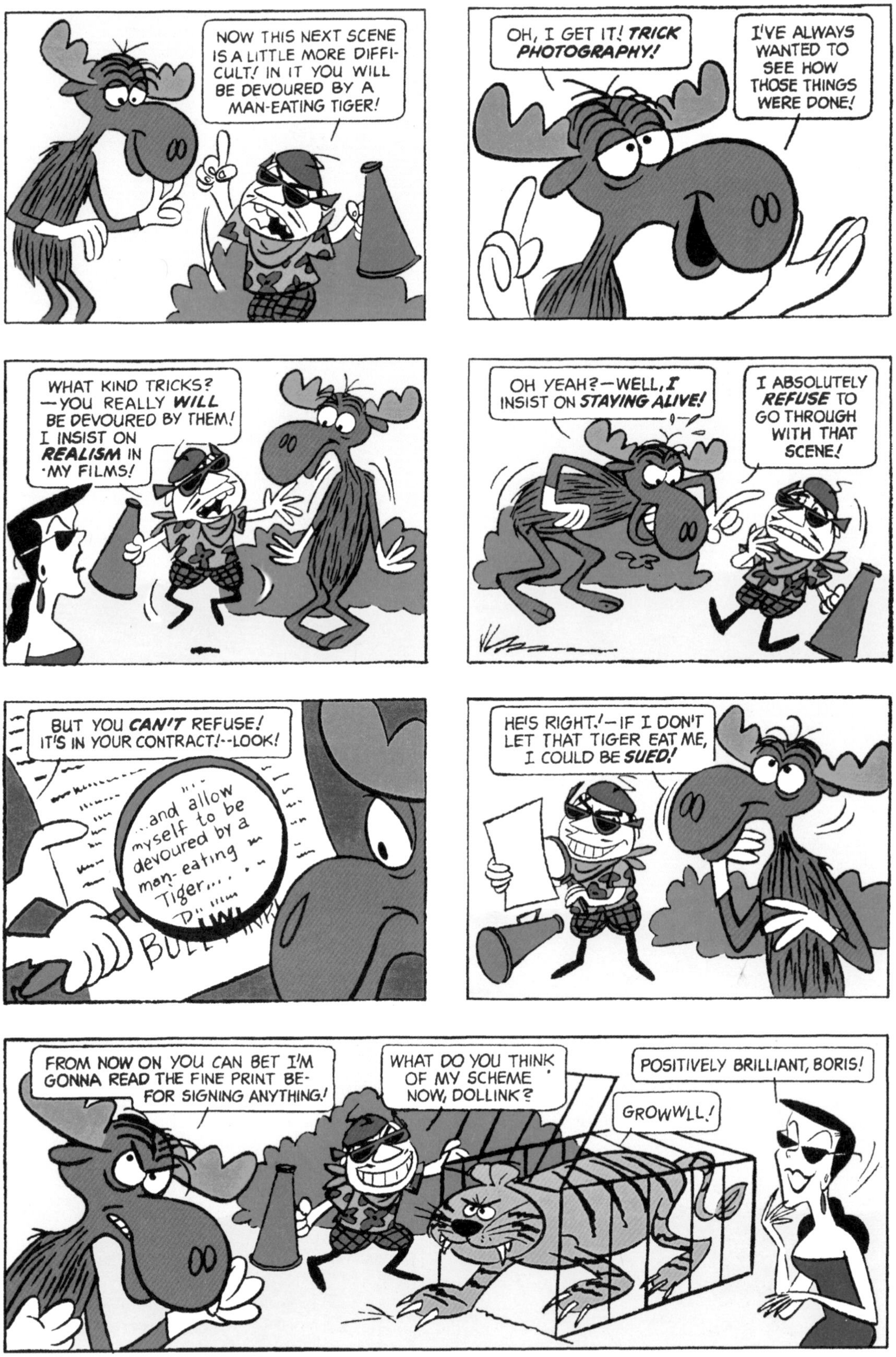

NOW THIS NEXT SCENE IS A LITTLE MORE DIFFICULT! IN IT YOU WILL BE DEVOURED BY A MAN-EATING TIGER!
OH, I GET IT! TRICK PHOTOGRAPHY!
I'VE ALWAYS WANTED TO SEE HOW THOSE THINGS WERE DONE!
WHAT KIND TRICKS? —YOU REALLY WILL BE DEVOURED BY THEM! I INSIST ON REALISM IN MY FILMS!
OH YEAH?—WELL, I INSIST ON STAYING ALIVE!
I ABSOLUTELY REFUSE TO GO THROUGH WITH THAT SCENE!
BUT YOU CAN'T REFUSE! IT'S IN YOUR CONTRACT!--LOOK!
...and allow myself to be devoured by a man-eating Tiger...
HE'S RIGHT!—IF I DON'T LET THAT TIGER EAT ME, I COULD BE SUED!
FROM NOW ON YOU CAN BET I'M GONNA READ THE FINE PRINT BEFOR SIGNING ANYTHING!
WHAT DO YOU THINK OF MY SCHEME NOW, DOLLINK?
GROWWLL!
POSITIVELY BRILLIANT, BORIS!

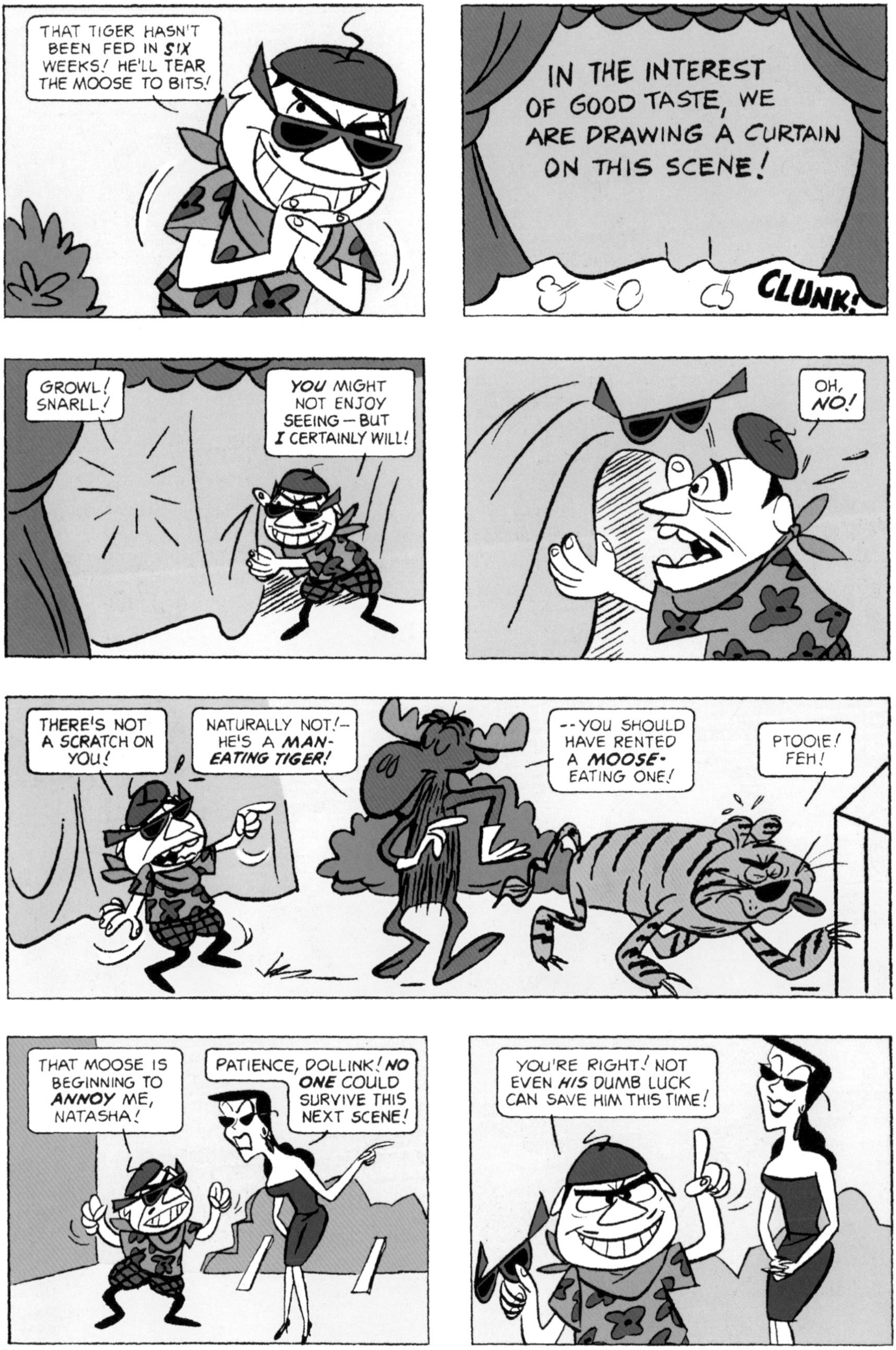
THAT TIGER HASN'T BEEN FED IN SIX WEEKS! HE'LL TEAR THE MOOSE TO BITS!
IN THE INTEREST OF GOOD TASTE, WE ARE DRAWING A CURTAIN ON THIS SCENE!
CLUNK!
GROWL! SNARLL!
YOU MIGHT NOT ENJOY SEEING—BUT I CERTAINLY WILL!
OH, NO!
THERE'S NOT A SCRATCH ON YOU!
NATURALLY NOT!— HE'S A MAN-EATING TIGER!
--YOU SHOULD HAVE RENTED A MOOSE-EATING ONE!
PTOOIE! FEH!
THAT MOOSE IS BEGINNING TO ANNOY ME, NATASHA!
PATIENCE, DOLLINK! NO ONE COULD SURVIVE THIS NEXT SCENE!
YOU'RE RIGHT! NOT EVEN HIS DUMB LUCK CAN SAVE HIM THIS TIME!

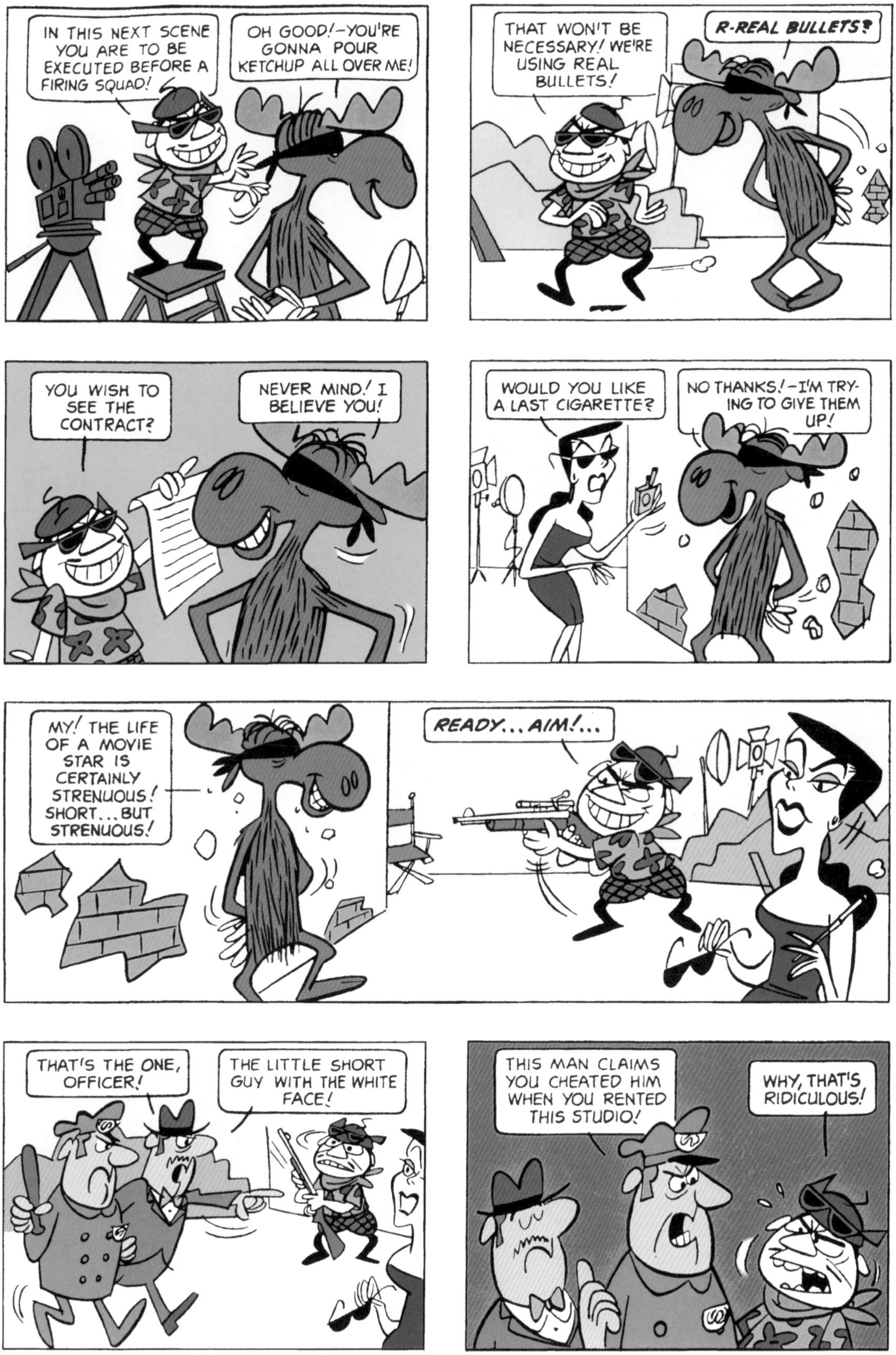
IN THIS NEXT SCENE YOU ARE TO BE EXECUTED BEFORE A FIRING SQUAD!
OH GOOD!—YOU'RE GONNA POUR KETCHUP ALL OVER ME!
THAT WON'T BE NECESSARY! WE'RE USING REAL BULLETS!
R-REAL BULLETS?
YOU WISH TO SEE THE CONTRACT?
NEVER MIND! I BELIEVE YOU!
WOULD YOU LIKE A LAST CIGARETTE?
NO THANKS!—I'M TRYING TO GIVE THEM UP!
MY! THE LIFE OF A MOVIE STAR IS CERTAINLY STRENUOUS! SHORT... BUT STRENUOUS!
READY... AIM!...
THAT'S THE ONE, OFFICER!
THE LITTLE SHORT GUY WITH THE WHITE FACE!
THIS MAN CLAIMS YOU CHEATED HIM WHEN YOU RENTED THIS STUDIO!
WHY, THAT'S RIDICULOUS!

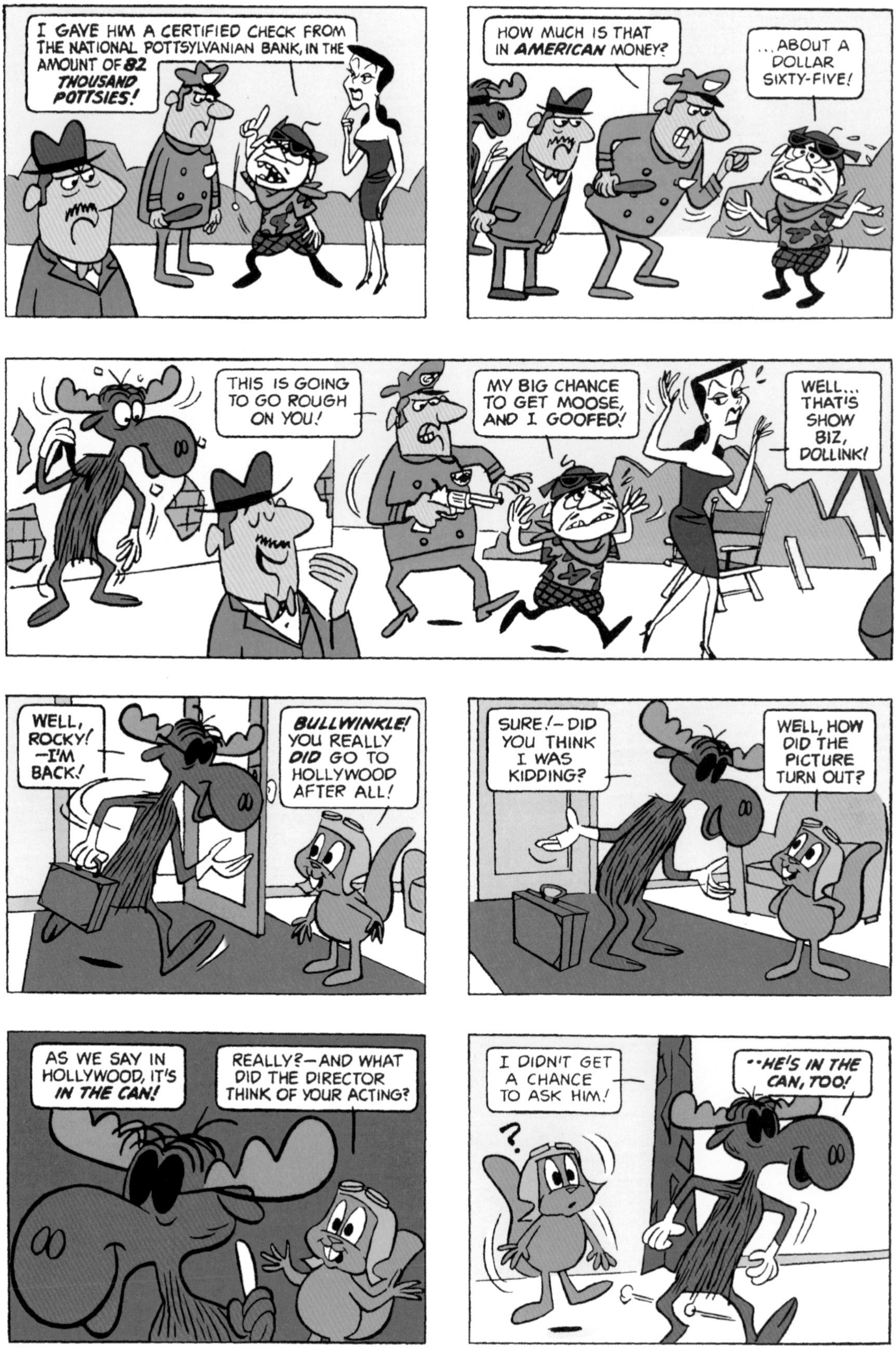
I GAVE HIM A CERTIFIED CHECK FROM THE NATIONAL POTTSYLVANIAN BANK, IN THE AMOUNT OF 82 THOUSAND POTTSIES!
HOW MUCH IS THAT IN AMERICAN MONEY?
...ABOUT A DOLLAR SIXTY-FIVE!
THIS IS GOING TO GO ROUGH ON YOU!
MY BIG CHANCE TO GET MOOSE, AND I GOOFED!
WELL... THAT'S SHOW BIZ, DOLLINK!
WELL, ROCKY! —I'M BACK!
BULLWINKLE! YOU REALLY DID GO TO HOLLYWOOD AFTER ALL!
SURE!—DID YOU THINK I WAS KIDDING?
WELL, HOW DID THE PICTURE TURN OUT?
AS WE SAY IN HOLLYWOOD, IT'S IN THE CAN!
REALLY?—AND WHAT DID THE DIRECTOR THINK OF YOUR ACTING?
I DIDN'T GET A CHANCE TO ASK HIM!
••HE'S IN THE CAN, TOO!
?

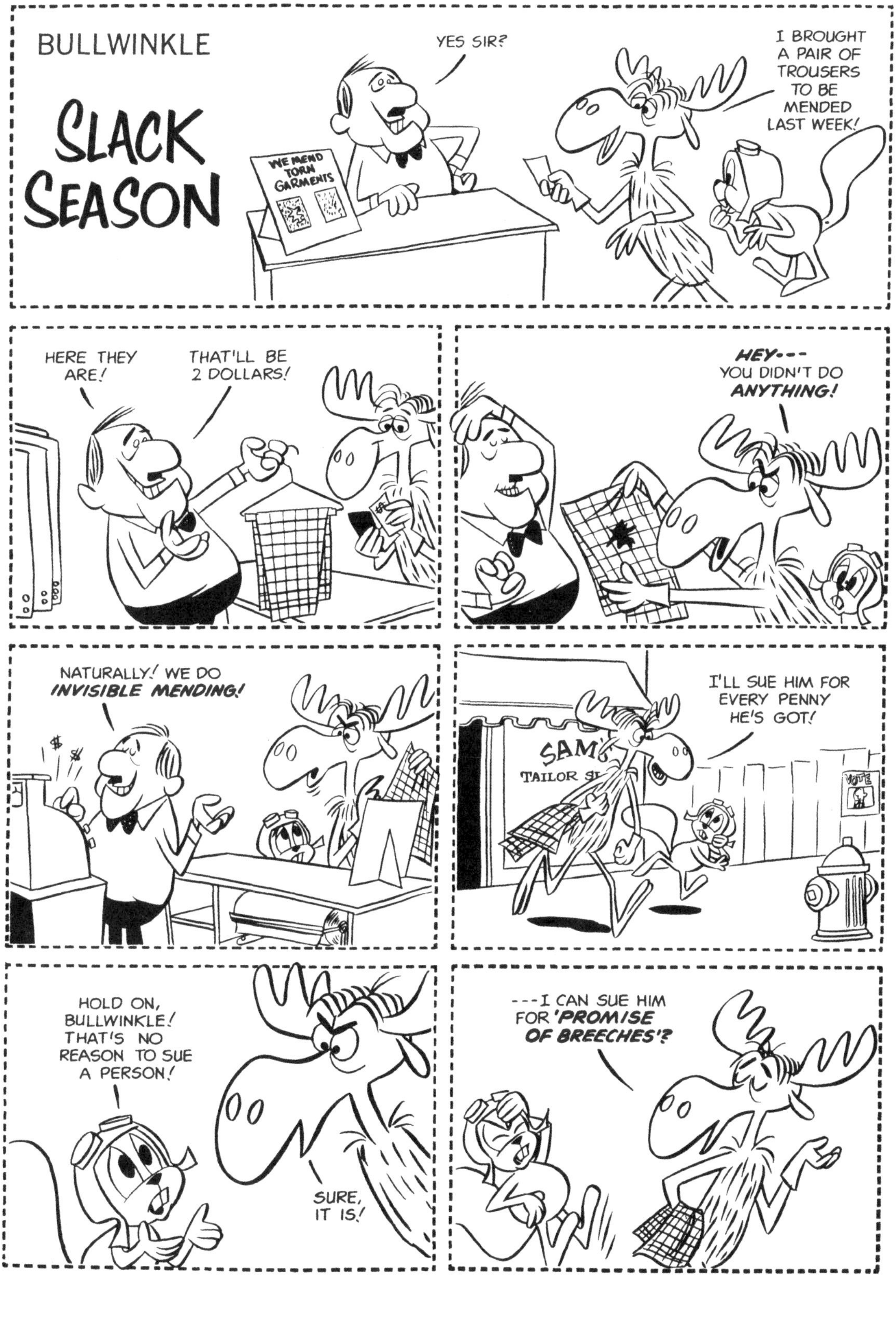
BULLWINKLE
SLACK SEASON
YES SIR?
I BROUGHT A PAIR OF TROUSERS TO BE MENDED LAST WEEK!
WE MEND TORN GARMENTS
HERE THEY ARE!
THAT'LL BE 2 DOLLARS!
HEY--- YOU DIDN'T DO ANYTHING!
NATURALLY! WE DO INVISIBLE MENDING!
I'LL SUE HIM FOR EVERY PENNY HE'S GOT!
VOTE
HOLD ON, BULLWINKLE! THAT'S NO REASON TO SUE A PERSON!
SURE, IT IS!
---I CAN SUE HIM FOR 'PROMISE OF BREECHES'?

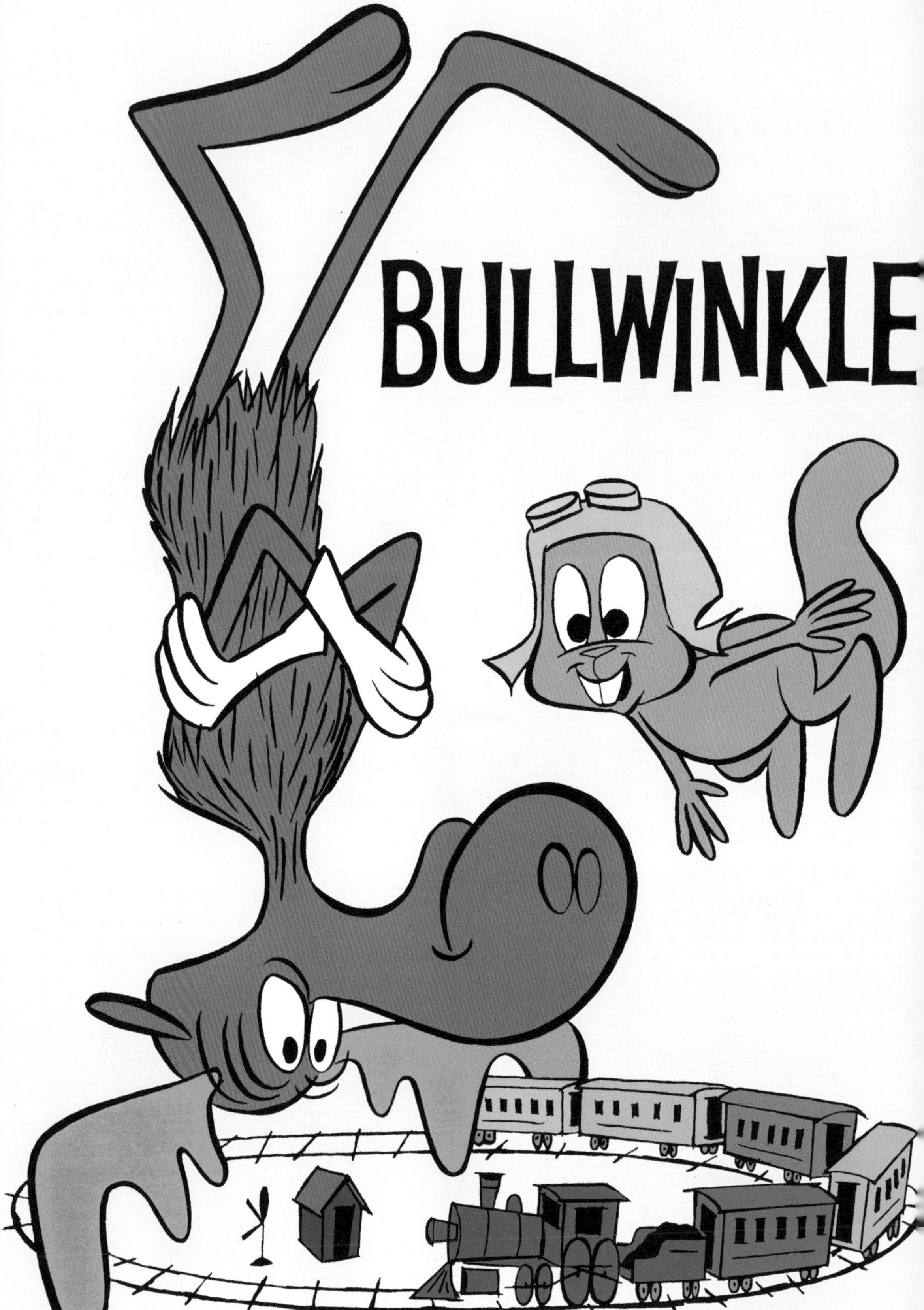
BULLWINKLE

ISSUE #2 · GOLD KEY · FEBRUARY 1963

Bullwinkle and Rocky
PHANTOM OF THE SOAP OPERA
HEY, BULLWINKLE! IT'S MISTER SOAP OF THE SOAP OPERA HOUSE! HE WANTS US TO COME DOWN AND INVESTIGATE STRANGE GOINGS-ON!
TELL HIM WE'RE HIS FOR A SONG!
SOAP OPERA HOUSE
I'LL TALK TO MISTER SOAP! SEE WHAT YOU CAN LEARN ON YOUR OWN!
I'LL MINGLE WITH THE CROWD, ROCK!
COMING SOON: Th MAGIC FLUKE
MADAME BUTTERFLY
CLEANEST SHOW IN TOWN
TONIGHT CARMEN MONOXIDE with MARIA CALLOUS
...ONLY THERE'S NO CROWD TO MINGLE WITH!
THAT'S BECAUSE NOBODY SHOWED UP! THEY'RE SCARED OF THE STRANGE GOINGS-ON!
HERE'S YOUR SEAT, SONNY BOY!
STRANGE GOINGS-ON LIKE WHAT, USHER?
LIKE YOU TUMBLING DOWN COAL CHUTE!
HA! HA! THAT'S WHAT YOU CALL CHUTE-ING THE WORKS!
CRASH! TUMBLE
BULLWINKLE #2-6211

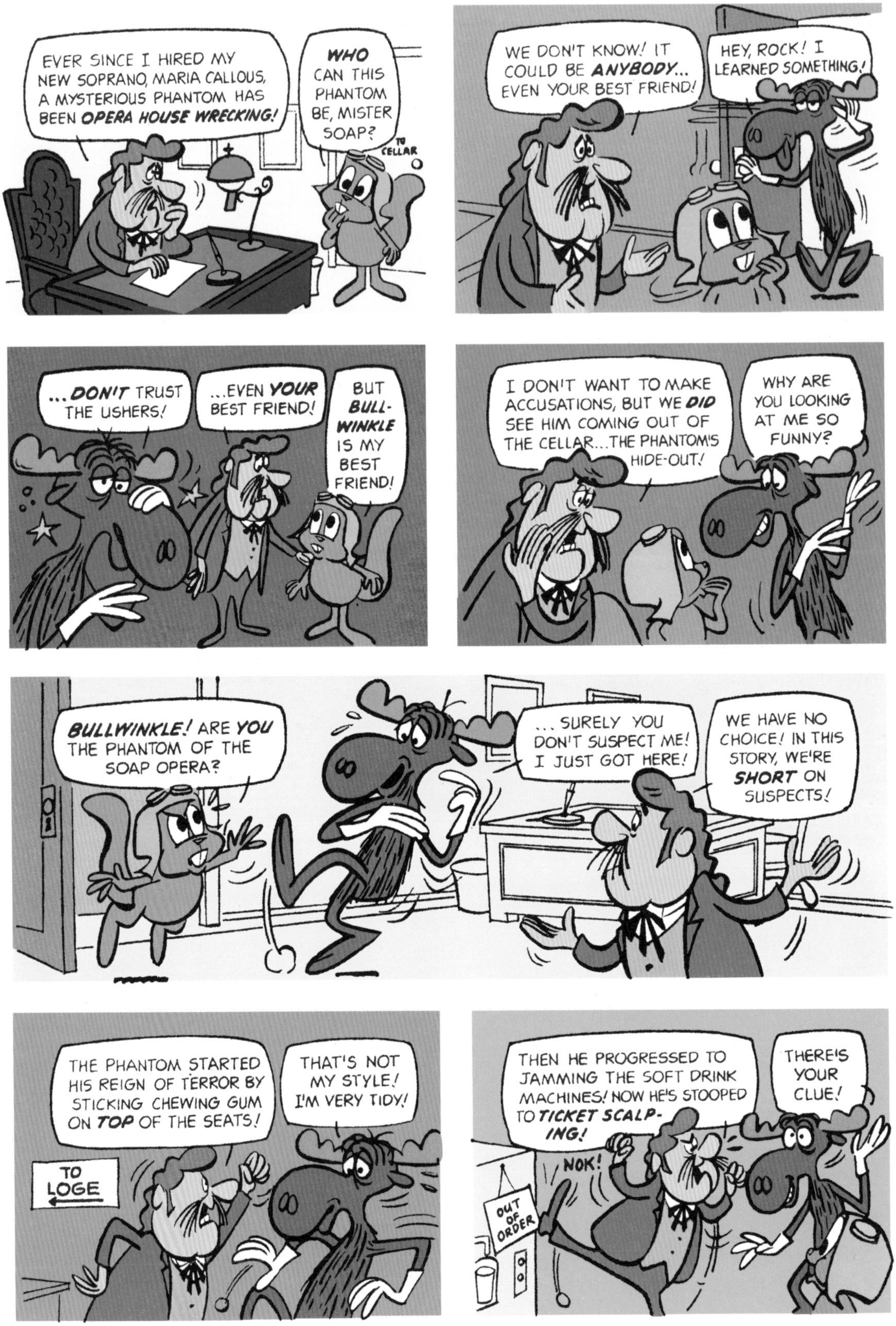
EVER SINCE I HIRED MY NEW SOPRANO, MARIA CALLOUS, A MYSTERIOUS PHANTOM HAS BEEN OPERA HOUSE WRECKING!
WHO CAN THIS PHANTOM BE, MISTER SOAP?
TO CELLAR
WE DON'T KNOW! IT COULD BE ANYBODY... EVEN YOUR BEST FRIEND!
HEY, ROCK! I LEARNED SOMETHING!
...DON'T TRUST THE USHERS!
...EVEN YOUR BEST FRIEND!
BUT BULLWINKLE IS MY BEST FRIEND!
I DON'T WANT TO MAKE ACCUSATIONS, BUT WE DID SEE HIM COMING OUT OF THE CELLAR...THE PHANTOM'S HIDE-OUT!
WHY ARE YOU LOOKING AT ME SO FUNNY?
BULLWINKLE! ARE YOU THE PHANTOM OF THE SOAP OPERA?
...SURELY YOU DON'T SUSPECT ME! I JUST GOT HERE!
WE HAVE NO CHOICE! IN THIS STORY, WE'RE SHORT ON SUSPECTS!
THE PHANTOM STARTED HIS REIGN OF TERROR BY STICKING CHEWING GUM ON TOP OF THE SEATS!
THAT'S NOT MY STYLE! I'M VERY TIDY!
TO LOGE
THEN HE PROGRESSED TO JAMMING THE SOFT DRINK MACHINES! NOW HE'S STOOPED TO TICKET SCALPING!
THERE'S YOUR CLUE!
NOK!
OUT OF ORDER

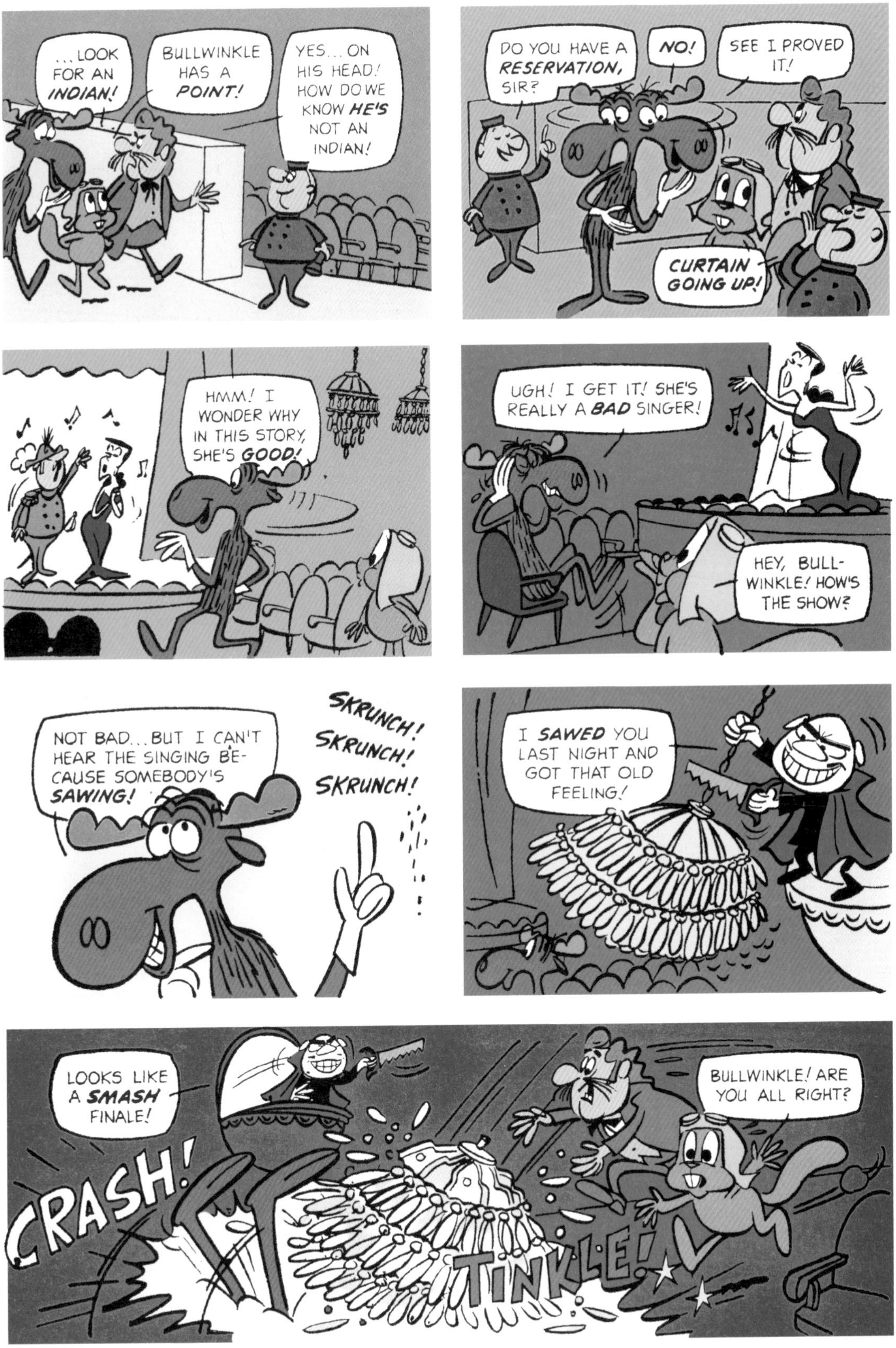
...LOOK FOR AN INDIAN!
BULLWINKLE HAS A POINT!
YES...ON HIS HEAD! HOW DO WE KNOW HE'S NOT AN INDIAN!
DO YOU HAVE A RESERVATION, SIR?
NO!
SEE I PROVED IT!
CURTAIN GOING UP!
HMM! I WONDER WHY IN THIS STORY, SHE'S GOOD!
UGH! I GET IT! SHE'S REALLY A BAD SINGER!
HEY, BULL-WINKLE! HOW'S THE SHOW?
NOT BAD...BUT I CAN'T HEAR THE SINGING BE-CAUSE SOMEBODY'S SAWING!
SKRUNCH! SKRUNCH! SKRUNCH!
I SAWED YOU LAST NIGHT AND GOT THAT OLD FEELING!
LOOKS LIKE A SMASH FINALE!
BULLWINKLE! ARE YOU ALL RIGHT?
CRASH!
TINKLE!

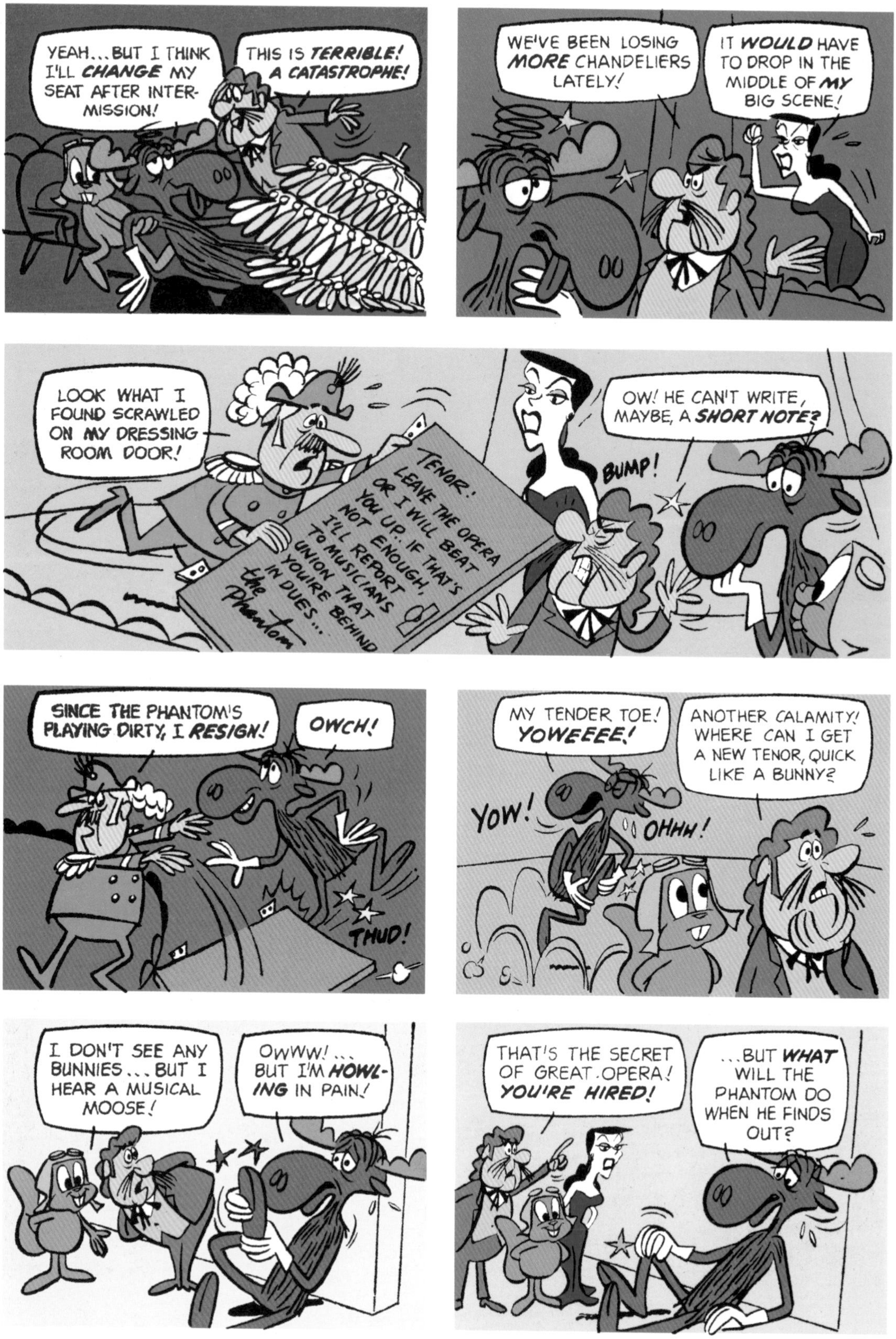

YEAH...BUT I THINK I'LL CHANGE MY SEAT AFTER INTER-MISSION!
THIS IS TERRIBLE! A CATASTROPHE!
WE'VE BEEN LOSING MORE CHANDELIERS LATELY!
IT WOULD HAVE TO DROP IN THE MIDDLE OF MY BIG SCENE!
LOOK WHAT I FOUND SCRAWLED ON MY DRESSING ROOM DOOR!
TENOR: LEAVE THE OPERA OR I WILL BEAT YOU UP. IF THAT'S NOT ENOUGH, I'LL REPORT TO MUSICIANS UNION THAT YOU'RE BEHIND IN DUES... the Phantom
OW! HE CAN'T WRITE, MAYBE, A SHORT NOTE?
BUMP!
SINCE THE PHANTOM'S PLAYING DIRTY, I RESIGN!
OWCH!
THUD!
MY TENDER TOE! YOWEEEE!
ANOTHER CALAMITY! WHERE CAN I GET A NEW TENOR, QUICK LIKE A BUNNY?
YOW!
OHHH!
I DON'T SEE ANY BUNNIES... BUT I HEAR A MUSICAL MOOSE!
OWWW!... BUT I'M HOWL-ING IN PAIN!
THAT'S THE SECRET OF GREAT OPERA! YOU'RE HIRED!
...BUT WHAT WILL THE PHANTOM DO WHEN HE FINDS OUT?

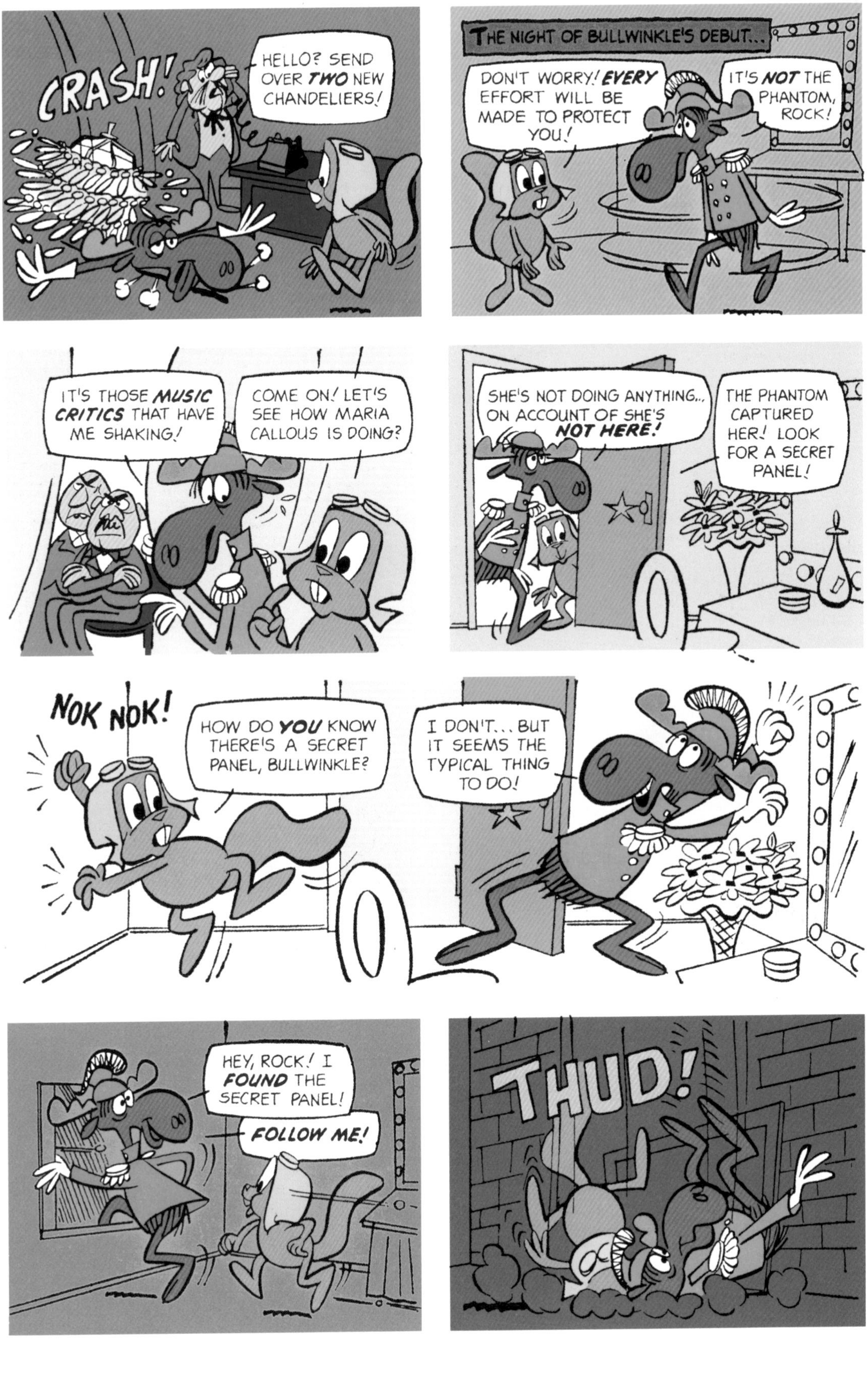
CRASH!
HELLO? SEND OVER **TWO** NEW CHANDELIERS!
THE NIGHT OF BULLWINKLE'S DEBUT...
DON'T WORRY! **EVERY** EFFORT WILL BE MADE TO PROTECT YOU!
IT'S **NOT** THE PHANTOM, ROCK!
IT'S THOSE **MUSIC CRITICS** THAT HAVE ME SHAKING!
COME ON! LET'S SEE HOW MARIA CALLOUS IS DOING?
SHE'S NOT DOING ANYTHING... ON ACCOUNT OF SHE'S **NOT HERE!**
THE PHANTOM CAPTURED HER! LOOK FOR A SECRET PANEL!
NOK NOK!
HOW DO **YOU** KNOW THERE'S A SECRET PANEL, BULLWINKLE?
I DON'T... BUT IT SEEMS THE TYPICAL THING TO DO!
HEY, ROCK! I **FOUND** THE SECRET PANEL!
FOLLOW ME!
THUD!

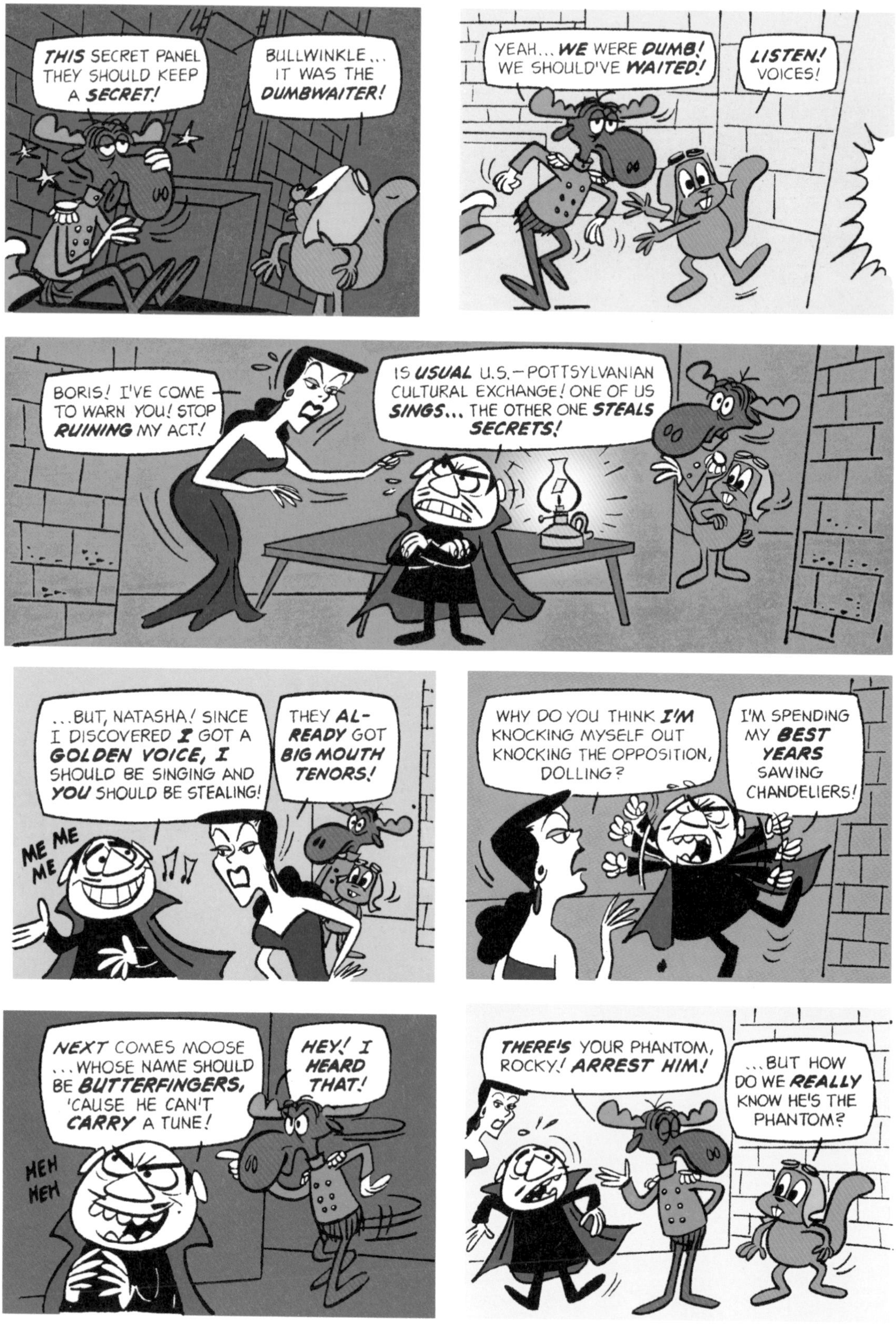
THIS SECRET PANEL THEY SHOULD KEEP A SECRET!
BULLWINKLE... IT WAS THE DUMBWAITER!
YEAH... WE WERE DUMB! WE SHOULD'VE WAITED!
LISTEN! VOICES!
BORIS! I'VE COME TO WARN YOU! STOP RUINING MY ACT!
IS USUAL U.S.–POTTSYLVANIAN CULTURAL EXCHANGE! ONE OF US SINGS... THE OTHER ONE STEALS SECRETS!
...BUT, NATASHA! SINCE I DISCOVERED I GOT A GOLDEN VOICE, I SHOULD BE SINGING AND YOU SHOULD BE STEALING!
THEY AL-READY GOT BIG MOUTH TENORS!
ME ME ME
WHY DO YOU THINK I'M KNOCKING MYSELF OUT KNOCKING THE OPPOSITION, DOLLING?
I'M SPENDING MY BEST YEARS SAWING CHANDELIERS!
NEXT COMES MOOSE ...WHOSE NAME SHOULD BE BUTTERFINGERS, 'CAUSE HE CAN'T CARRY A TUNE!
HEY! I HEARD THAT!
MEH MEH
THERE'S YOUR PHANTOM, ROCKY! ARREST HIM!
...BUT HOW DO WE REALLY KNOW HE'S THE PHANTOM?

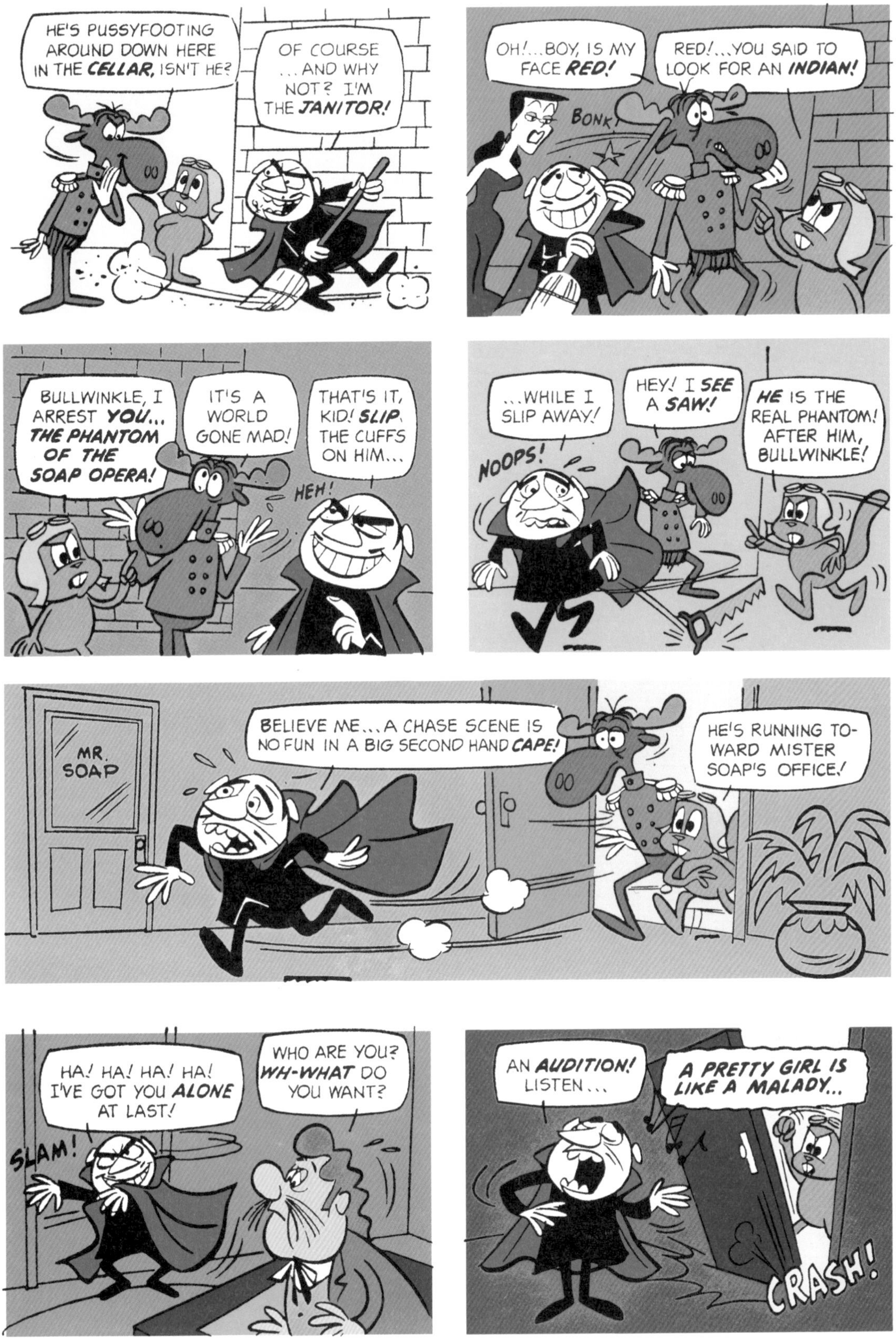
HE'S PUSSYFOOTING AROUND DOWN HERE IN THE CELLAR, ISN'T HE?
OF COURSE ... AND WHY NOT? I'M THE JANITOR!
OH!...BOY, IS MY FACE RED!
RED!...YOU SAID TO LOOK FOR AN INDIAN!
BONK!
BULLWINKLE, I ARREST YOU... THE PHANTOM OF THE SOAP OPERA!
IT'S A WORLD GONE MAD!
THAT'S IT, KID! SLIP THE CUFFS ON HIM...
HEH!
...WHILE I SLIP AWAY!
HEY! I SEE A SAW!
HE IS THE REAL PHANTOM! AFTER HIM, BULLWINKLE!
NOOPS!
MR. SOAP
BELIEVE ME... A CHASE SCENE IS NO FUN IN A BIG SECOND HAND CAPE!
HE'S RUNNING TOWARD MISTER SOAP'S OFFICE!
HA! HA! HA! HA! I'VE GOT YOU ALONE AT LAST!
WHO ARE YOU? WH-WHAT DO YOU WANT?
SLAM!
AN AUDITION! LISTEN...
A PRETTY GIRL IS LIKE A MALADY...
CRASH!

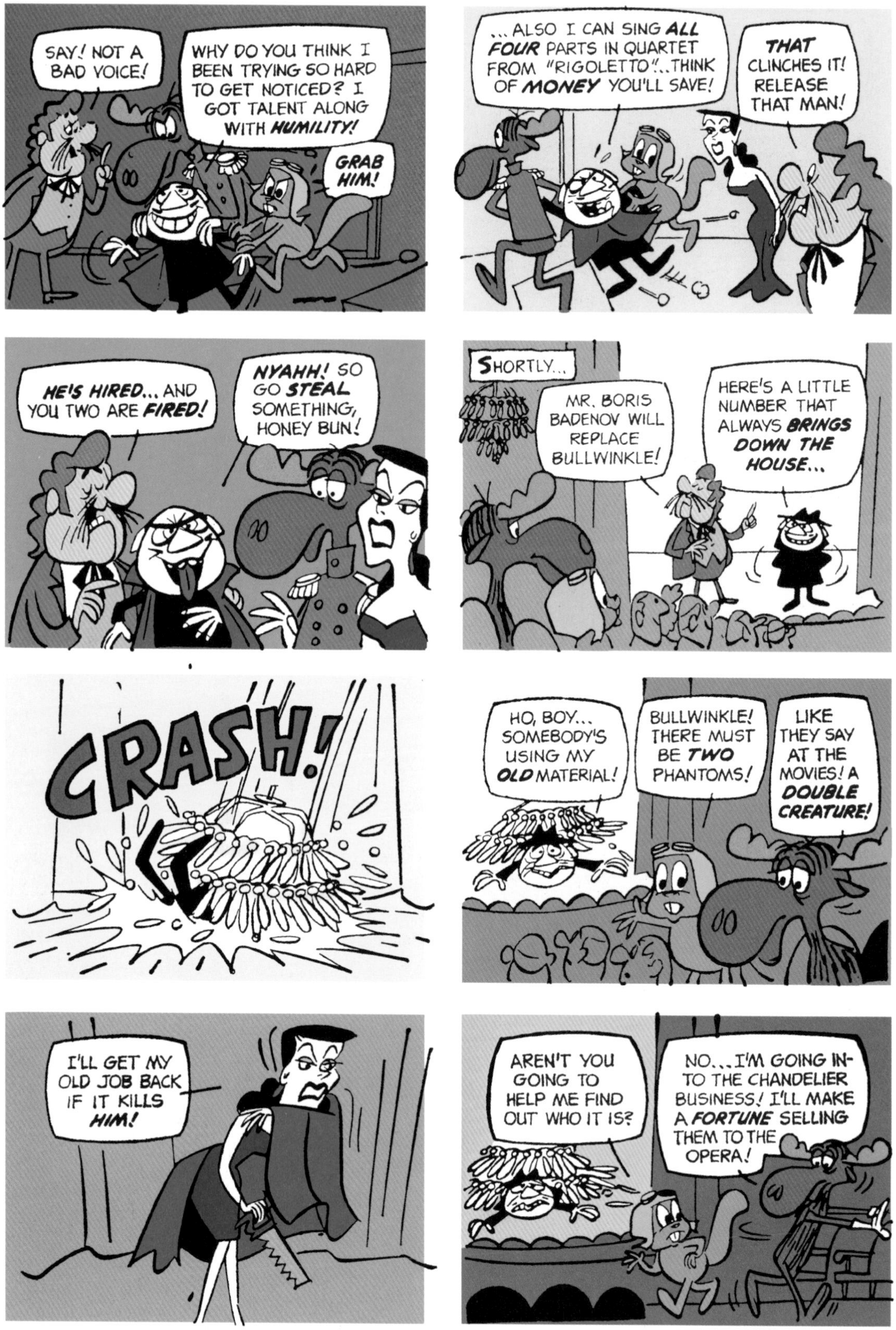
SAY! NOT A BAD VOICE!
WHY DO YOU THINK I BEEN TRYING SO HARD TO GET NOTICED? I GOT TALENT ALONG WITH HUMILITY!
GRAB HIM!
...ALSO I CAN SING ALL FOUR PARTS IN QUARTET FROM "RIGOLETTO"...THINK OF MONEY YOU'LL SAVE!
THAT CLINCHES IT! RELEASE THAT MAN!
HE'S HIRED... AND YOU TWO ARE FIRED!
NYAHH! SO GO STEAL SOMETHING, HONEY BUN!
SHORTLY...
MR. BORIS BADENOV WILL REPLACE BULLWINKLE!
HERE'S A LITTLE NUMBER THAT ALWAYS BRINGS DOWN THE HOUSE...
CRASH!
HO, BOY... SOMEBODY'S USING MY OLD MATERIAL!
BULLWINKLE! THERE MUST BE TWO PHANTOMS!
LIKE THEY SAY AT THE MOVIES! A DOUBLE CREATURE!
I'LL GET MY OLD JOB BACK IF IT KILLS HIM!
AREN'T YOU GOING TO HELP ME FIND OUT WHO IT IS?
NO...I'M GOING INTO THE CHANDELIER BUSINESS! I'LL MAKE A FORTUNE SELLING THEM TO THE OPERA!

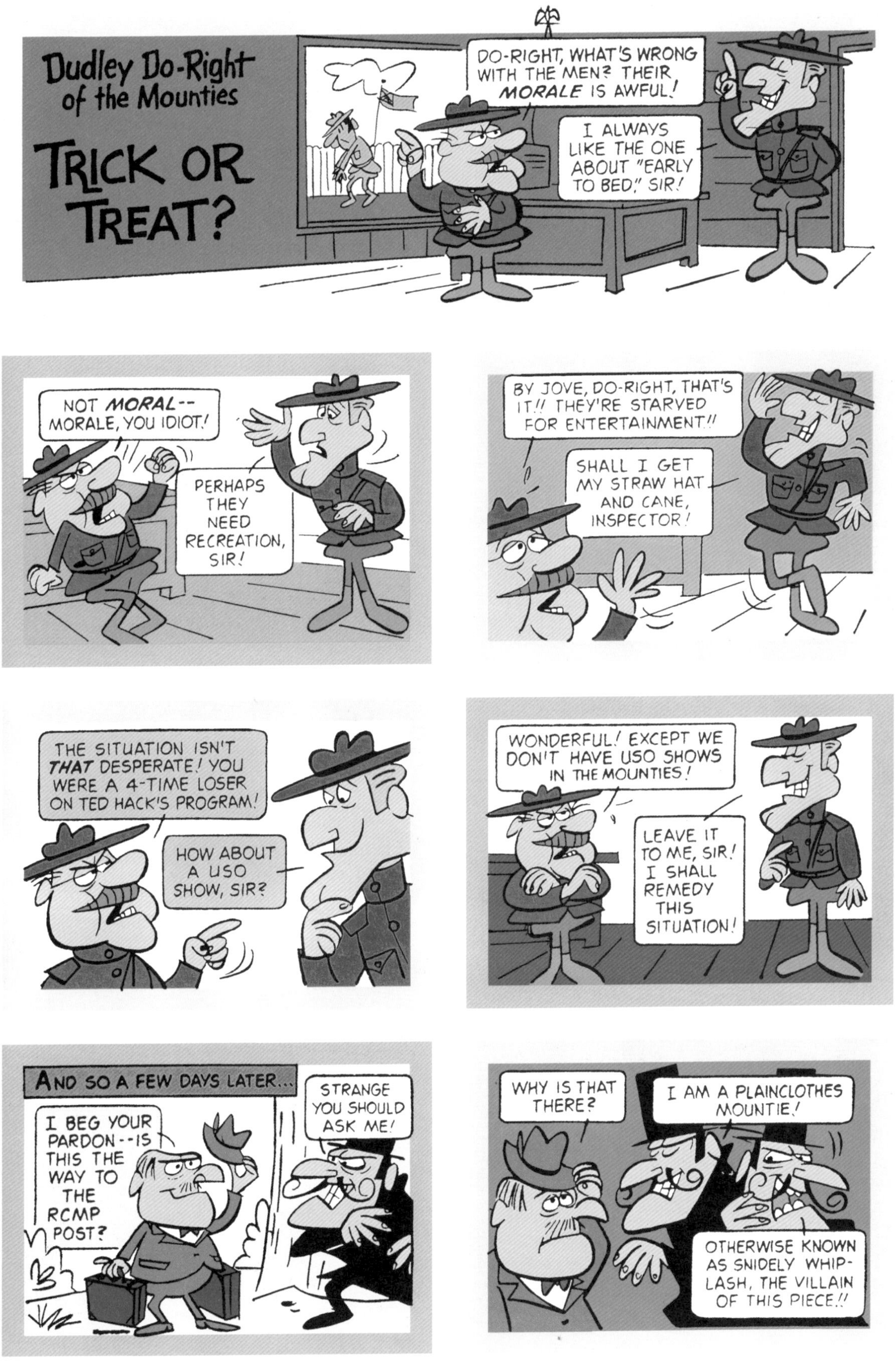

Dudley Do-Right of the Mounties
TRICK OR TREAT?
DO-RIGHT, WHAT'S WRONG WITH THE MEN? THEIR MORALE IS AWFUL!
I ALWAYS LIKE THE ONE ABOUT "EARLY TO BED," SIR!
NOT MORAL-- MORALE, YOU IDIOT!
PERHAPS THEY NEED RECREATION, SIR!
BY JOVE, DO-RIGHT, THAT'S IT!! THEY'RE STARVED FOR ENTERTAINMENT!!
SHALL I GET MY STRAW HAT AND CANE, INSPECTOR!
THE SITUATION ISN'T THAT DESPERATE! YOU WERE A 4-TIME LOSER ON TED HACK'S PROGRAM!
HOW ABOUT A USO SHOW, SIR?
WONDERFUL! EXCEPT WE DON'T HAVE USO SHOWS IN THE MOUNTIES!
LEAVE IT TO ME, SIR! I SHALL REMEDY THIS SITUATION!
AND SO A FEW DAYS LATER...
I BEG YOUR PARDON--IS THIS THE WAY TO THE RCMP POST?
STRANGE YOU SHOULD ASK ME!
WHY IS THAT THERE?
I AM A PLAINCLOTHES MOUNTIE!
OTHERWISE KNOWN AS SNIDELY WHIP-LASH, THE VILLAIN OF THIS PIECE!!

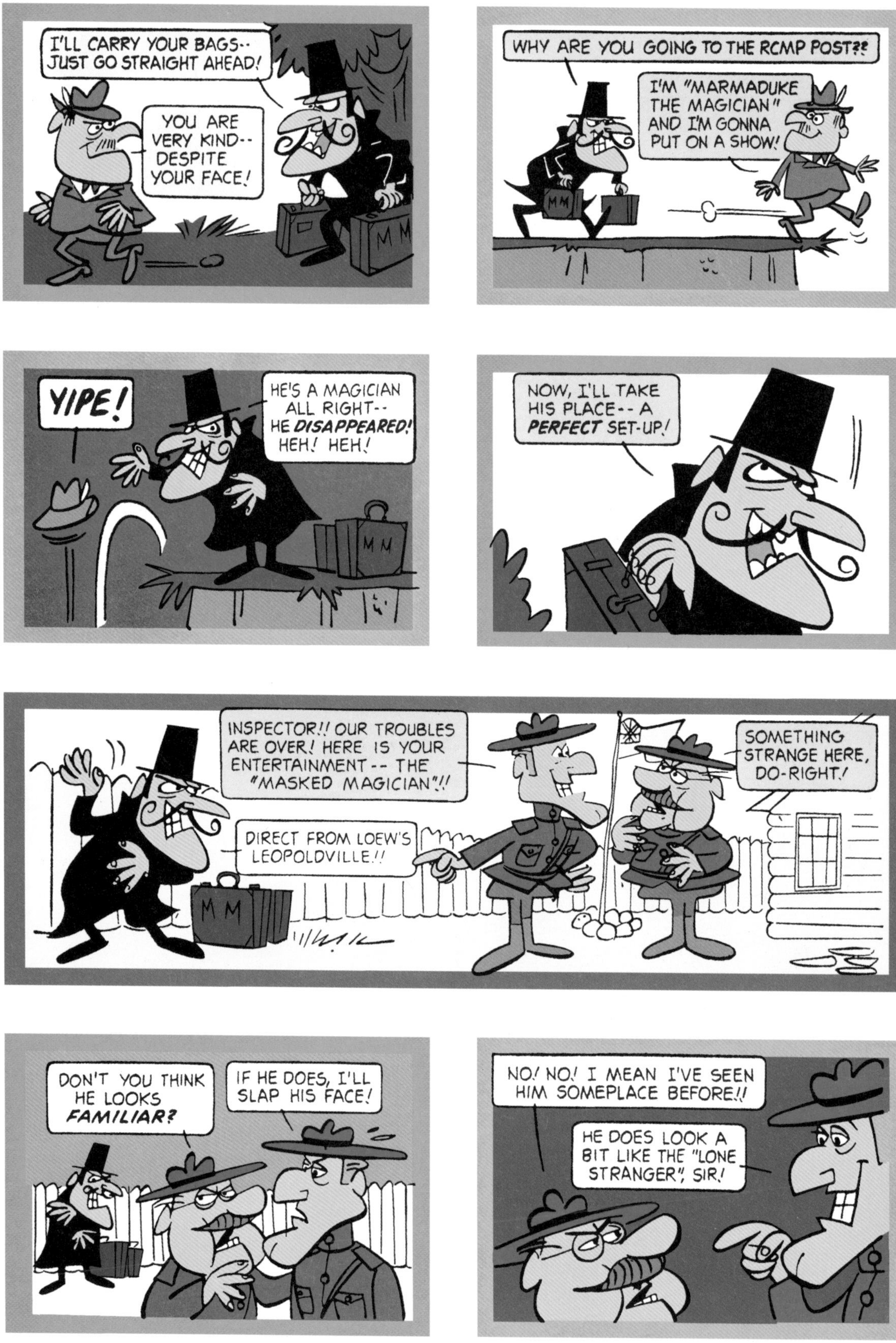
I'LL CARRY YOUR BAGS-- JUST GO STRAIGHT AHEAD!
YOU ARE VERY KIND-- DESPITE YOUR FACE!
WHY ARE YOU GOING TO THE RCMP POST??
I'M "MARMADUKE THE MAGICIAN" AND I'M GONNA PUT ON A SHOW!
MM
YIPE!
HE'S A MAGICIAN ALL RIGHT-- HE DISAPPEARED! HEH! HEH!
MM
NOW, I'LL TAKE HIS PLACE-- A PERFECT SET-UP!
INSPECTOR!! OUR TROUBLES ARE OVER! HERE IS YOUR ENTERTAINMENT-- THE "MASKED MAGICIAN"!!
DIRECT FROM LOEW'S LEOPOLDVILLE!!
SOMETHING STRANGE HERE, DO-RIGHT!
MM
DON'T YOU THINK HE LOOKS FAMILIAR?
IF HE DOES, I'LL SLAP HIS FACE!
NO! NO! I MEAN I'VE SEEN HIM SOMEPLACE BEFORE!!
HE DOES LOOK A BIT LIKE THE "LONE STRANGER", SIR!

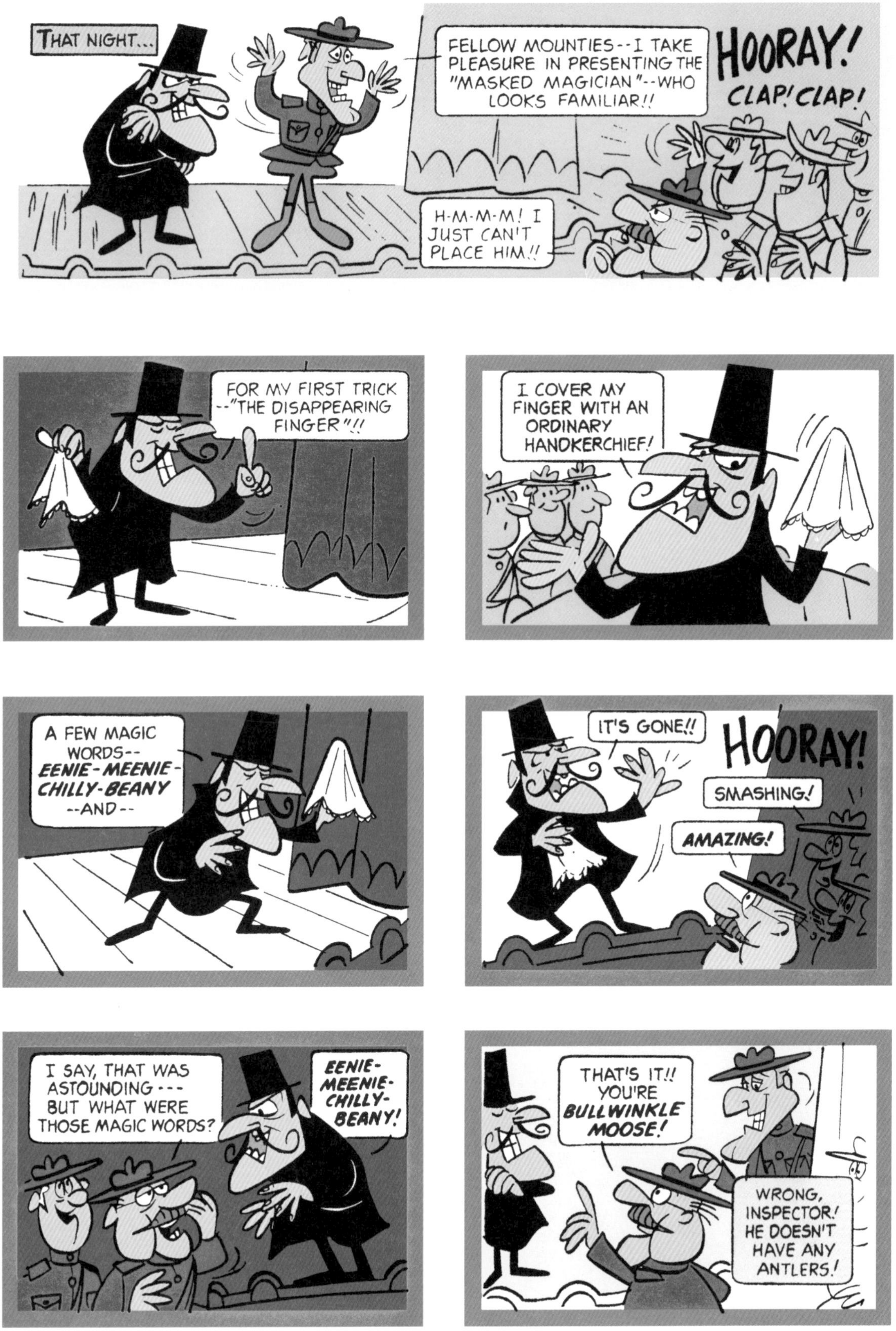
THAT NIGHT...
FELLOW MOUNTIES--I TAKE PLEASURE IN PRESENTING THE "MASKED MAGICIAN"--WHO LOOKS FAMILIAR!!
HOORAY!
CLAP! CLAP!
H-M-M-M! I JUST CAN'T PLACE HIM!!
FOR MY FIRST TRICK--"THE DISAPPEARING FINGER"!!
I COVER MY FINGER WITH AN ORDINARY HANDKERCHIEF!
A FEW MAGIC WORDS-- EENIE-MEENIE-CHILLY-BEANY --AND--
IT'S GONE!!
HOORAY!
SMASHING!
AMAZING!
I SAY, THAT WAS ASTOUNDING--- BUT WHAT WERE THOSE MAGIC WORDS?
EENIE-MEENIE-CHILLY-BEANY!
THAT'S IT!! YOU'RE BULLWINKLE MOOSE!
WRONG, INSPECTOR! HE DOESN'T HAVE ANY ANTLERS!

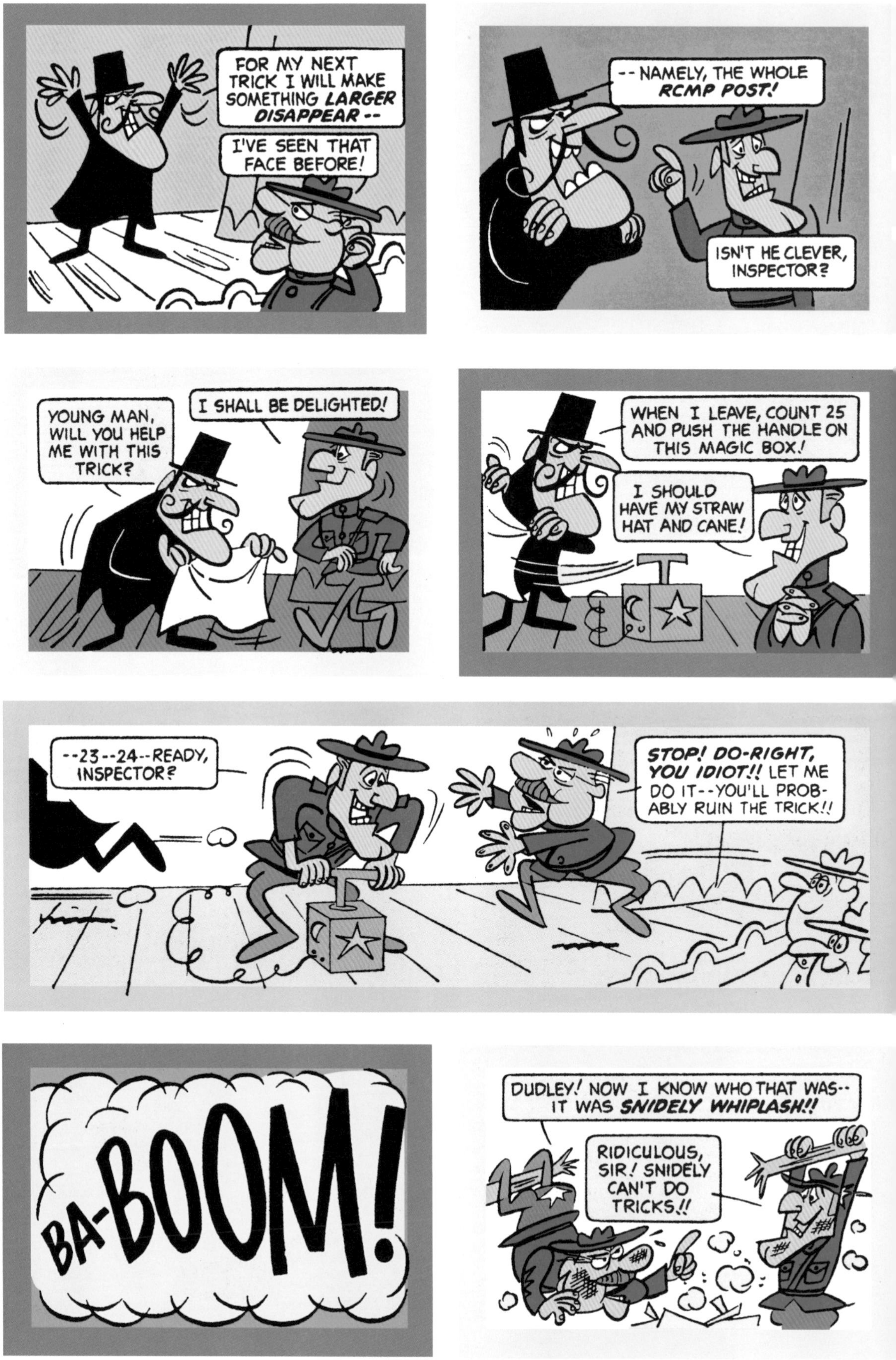

FOR MY NEXT TRICK I WILL MAKE SOMETHING LARGER DISAPPEAR --
I'VE SEEN THAT FACE BEFORE!
-- NAMELY, THE WHOLE RCMP POST!
ISN'T HE CLEVER, INSPECTOR?
YOUNG MAN, WILL YOU HELP ME WITH THIS TRICK?
I SHALL BE DELIGHTED!
WHEN I LEAVE, COUNT 25 AND PUSH THE HANDLE ON THIS MAGIC BOX!
I SHOULD HAVE MY STRAW HAT AND CANE!
--23--24--READY, INSPECTOR?
STOP! DO-RIGHT, YOU IDIOT!! LET ME DO IT--YOU'LL PROBABLY RUIN THE TRICK!!
BA-BOOM!
DUDLEY! NOW I KNOW WHO THAT WAS-- IT WAS SNIDELY WHIPLASH!!
RIDICULOUS, SIR! SNIDELY CAN'T DO TRICKS!!

WOODCHOPPER'S BALL

a fractured fairy tale

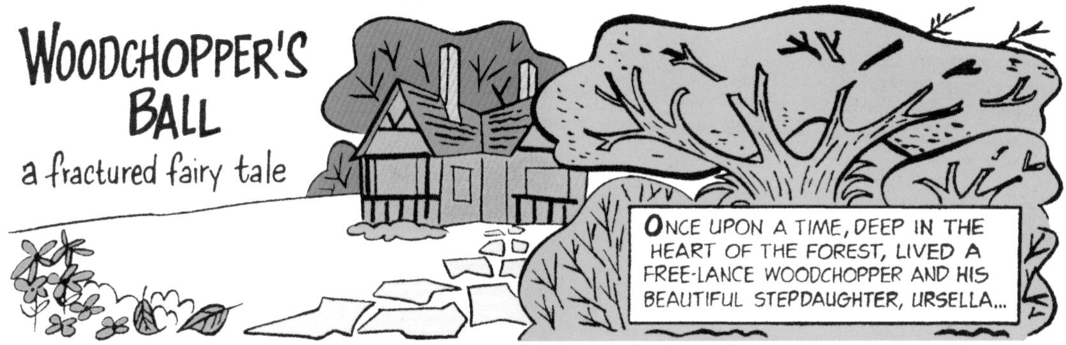
ONCE UPON A TIME, DEEP IN THE HEART OF THE FOREST, LIVED A FREE-LANCE WOODCHOPPER AND HIS BEAUTIFUL STEPDAUGHTER, URSELLA...

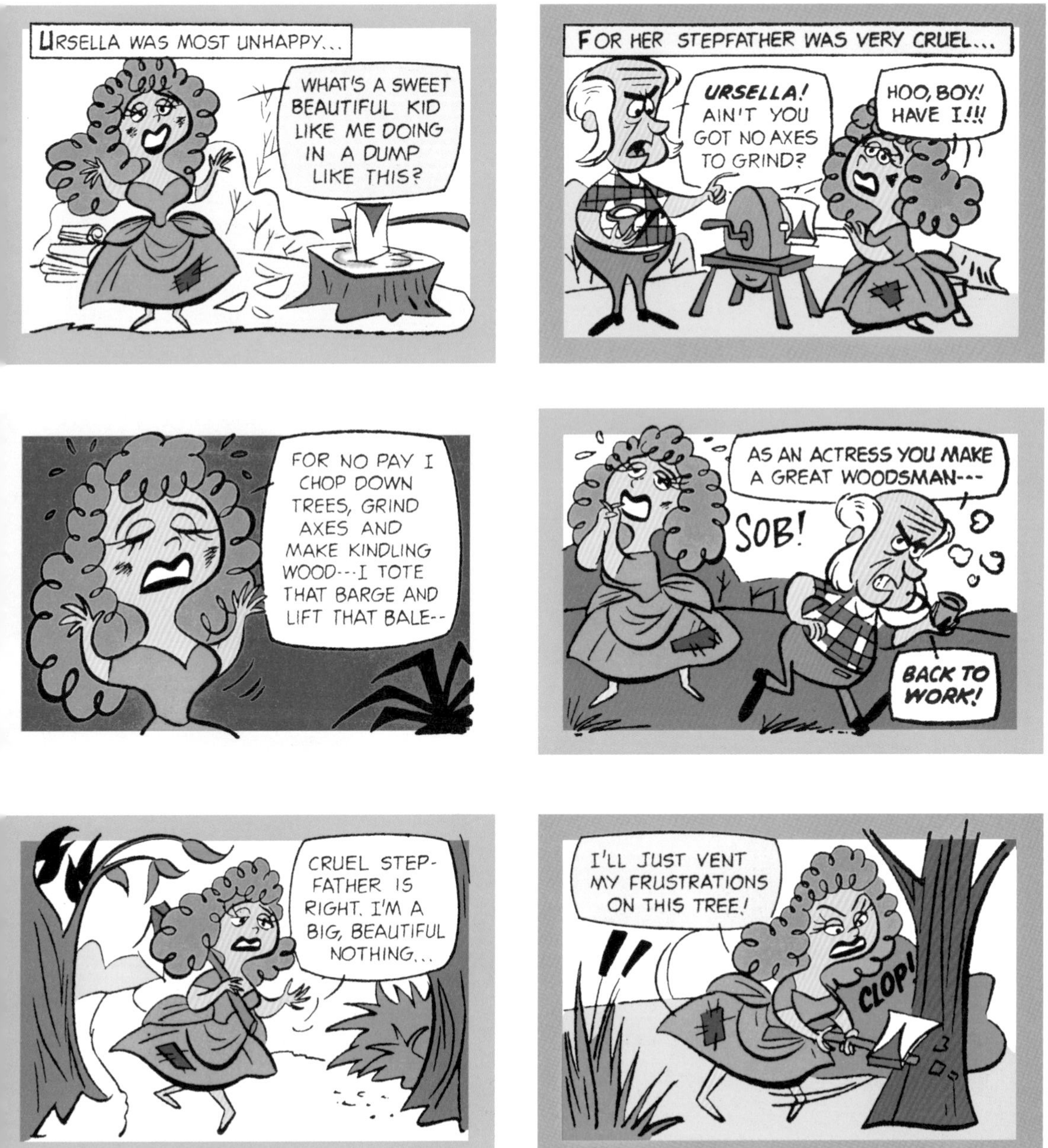
URSELLA WAS MOST UNHAPPY...
WHAT'S A SWEET BEAUTIFUL KID LIKE ME DOING IN A DUMP LIKE THIS?
FOR HER STEPFATHER WAS VERY CRUEL...
URSELLA! AIN'T YOU GOT NO AXES TO GRIND?
HOO, BOY! HAVE I!!!
FOR NO PAY I CHOP DOWN TREES, GRIND AXES AND MAKE KINDLING WOOD---I TOTE THAT BARGE AND LIFT THAT BALE--
SOB!
AS AN ACTRESS YOU MAKE A GREAT WOODSMAN---
BACK TO WORK!
CRUEL STEP-FATHER IS RIGHT. I'M A BIG, BEAUTIFUL NOTHING...
I'LL JUST VENT MY FRUSTRATIONS ON THIS TREE!
CLOP!

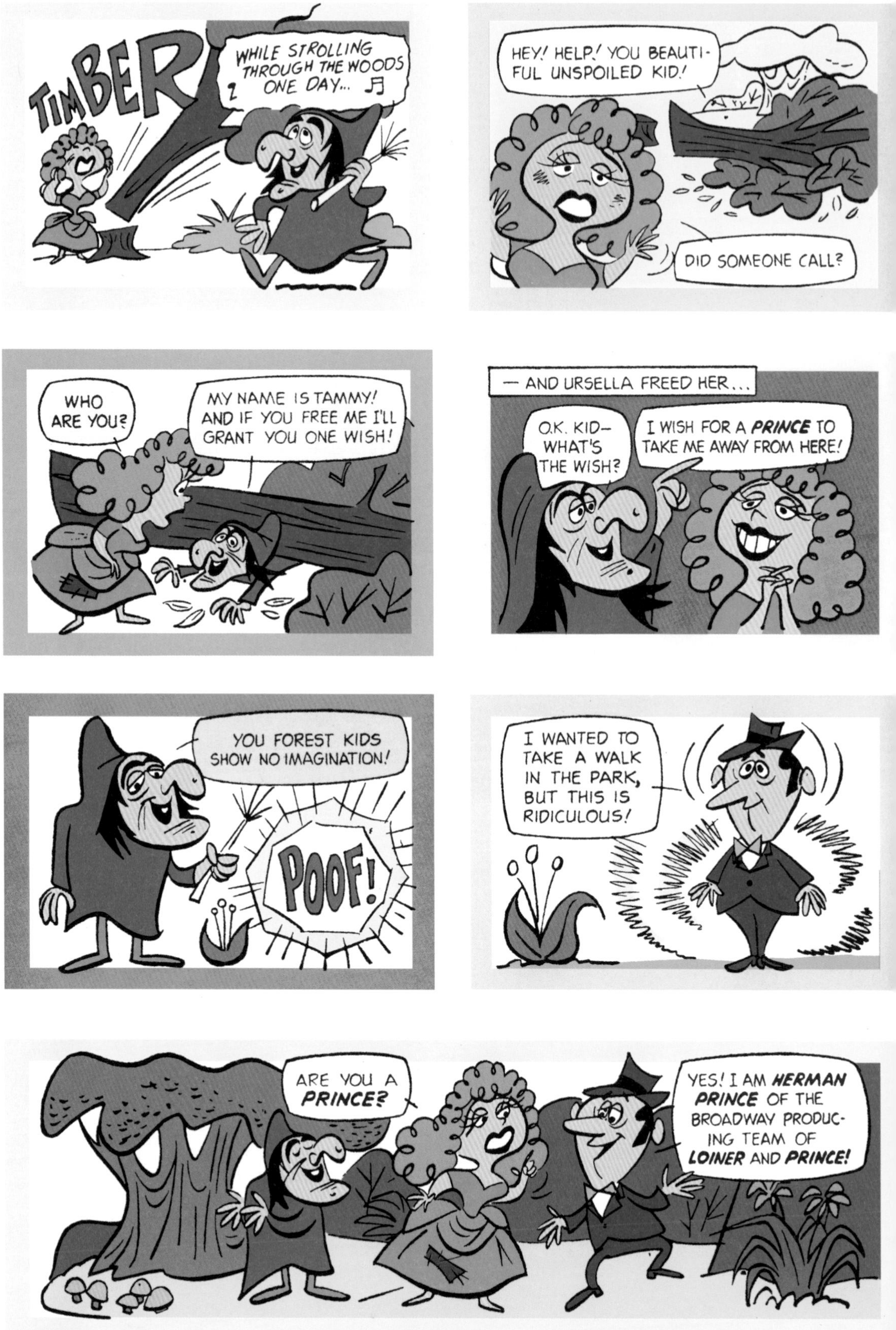
TIMBER
WHILE STROLLING THROUGH THE WOODS ONE DAY...
HEY! HELP! YOU BEAUTIFUL UNSPOILED KID!
DID SOMEONE CALL?
WHO ARE YOU?
MY NAME IS TAMMY! AND IF YOU FREE ME I'LL GRANT YOU ONE WISH!
— AND URSELLA FREED HER...
O.K. KID— WHAT'S THE WISH?
I WISH FOR A PRINCE TO TAKE ME AWAY FROM HERE!
YOU FOREST KIDS SHOW NO IMAGINATION!
POOF!
I WANTED TO TAKE A WALK IN THE PARK, BUT THIS IS RIDICULOUS!
ARE YOU A PRINCE?
YES! I AM HERMAN PRINCE OF THE BROADWAY PRODUCING TEAM OF LOINER AND PRINCE!

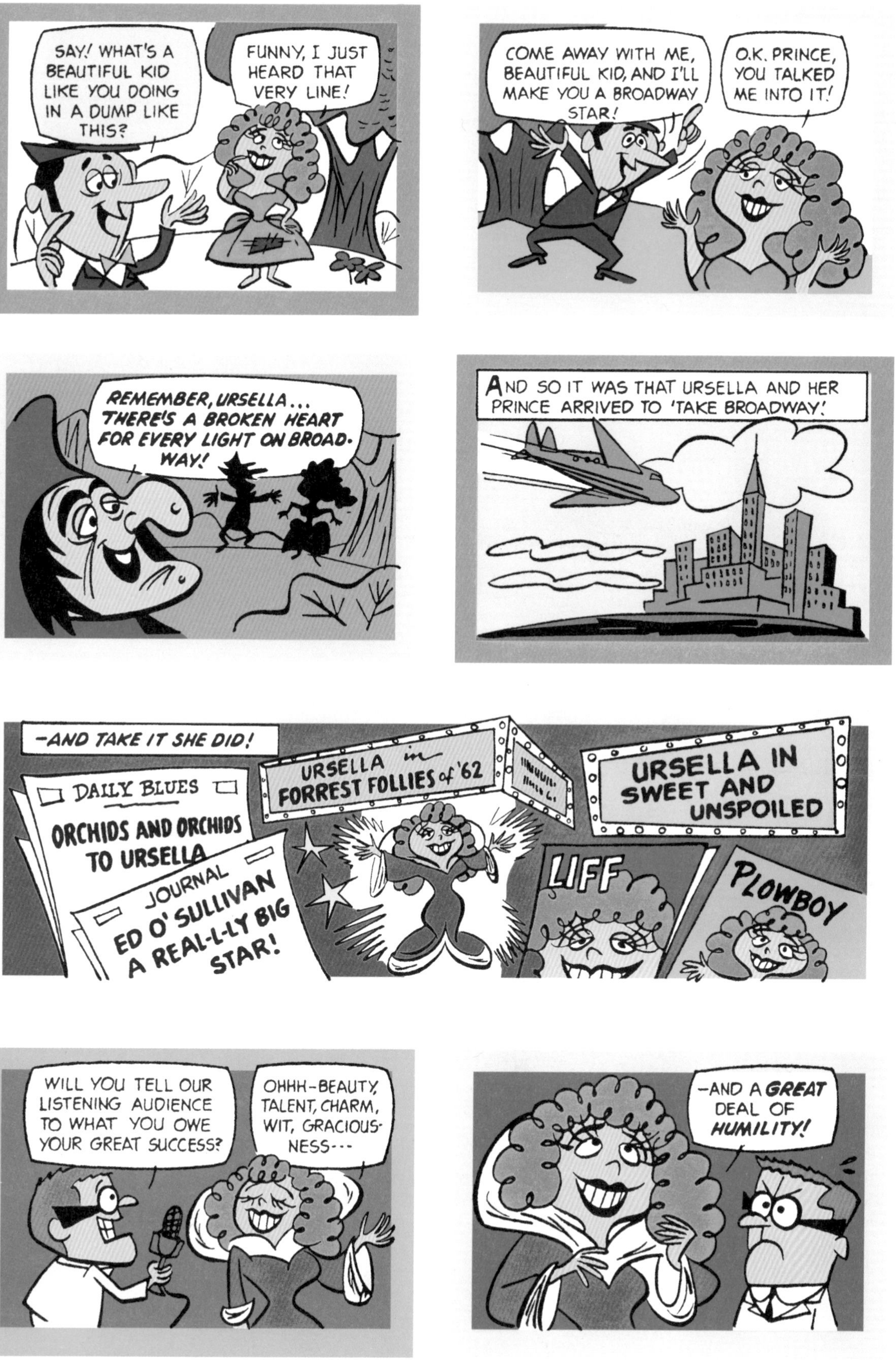
SAY! WHAT'S A BEAUTIFUL KID LIKE YOU DOING IN A DUMP LIKE THIS?
FUNNY, I JUST HEARD THAT VERY LINE!
COME AWAY WITH ME, BEAUTIFUL KID, AND I'LL MAKE YOU A BROADWAY STAR!
O.K. PRINCE, YOU TALKED ME INTO IT!
REMEMBER, URSELLA... THERE'S A BROKEN HEART FOR EVERY LIGHT ON BROADWAY!
AND SO IT WAS THAT URSELLA AND HER PRINCE ARRIVED TO 'TAKE BROADWAY.'
—AND TAKE IT SHE DID!
DAILY BLUES
ORCHIDS AND ORCHIDS TO URSELLA
JOURNAL
ED O' SULLIVAN A REAL-L-LY BIG STAR!
URSELLA in FORREST FOLLIES of '62
URSELLA IN SWEET AND UNSPOILED
LIFF
PLOWBOY
WILL YOU TELL OUR LISTENING AUDIENCE TO WHAT YOU OWE YOUR GREAT SUCCESS?
OHHH—BEAUTY, TALENT, CHARM, WIT, GRACIOUSNESS---
—AND A GREAT DEAL OF HUMILITY!

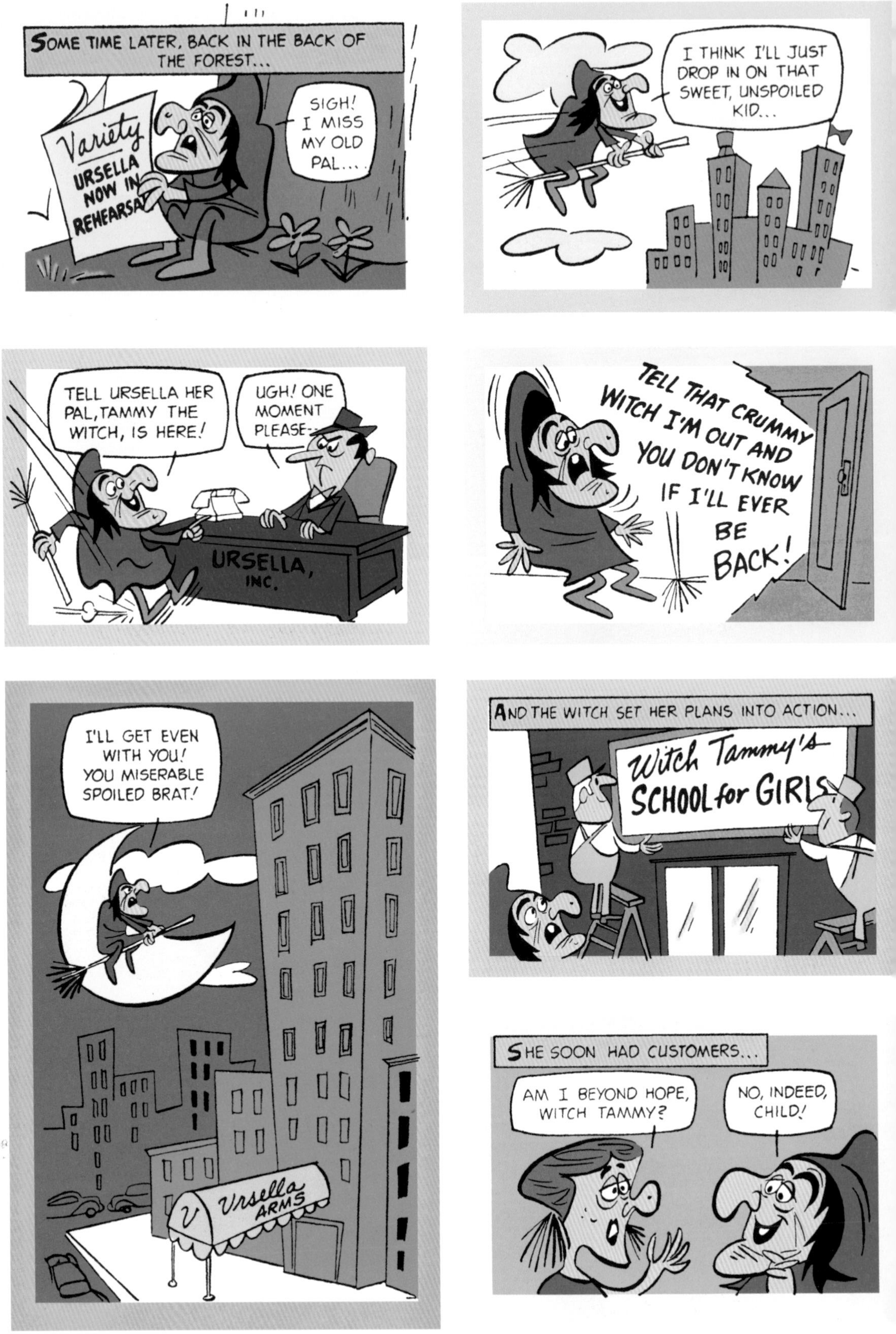
SOME TIME LATER, BACK IN THE BACK OF THE FOREST...
Variety
URSELLA NOW IN REHEARSA
SIGH! I MISS MY OLD PAL...
I THINK I'LL JUST DROP IN ON THAT SWEET, UNSPOILED KID...
TELL URSELLA HER PAL, TAMMY THE WITCH, IS HERE!
UGH! ONE MOMENT PLEASE--
URSELLA, INC.
TELL THAT CRUMMY WITCH I'M OUT AND YOU DON'T KNOW IF I'LL EVER BE BACK!
I'LL GET EVEN WITH YOU! YOU MISERABLE SPOILED BRAT!
Ursella ARMS
AND THE WITCH SET HER PLANS INTO ACTION...
Witch Tammy's SCHOOL for GIRLS
SHE SOON HAD CUSTOMERS...
AM I BEYOND HOPE, WITCH TAMMY?
NO, INDEED, CHILD!

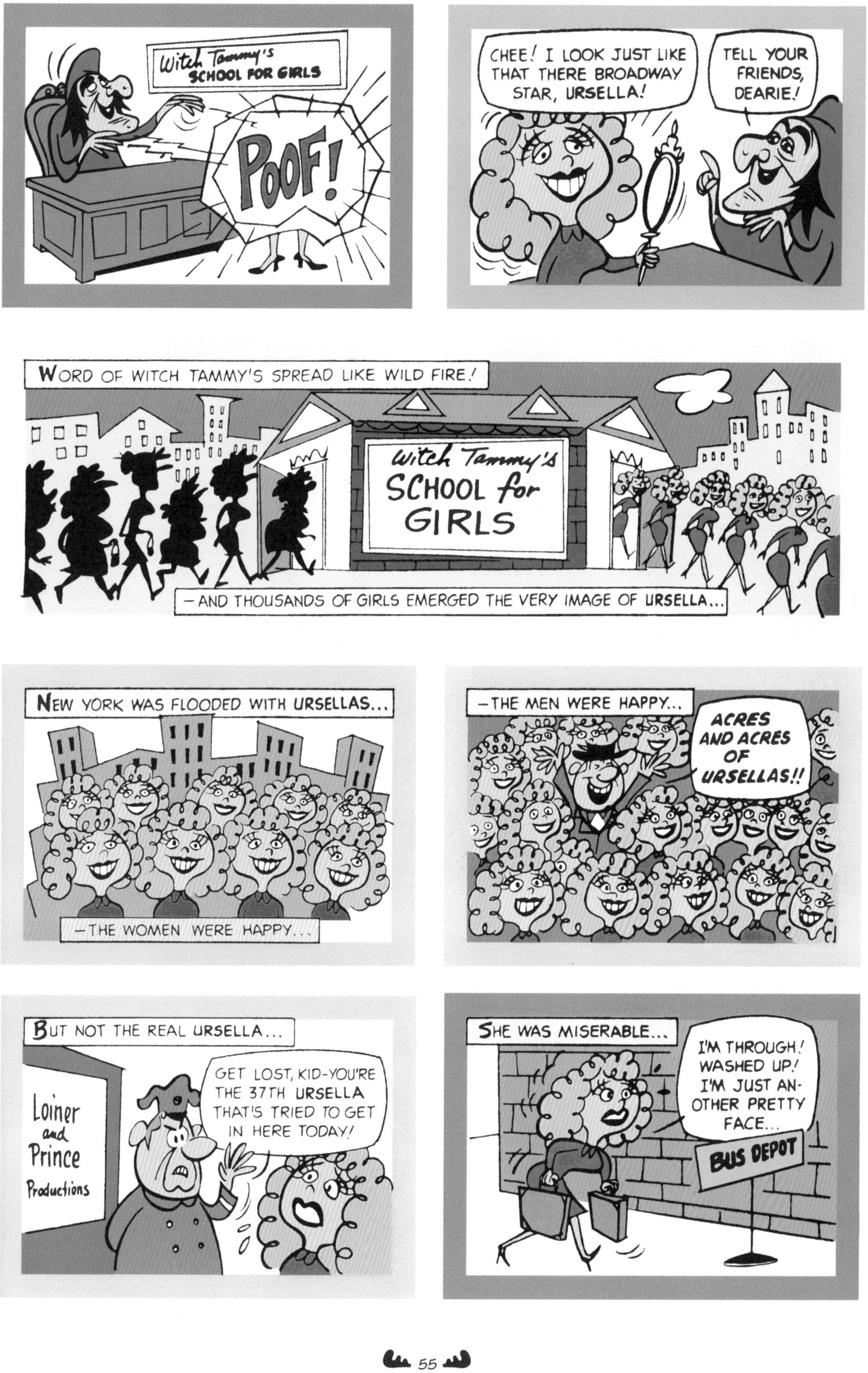
Witch Tammy's SCHOOL FOR GIRLS
POOF!
CHEE! I LOOK JUST LIKE THAT THERE BROADWAY STAR, URSELLA!
TELL YOUR FRIENDS, DEARIE!
WORD OF WITCH TAMMY'S SPREAD LIKE WILD FIRE!
Witch Tammy's SCHOOL for GIRLS
—AND THOUSANDS OF GIRLS EMERGED THE VERY IMAGE OF URSELLA...
NEW YORK WAS FLOODED WITH URSELLAS...
—THE WOMEN WERE HAPPY...
—THE MEN WERE HAPPY...
ACRES AND ACRES OF URSELLAS!!
BUT NOT THE REAL URSELLA...
Loiner and Prince Productions
GET LOST, KID-YOU'RE THE 37TH URSELLA THAT'S TRIED TO GET IN HERE TODAY!
SHE WAS MISERABLE...
I'M THROUGH! WASHED UP! I'M JUST AN-OTHER PRETTY FACE...
BUS DEPOT

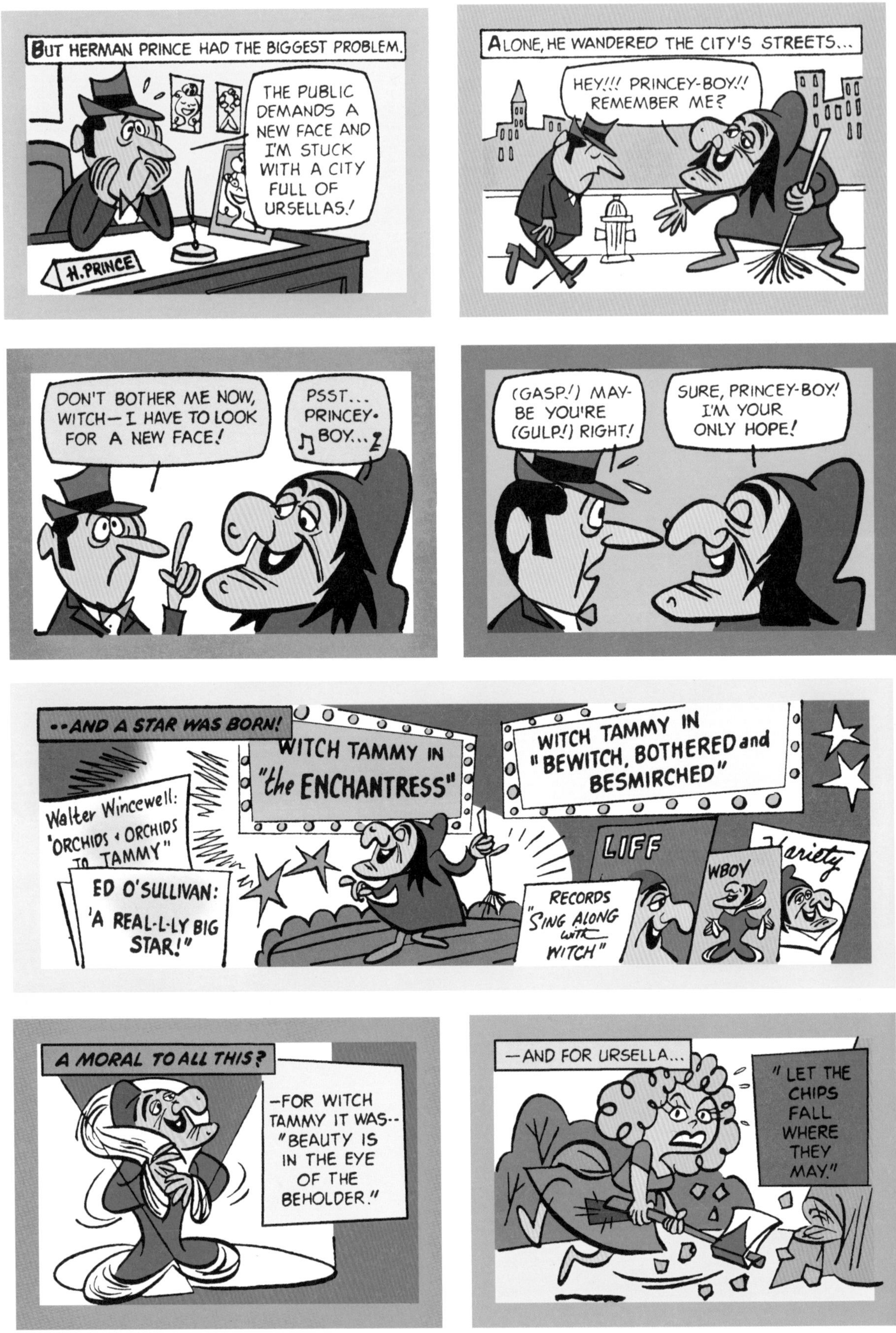
BUT HERMAN PRINCE HAD THE BIGGEST PROBLEM.
THE PUBLIC DEMANDS A NEW FACE AND I'M STUCK WITH A CITY FULL OF URSELLAS!
H. PRINCE
ALONE, HE WANDERED THE CITY'S STREETS...
HEY!!! PRINCEY-BOY!! REMEMBER ME?
DON'T BOTHER ME NOW, WITCH—I HAVE TO LOOK FOR A NEW FACE!
PSST... PRINCEY-BOY...
(GASP!) MAY-BE YOU'RE (GULP!) RIGHT!
SURE, PRINCEY-BOY! I'M YOUR ONLY HOPE!
--AND A STAR WAS BORN!
WITCH TAMMY IN "the ENCHANTRESS"
WITCH TAMMY IN "BEWITCH, BOTHERED and BESMIRCHED"
Walter Wincewell: 'ORCHIDS & ORCHIDS TO TAMMY"
ED O'SULLIVAN: 'A REAL-L-LY BIG STAR!"
LIFF
WBOY
Variety
RECORDS "SING ALONG with WITCH"
A MORAL TO ALL THIS?
—FOR WITCH TAMMY IT WAS-- "BEAUTY IS IN THE EYE OF THE BEHOLDER."
—AND FOR URSELLA...
"LET THE CHIPS FALL WHERE THEY MAY."

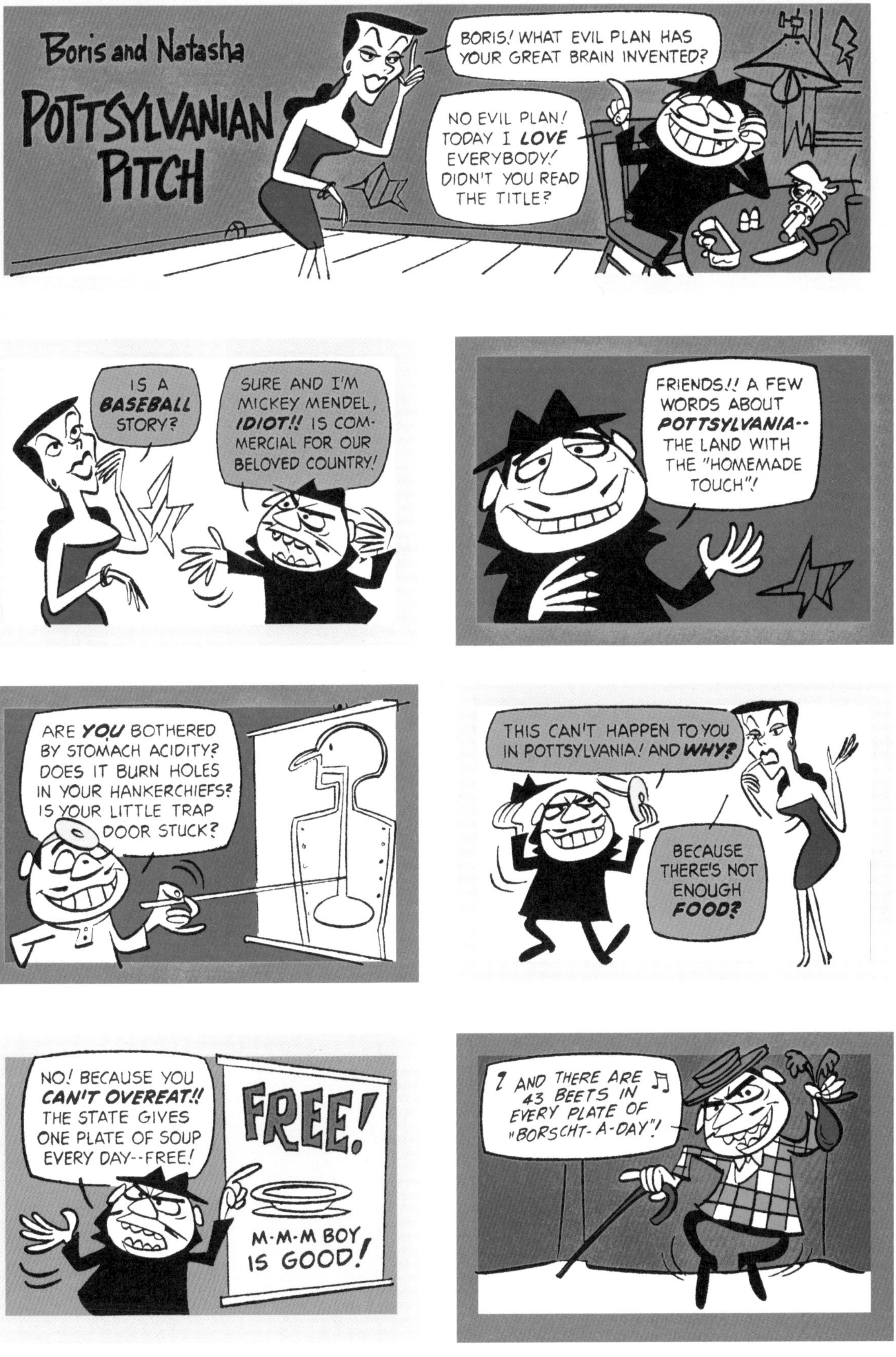

Boris and Natasha
POTTSYLVANIAN PITCH
BORIS! WHAT EVIL PLAN HAS YOUR GREAT BRAIN INVENTED?
NO EVIL PLAN! TODAY I **LOVE** EVERYBODY! DIDN'T YOU READ THE TITLE?
IS A **BASEBALL** STORY?
SURE AND I'M MICKEY MENDEL, **IDIOT!!** IS COMMERCIAL FOR OUR BELOVED COUNTRY!
FRIENDS!! A FEW WORDS ABOUT **POTTSYLVANIA**--THE LAND WITH THE "HOMEMADE TOUCH"!
ARE **YOU** BOTHERED BY STOMACH ACIDITY? DOES IT BURN HOLES IN YOUR HANKERCHIEFS? IS YOUR LITTLE TRAP DOOR STUCK?
THIS CAN'T HAPPEN TO YOU IN POTTSYLVANIA! AND **WHY?**
BECAUSE THERE'S NOT ENOUGH **FOOD?**
NO! BECAUSE YOU **CAN'T OVEREAT!!** THE STATE GIVES ONE PLATE OF SOUP EVERY DAY--FREE!
FREE!
M-M-M BOY IS GOOD!
♪ AND THERE ARE 43 BEETS IN EVERY PLATE OF "BORSCHT-A-DAY"! ♫

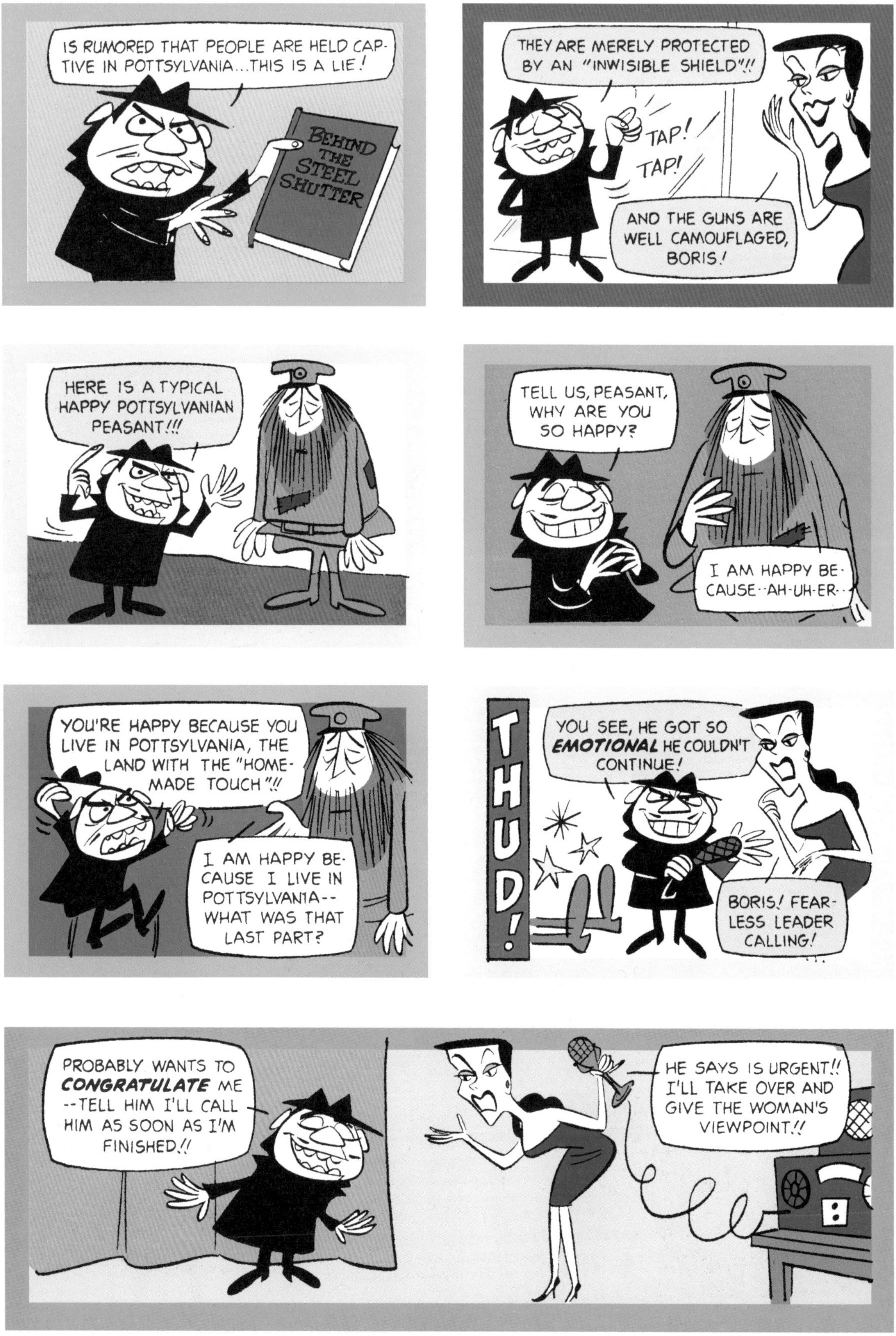

IS RUMORED THAT PEOPLE ARE HELD CAPTIVE IN POTTSYLVANIA...THIS IS A LIE!
BEHIND THE STEEL SHUTTER
THEY ARE MERELY PROTECTED BY AN "INWISIBLE SHIELD"!!
TAP! TAP!
AND THE GUNS ARE WELL CAMOUFLAGED, BORIS!
HERE IS A TYPICAL HAPPY POTTSYLVANIAN PEASANT!!!
TELL US, PEASANT, WHY ARE YOU SO HAPPY?
I AM HAPPY BECAUSE--AH-UH-ER--
YOU'RE HAPPY BECAUSE YOU LIVE IN POTTSYLVANIA, THE LAND WITH THE "HOME-MADE TOUCH"!!
I AM HAPPY BECAUSE I LIVE IN POTTSYLVANIA-- WHAT WAS THAT LAST PART?
THUD!
YOU SEE, HE GOT SO **EMOTIONAL** HE COULDN'T CONTINUE!
BORIS! FEARLESS LEADER CALLING!
PROBABLY WANTS TO **CONGRATULATE** ME --TELL HIM I'LL CALL HIM AS SOON AS I'M FINISHED!!
HE SAYS IS URGENT!! I'LL TAKE OVER AND GIVE THE WOMAN'S VIEWPOINT!!

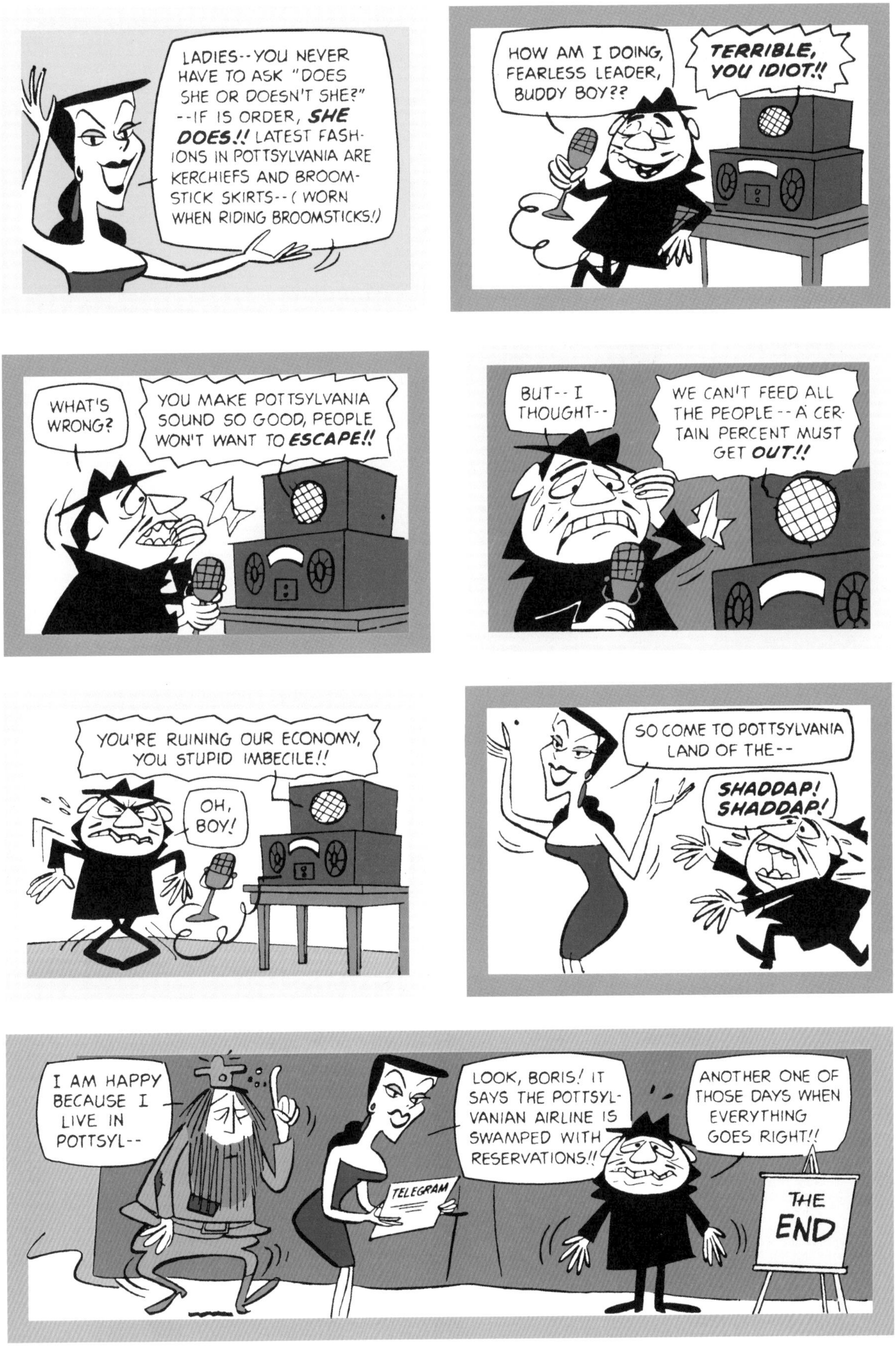
LADIES--YOU NEVER HAVE TO ASK "DOES SHE OR DOESN'T SHE?" --IF IS ORDER, SHE DOES!! LATEST FASHIONS IN POTTSYLVANIA ARE KERCHIEFS AND BROOMSTICK SKIRTS--(WORN WHEN RIDING BROOMSTICKS!)
HOW AM I DOING, FEARLESS LEADER, BUDDY BOY??
TERRIBLE, YOU IDIOT!!
WHAT'S WRONG?
YOU MAKE POTTSYLVANIA SOUND SO GOOD, PEOPLE WON'T WANT TO ESCAPE!!
BUT--I THOUGHT--
WE CAN'T FEED ALL THE PEOPLE--A CERTAIN PERCENT MUST GET OUT!!
YOU'RE RUINING OUR ECONOMY, YOU STUPID IMBECILE!!
OH, BOY!
SO COME TO POTTSYLVANIA LAND OF THE--
SHADDAP! SHADDAP!
I AM HAPPY BECAUSE I LIVE IN POTTSYL--
LOOK, BORIS! IT SAYS THE POTTSYLVANIAN AIRLINE IS SWAMPED WITH RESERVATIONS!!
TELEGRAM
ANOTHER ONE OF THOSE DAYS WHEN EVERYTHING GOES RIGHT!!
THE END

Ridiculous isn't it?

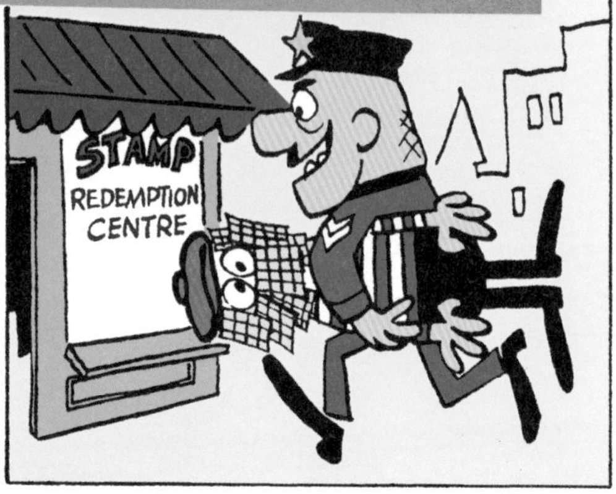
STAMP
REDEMPTION
CENTRE

Folks in California have a great sense of humor. When a gunman held up a grocery store in Fresno, he masked his face with trading stamps. So help me!

In case you've been wondering, an ornithologist from the Smithsonian Institution has just discovered that the Purple Grackle preens its feathers with an acid extracted from walnuts!

Jellyfish are 95 per cent water and 4 per cent salt. But Japanese folks have found a way of drying, preserving and cooking the remaining 1 per cent.

Here is the latest item from the proposed national budget! Scientists are asking for $1,200,000 to find out why infant monkeys love their mothers.

Over in England there's a fellow who played the piano for more than five days, non-stop! He played more than 3,000 pieces and claims he broke the record.

You kiddies who are interested in becoming astronauts better read this item first: A California scientist is suggesting that astronauts be frozen in suspended animation for long trips to other galaxies.

Among the many products they make from wood are yeast, alcohol, glue, plastics—and even vanilla flavoring for ice-cream! Better watch out for splinters the next time you order a sundae.

Pigs have their troubles too! College researchers report that worried porkers can get ulcers just like us humans.

One drugstore chain guarantees speedy service at its lunch counters. If they don't serve your order within four minutes your meal is on the house!

Most of the world's milk comes from cows but investigators tell us that mankind also used milk from horses, sheep, goats, donkeys, reindeer, camels, llamas, yaks, and even water buffaloes!

Fellow taxpayers arise! A late bulletin from Washington reports that the Treasury Department is burning money. They often destroy $25,000,000 a day in worn-out bills, of course.

When New York hired a new traffic commissioner, he left the family car back in Baltimore! He claimed there was no place to park in the big town.

So you think the auto has replaced the horse, hey? Well, latest reports reveal that auto traffic in the heart of London averages six miles per hour. Back in 1908 horse-drawn traffic moved at better than 14 mph! How about that!

A restaurant in Alaska features a bowl of clam chowder for 50 cents! You can get a "Texas-sized" cup of chowder for 25 cents.

To protect its messengers against attack a London banking house is supplying them with shock-resistant, dent-proof derbies.

An Arkansas drive-in movie has installed a battery of washing machines! Customers can watch the feature and then pick up their laundry after the show.

An English dental expert has estimated that 20 per cent of all kids walk around with their mouths open! No wonder it's so noisy.

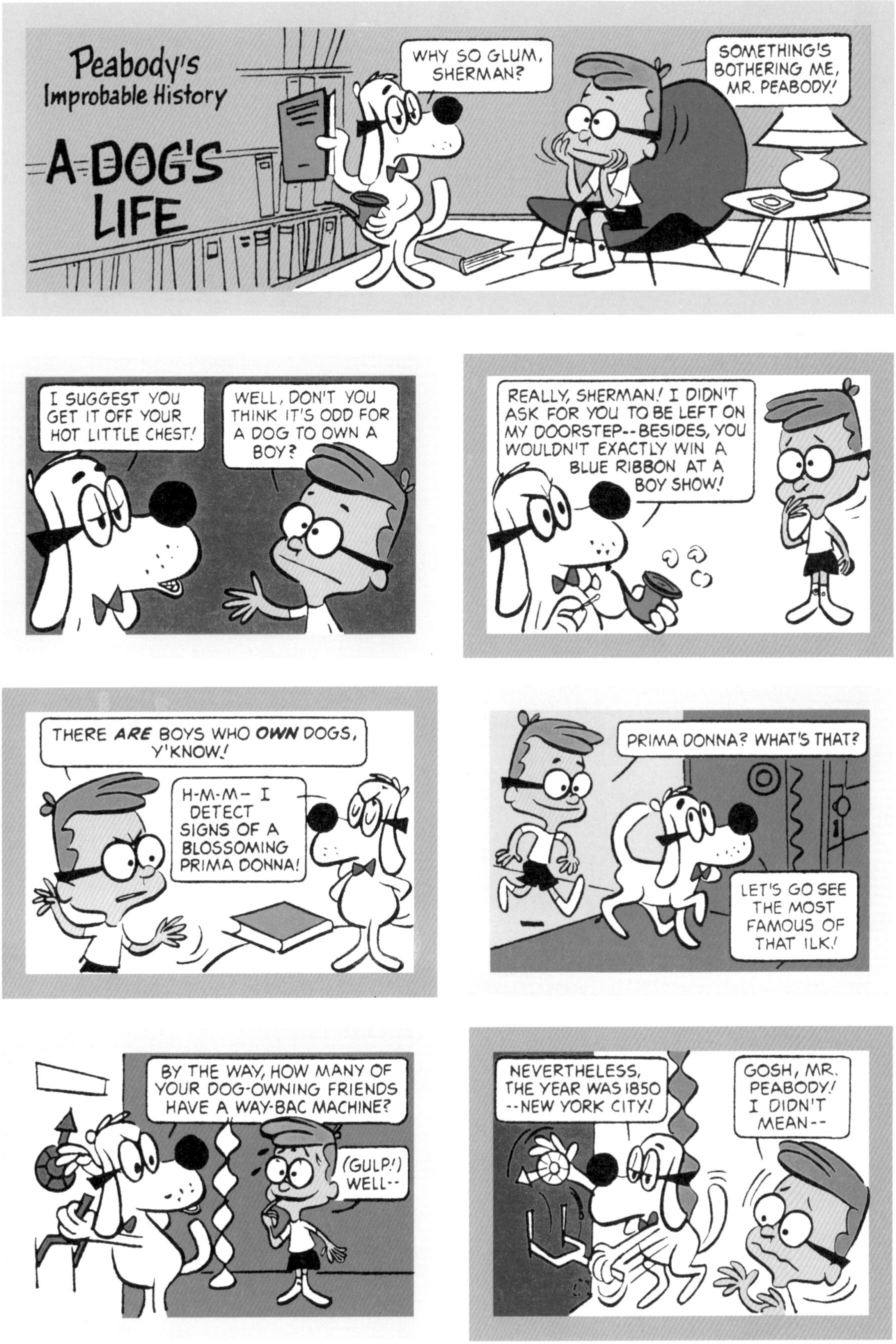
Peabody's Improbable History
A DOG'S LIFE
WHY SO GLUM, SHERMAN?
SOMETHING'S BOTHERING ME, MR. PEABODY!
I SUGGEST YOU GET IT OFF YOUR HOT LITTLE CHEST!
WELL, DON'T YOU THINK IT'S ODD FOR A DOG TO OWN A BOY?
REALLY, SHERMAN! I DIDN'T ASK FOR YOU TO BE LEFT ON MY DOORSTEP--BESIDES, YOU WOULDN'T EXACTLY WIN A BLUE RIBBON AT A BOY SHOW!
THERE ARE BOYS WHO OWN DOGS, Y'KNOW!
H-M-M-- I DETECT SIGNS OF A BLOSSOMING PRIMA DONNA!
PRIMA DONNA? WHAT'S THAT?
LET'S GO SEE THE MOST FAMOUS OF THAT ILK!
BY THE WAY, HOW MANY OF YOUR DOG-OWNING FRIENDS HAVE A WAY-BAC MACHINE?
(GULP!) WELL--
NEVERTHELESS, THE YEAR WAS 1850 --NEW YORK CITY!
GOSH, MR. PEABODY! I DIDN'T MEAN--

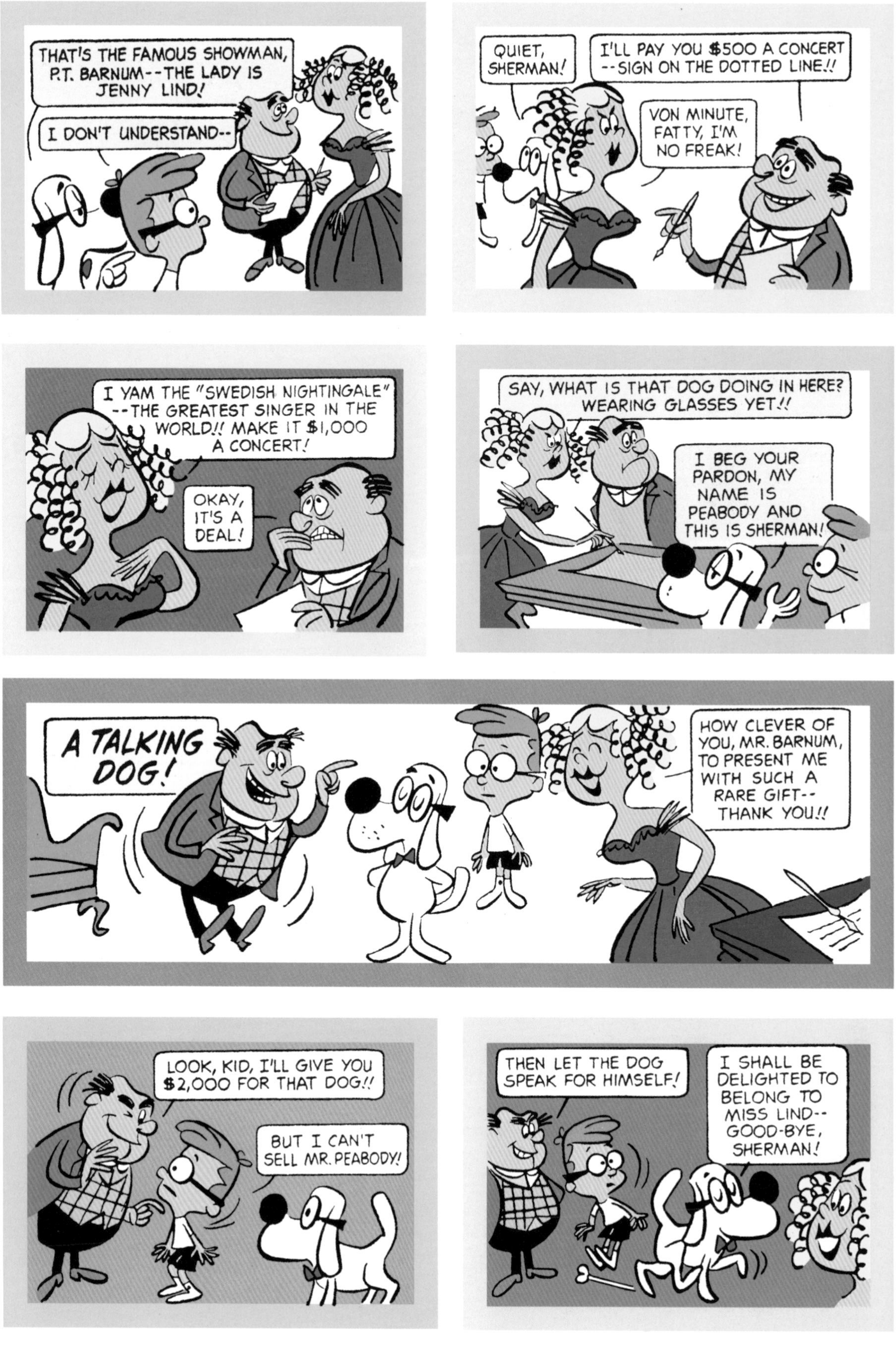
THAT'S THE FAMOUS SHOWMAN, P.T. BARNUM--THE LADY IS JENNY LIND!
I DON'T UNDERSTAND--
QUIET, SHERMAN!
I'LL PAY YOU $500 A CONCERT --SIGN ON THE DOTTED LINE!!
VON MINUTE, FATTY, I'M NO FREAK!
I YAM THE "SWEDISH NIGHTINGALE" --THE GREATEST SINGER IN THE WORLD!! MAKE IT $1,000 A CONCERT!
OKAY, IT'S A DEAL!
SAY, WHAT IS THAT DOG DOING IN HERE? WEARING GLASSES YET!!
I BEG YOUR PARDON, MY NAME IS PEABODY AND THIS IS SHERMAN!
A TALKING DOG!
HOW CLEVER OF YOU, MR. BARNUM, TO PRESENT ME WITH SUCH A RARE GIFT--THANK YOU!!
LOOK, KID, I'LL GIVE YOU $2,000 FOR THAT DOG!!
BUT I CAN'T SELL MR. PEABODY!
THEN LET THE DOG SPEAK FOR HIMSELF!
I SHALL BE DELIGHTED TO BELONG TO MISS LIND--GOOD-BYE, SHERMAN!

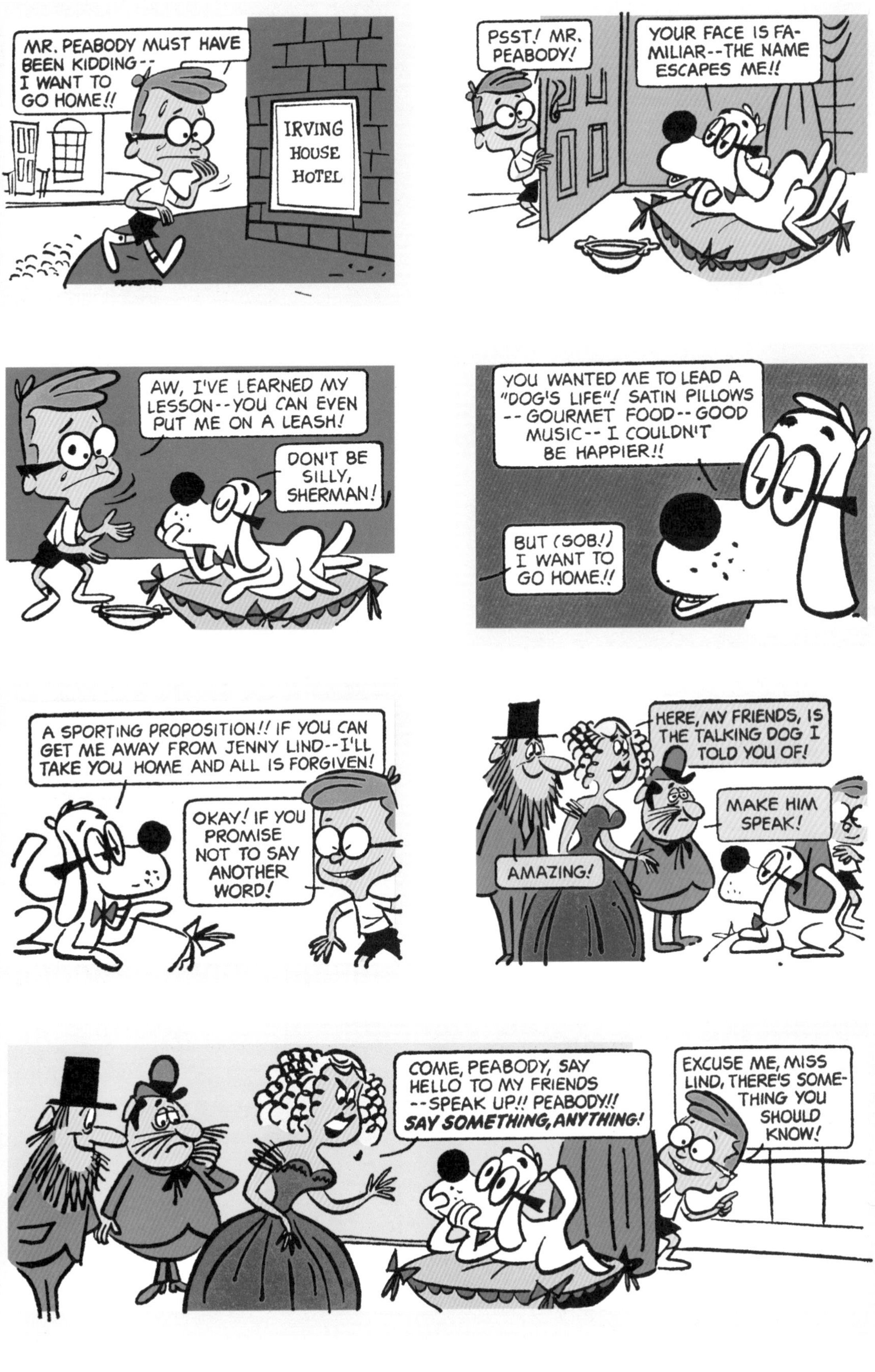
MR. PEABODY MUST HAVE BEEN KIDDING-- I WANT TO GO HOME!!
IRVING HOUSE HOTEL
PSST! MR. PEABODY!
YOUR FACE IS FA-MILIAR--THE NAME ESCAPES ME!!
AW, I'VE LEARNED MY LESSON--YOU CAN EVEN PUT ME ON A LEASH!
DON'T BE SILLY, SHERMAN!
YOU WANTED ME TO LEAD A "DOG'S LIFE"! SATIN PILLOWS --GOURMET FOOD--GOOD MUSIC--I COULDN'T BE HAPPIER!!
BUT (SOB!) I WANT TO GO HOME!!
A SPORTING PROPOSITION!! IF YOU CAN GET ME AWAY FROM JENNY LIND--I'LL TAKE YOU HOME AND ALL IS FORGIVEN!
OKAY! IF YOU PROMISE NOT TO SAY ANOTHER WORD!
HERE, MY FRIENDS, IS THE TALKING DOG I TOLD YOU OF!
MAKE HIM SPEAK!
AMAZING!
COME, PEABODY, SAY HELLO TO MY FRIENDS --SPEAK UP!! PEABODY!! SAY SOMETHING, ANYTHING!
EXCUSE ME, MISS LIND, THERE'S SOME-THING YOU SHOULD KNOW!

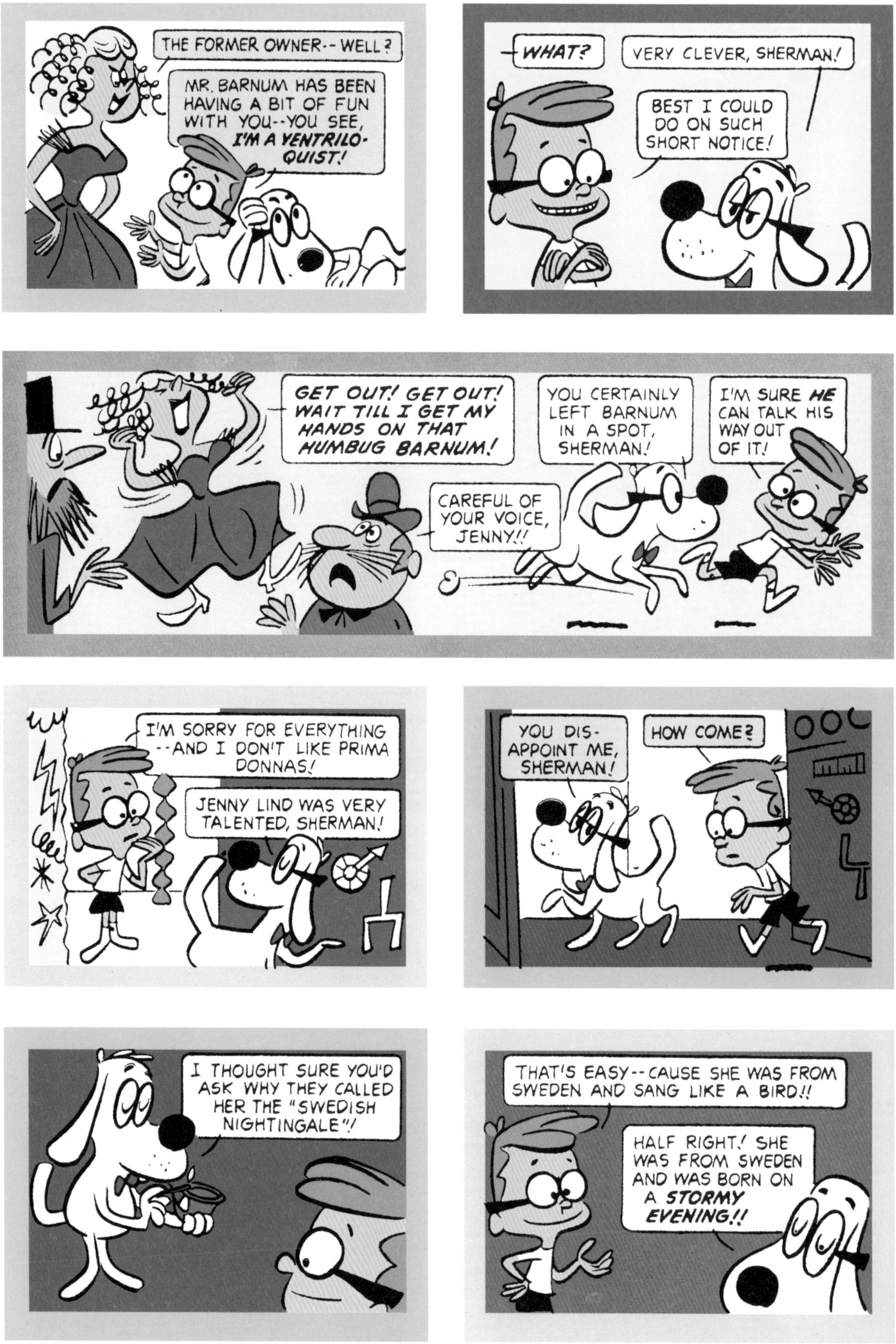

THE FORMER OWNER-- WELL?
MR. BARNUM HAS BEEN HAVING A BIT OF FUN WITH YOU--YOU SEE, I'M A VENTRILO-QUIST!
WHAT?
VERY CLEVER, SHERMAN!
BEST I COULD DO ON SUCH SHORT NOTICE!
GET OUT! GET OUT! WAIT TILL I GET MY HANDS ON THAT HUMBUG BARNUM!
CAREFUL OF YOUR VOICE, JENNY!!
YOU CERTAINLY LEFT BARNUM IN A SPOT, SHERMAN!
I'M SURE HE CAN TALK HIS WAY OUT OF IT!
I'M SORRY FOR EVERYTHING --AND I DON'T LIKE PRIMA DONNAS!
JENNY LIND WAS VERY TALENTED, SHERMAN!
YOU DIS-APPOINT ME, SHERMAN!
HOW COME?
I THOUGHT SURE YOU'D ASK WHY THEY CALLED HER THE "SWEDISH NIGHTINGALE"!
THAT'S EASY--CAUSE SHE WAS FROM SWEDEN AND SANG LIKE A BIRD!!
HALF RIGHT! SHE WAS FROM SWEDEN AND WAS BORN ON A STORMY EVENING!!

Bullwinkle and Rocky
BAT-BALL BATTY

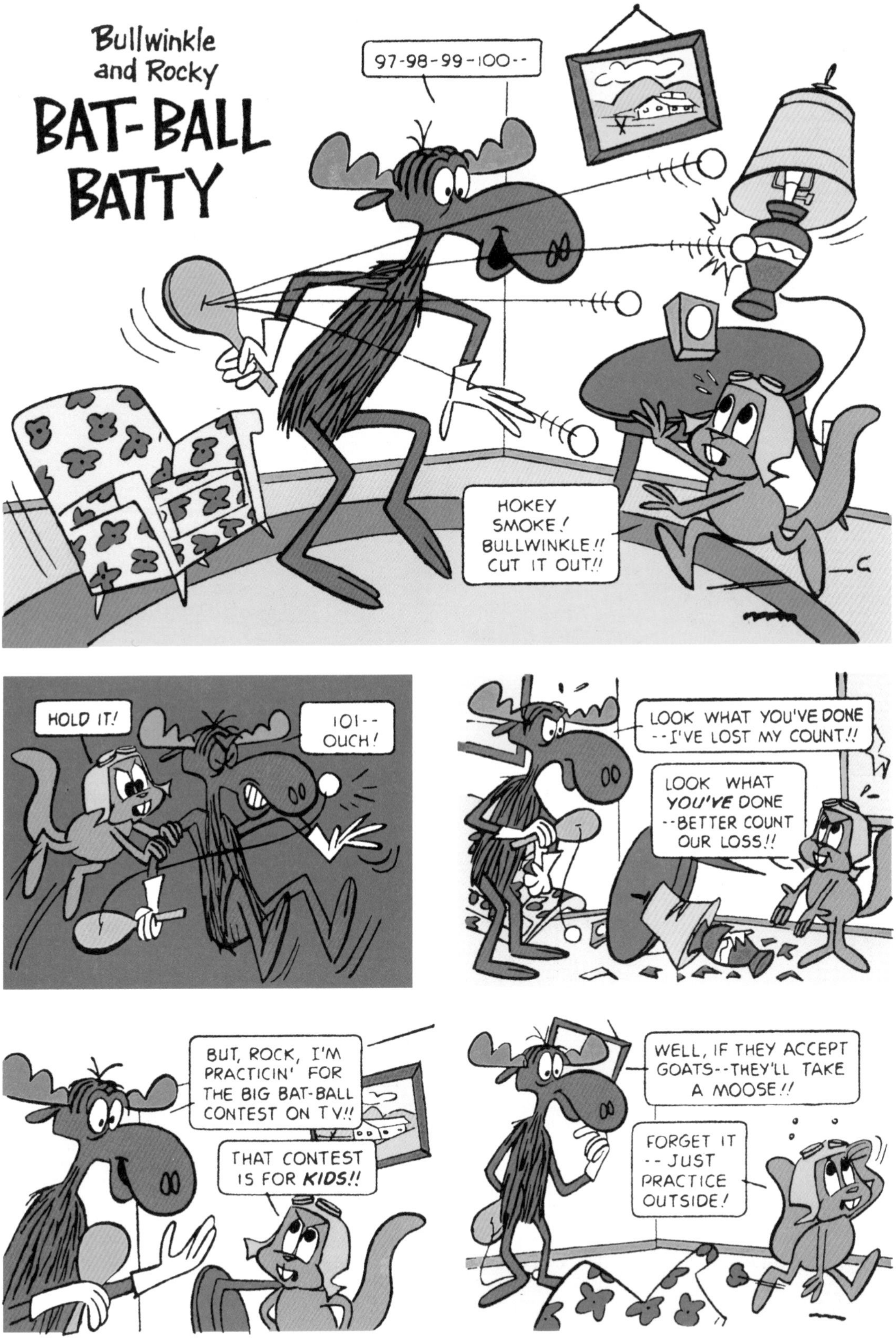
97-98-99-100--
HOKEY SMOKE! BULLWINKLE!! CUT IT OUT!!
HOLD IT!
101-- OUCH!
LOOK WHAT YOU'VE DONE --I'VE LOST MY COUNT!!
LOOK WHAT YOU'VE DONE --BETTER COUNT OUR LOSS!!
BUT, ROCK, I'M PRACTICIN' FOR THE BIG BAT-BALL CONTEST ON TV!!
THAT CONTEST IS FOR KIDS!!
WELL, IF THEY ACCEPT GOATS--THEY'LL TAKE A MOOSE!!
FORGET IT -- JUST PRACTICE OUTSIDE!

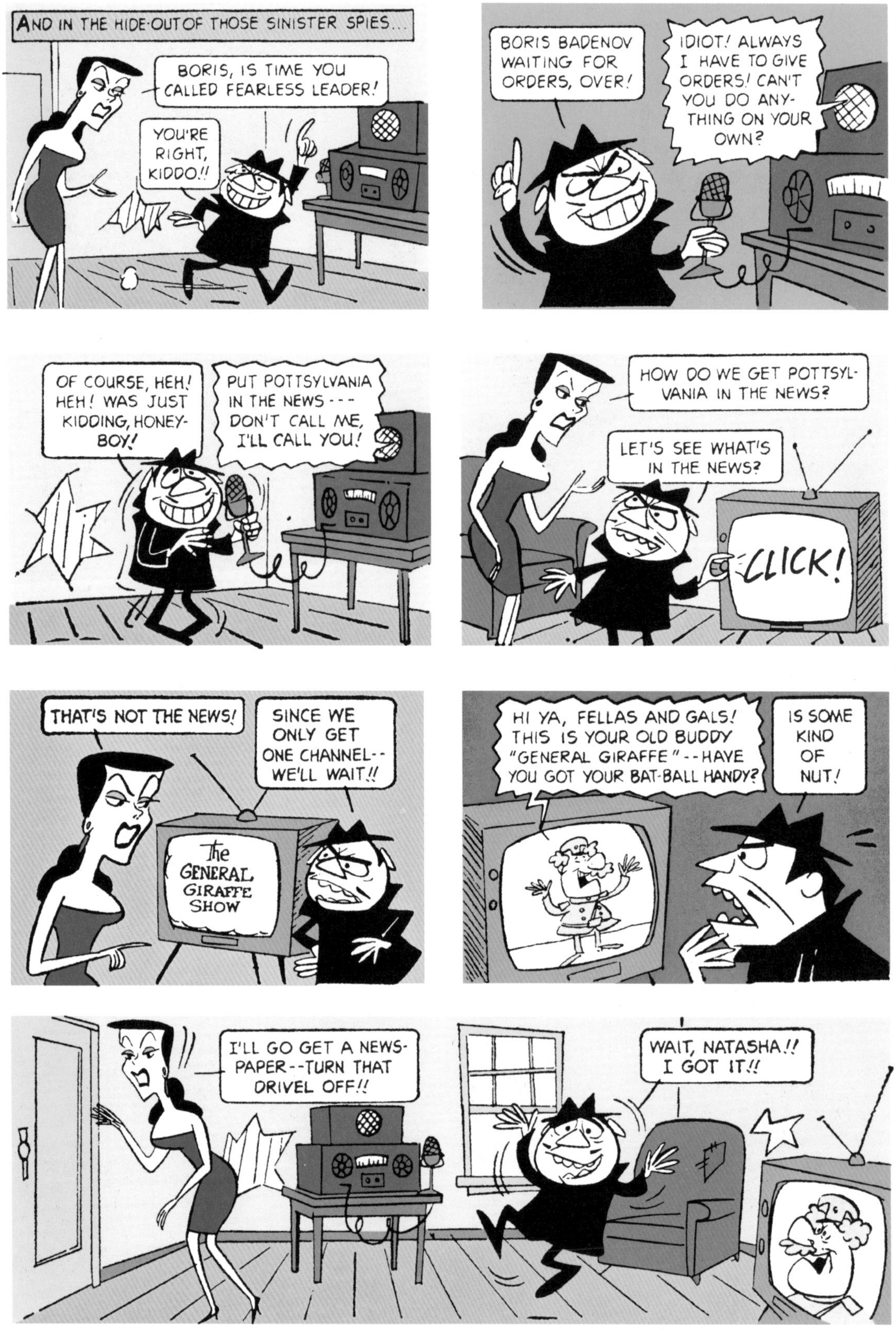

AND IN THE HIDE-OUT OF THOSE SINISTER SPIES...
BORIS, IS TIME YOU CALLED FEARLESS LEADER!
YOU'RE RIGHT, KIDDO!!
BORIS BADENOV WAITING FOR ORDERS, OVER!
IDIOT! ALWAYS I HAVE TO GIVE ORDERS! CAN'T YOU DO ANY-THING ON YOUR OWN?
OF COURSE, HEH! HEH! WAS JUST KIDDING, HONEY-BOY!
PUT POTTSYLVANIA IN THE NEWS --- DON'T CALL ME, I'LL CALL YOU!
HOW DO WE GET POTTSYL-VANIA IN THE NEWS?
LET'S SEE WHAT'S IN THE NEWS?
CLICK!
THAT'S NOT THE NEWS!
SINCE WE ONLY GET ONE CHANNEL-- WE'LL WAIT!!
The GENERAL GIRAFFE SHOW
HI YA, FELLAS AND GALS! THIS IS YOUR OLD BUDDY "GENERAL GIRAFFE" --HAVE YOU GOT YOUR BAT-BALL HANDY?
IS SOME KIND OF NUT!
I'LL GO GET A NEWS-PAPER--TURN THAT DRIVEL OFF!!
WAIT, NATASHA!! I GOT IT!!

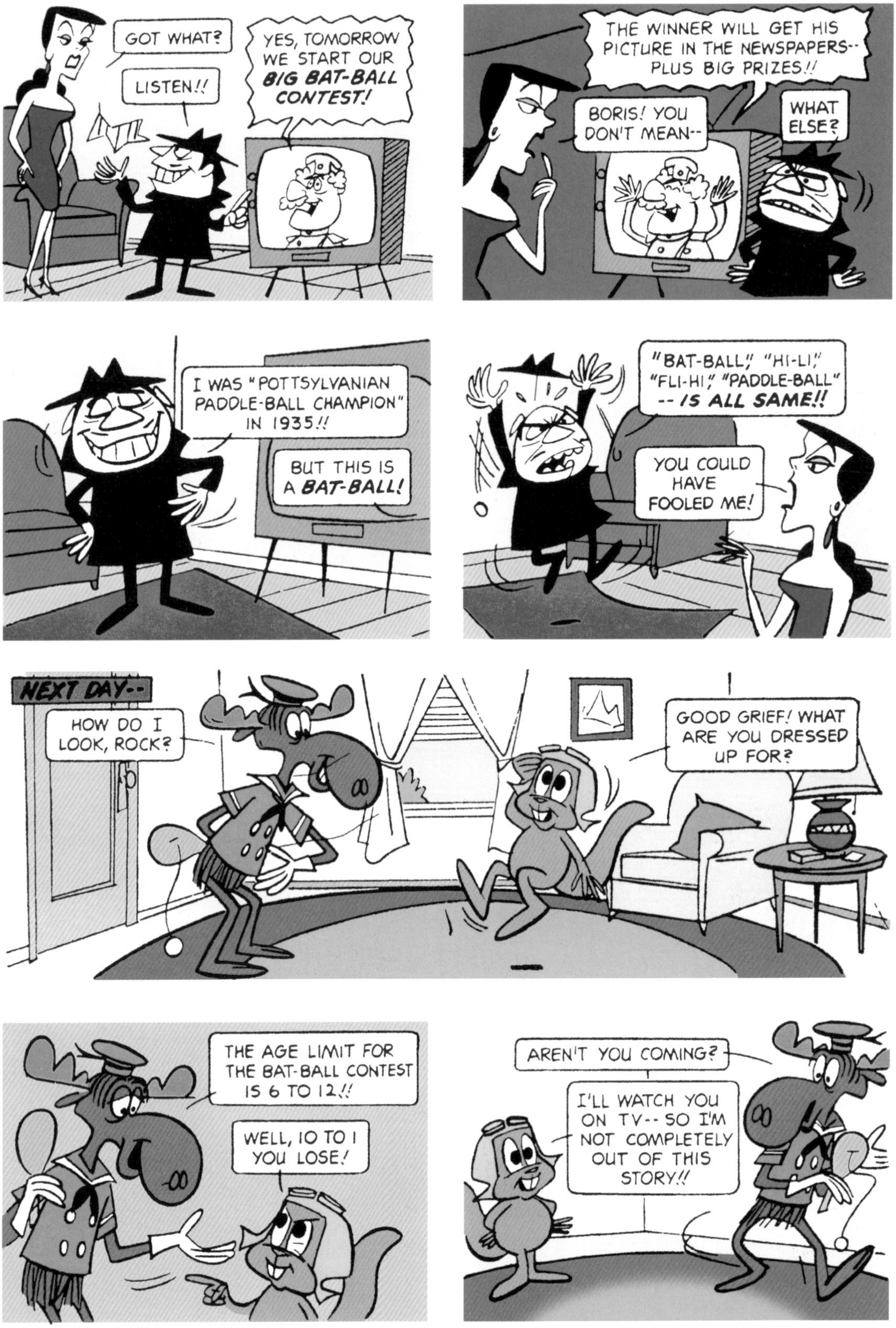
GOT WHAT?
LISTEN!!
YES, TOMORROW WE START OUR BIG BAT-BALL CONTEST!
THE WINNER WILL GET HIS PICTURE IN THE NEWSPAPERS-- PLUS BIG PRIZES!!
BORIS! YOU DON'T MEAN--
WHAT ELSE?
I WAS "POTTSYLVANIAN PADDLE-BALL CHAMPION" IN 1935!!
BUT THIS IS A BAT-BALL!
"BAT-BALL," "HI-LI," "FLI-HI," "PADDLE-BALL" -- IS ALL SAME!!
YOU COULD HAVE FOOLED ME!
NEXT DAY--
HOW DO I LOOK, ROCK?
GOOD GRIEF! WHAT ARE YOU DRESSED UP FOR?
THE AGE LIMIT FOR THE BAT-BALL CONTEST IS 6 TO 12!!
WELL, 10 TO 1 YOU LOSE!
AREN'T YOU COMING?
I'LL WATCH YOU ON TV-- SO I'M NOT COMPLETELY OUT OF THIS STORY!!

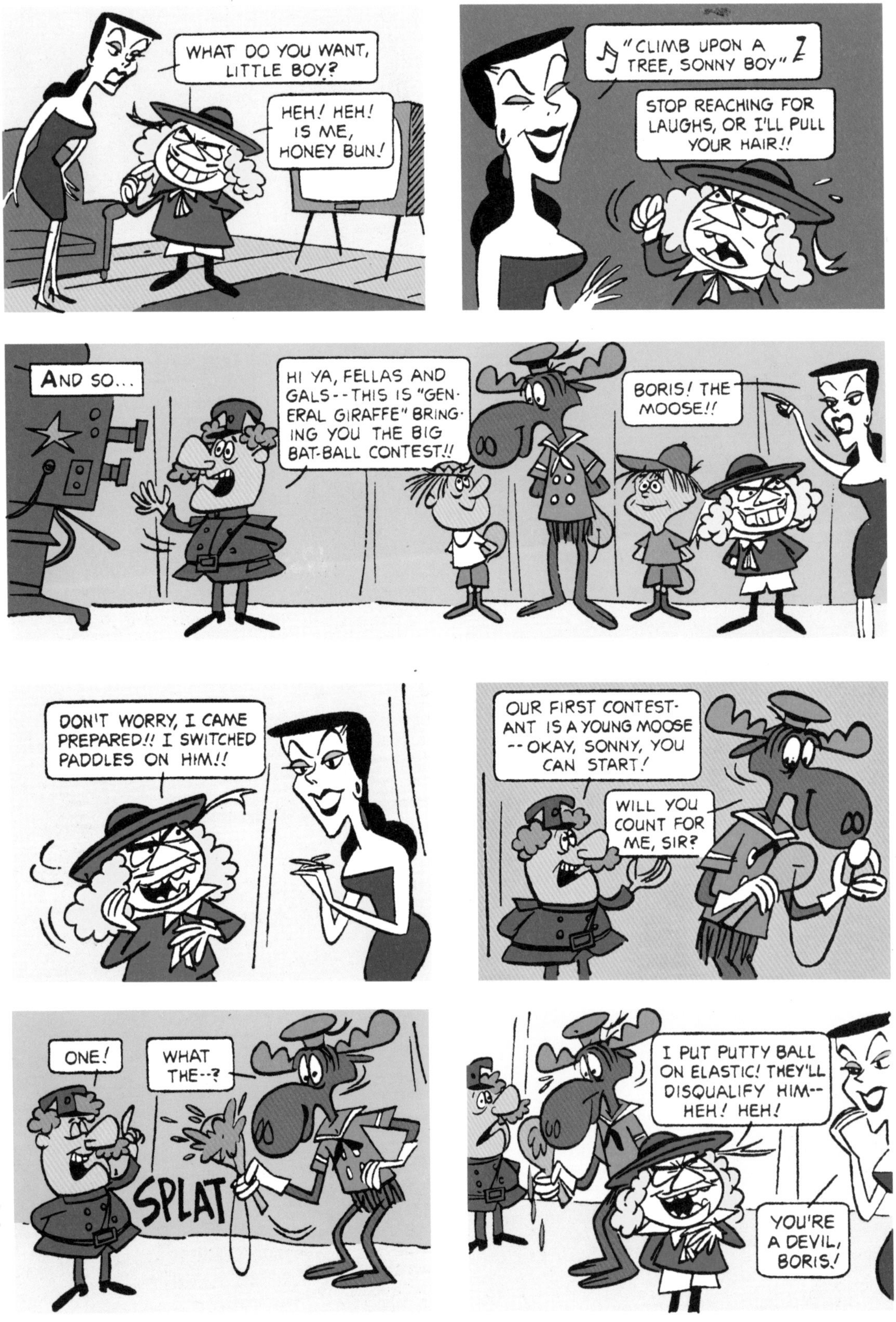

WHAT DO YOU WANT, LITTLE BOY?
HEH! HEH! IS ME, HONEY BUN!
"CLIMB UPON A TREE, SONNY BOY"
STOP REACHING FOR LAUGHS, OR I'LL PULL YOUR HAIR!!
AND SO...
HI YA, FELLAS AND GALS--THIS IS "GENERAL GIRAFFE" BRINGING YOU THE BIG BAT-BALL CONTEST!!
BORIS! THE MOOSE!!
DON'T WORRY, I CAME PREPARED!! I SWITCHED PADDLES ON HIM!!
OUR FIRST CONTESTANT IS A YOUNG MOOSE --OKAY, SONNY, YOU CAN START!
WILL YOU COUNT FOR ME, SIR?
ONE!
WHAT THE--?
SPLAT
I PUT PUTTY BALL ON ELASTIC! THEY'LL DISQUALIFY HIM--HEH! HEH!
YOU'RE A DEVIL, BORIS!

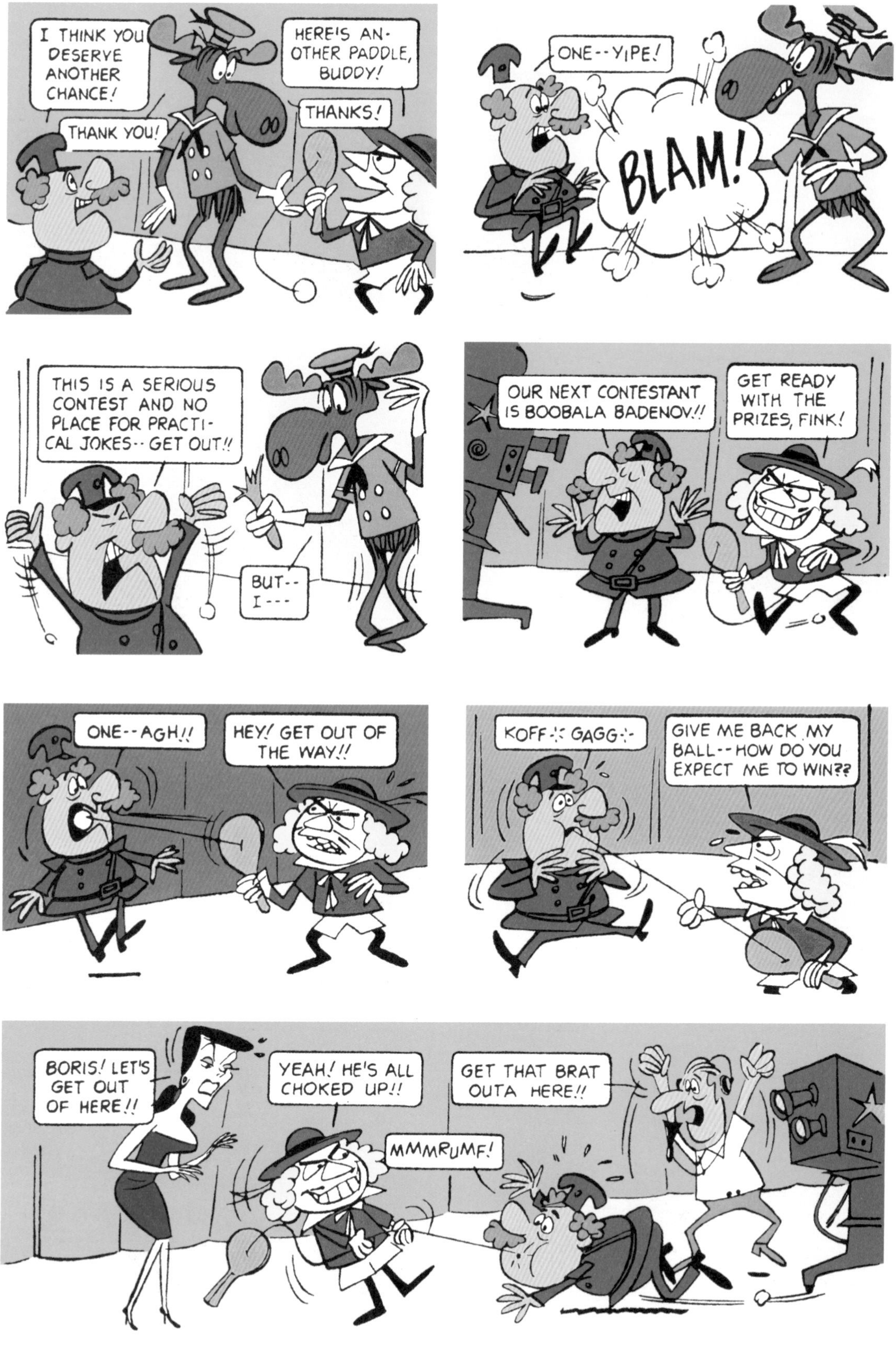
I THINK YOU DESERVE ANOTHER CHANCE!
THANK YOU!
HERE'S AN-OTHER PADDLE, BUDDY!
THANKS!
ONE--YIPE!
BLAM!
THIS IS A SERIOUS CONTEST AND NO PLACE FOR PRACTI-CAL JOKES-- GET OUT!!
BUT-- I---
OUR NEXT CONTESTANT IS BOOBALA BADENOV!!
GET READY WITH THE PRIZES, FINK!
ONE--AGH!!
HEY! GET OUT OF THE WAY!!
KOFF GAGG
GIVE ME BACK MY BALL--HOW DO YOU EXPECT ME TO WIN??
BORIS! LET'S GET OUT OF HERE!!
YEAH! HE'S ALL CHOKED UP!!
MMMRUMF!
GET THAT BRAT OUTA HERE!!

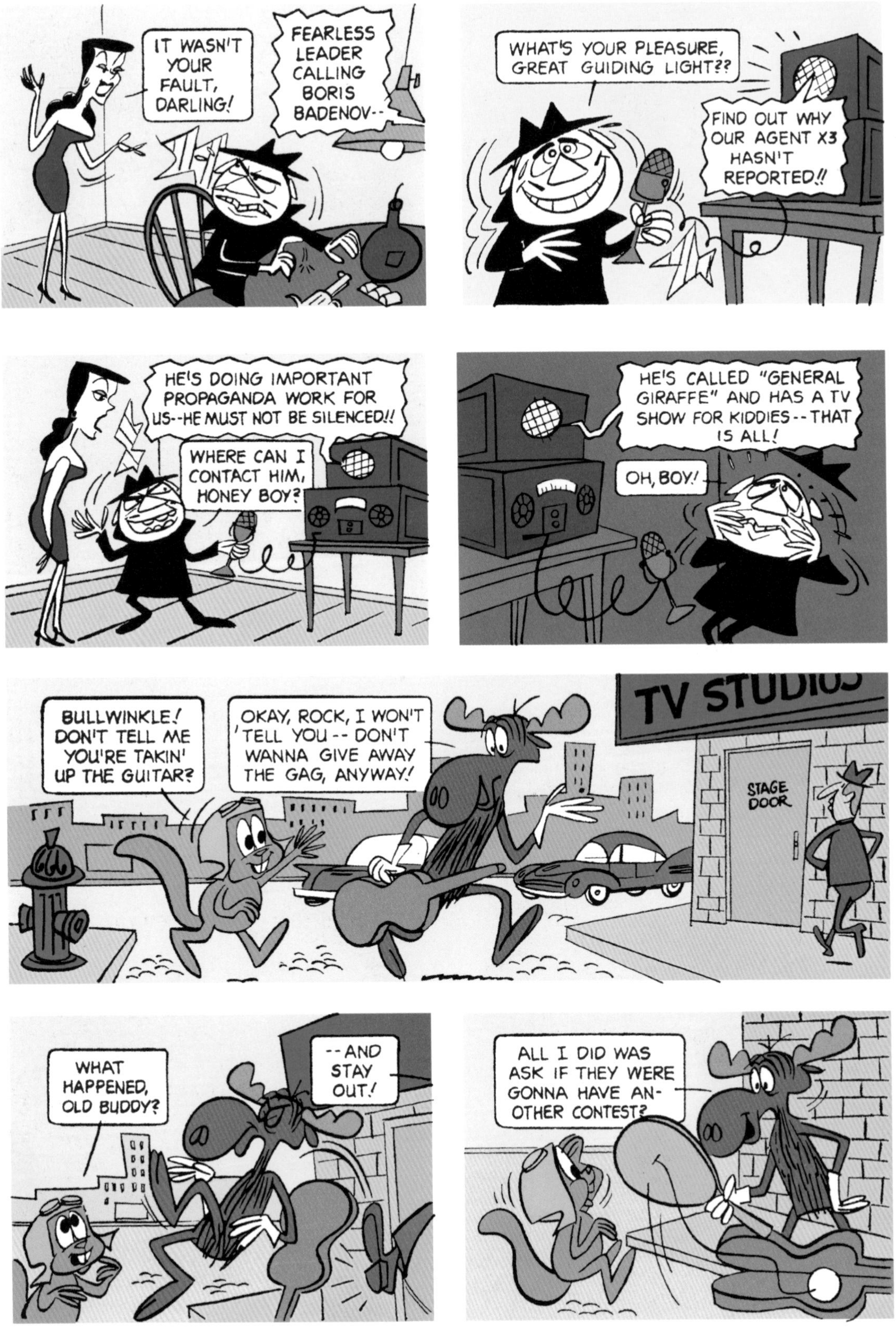
IT WASN'T YOUR FAULT, DARLING!
FEARLESS LEADER CALLING BORIS BADENOV--
WHAT'S YOUR PLEASURE, GREAT GUIDING LIGHT??
FIND OUT WHY OUR AGENT X3 HASN'T REPORTED!!
HE'S DOING IMPORTANT PROPAGANDA WORK FOR US--HE MUST NOT BE SILENCED!!
WHERE CAN I CONTACT HIM, HONEY BOY?
HE'S CALLED "GENERAL GIRAFFE" AND HAS A TV SHOW FOR KIDDIES--THAT IS ALL!
OH, BOY!
TV STUDIOS
BULLWINKLE! DON'T TELL ME YOU'RE TAKIN' UP THE GUITAR?
OKAY, ROCK, I WON'T TELL YOU -- DON'T WANNA GIVE AWAY THE GAG, ANYWAY!
STAGE DOOR
WHAT HAPPENED, OLD BUDDY?
--AND STAY OUT!
ALL I DID WAS ASK IF THEY WERE GONNA HAVE AN-OTHER CONTEST?

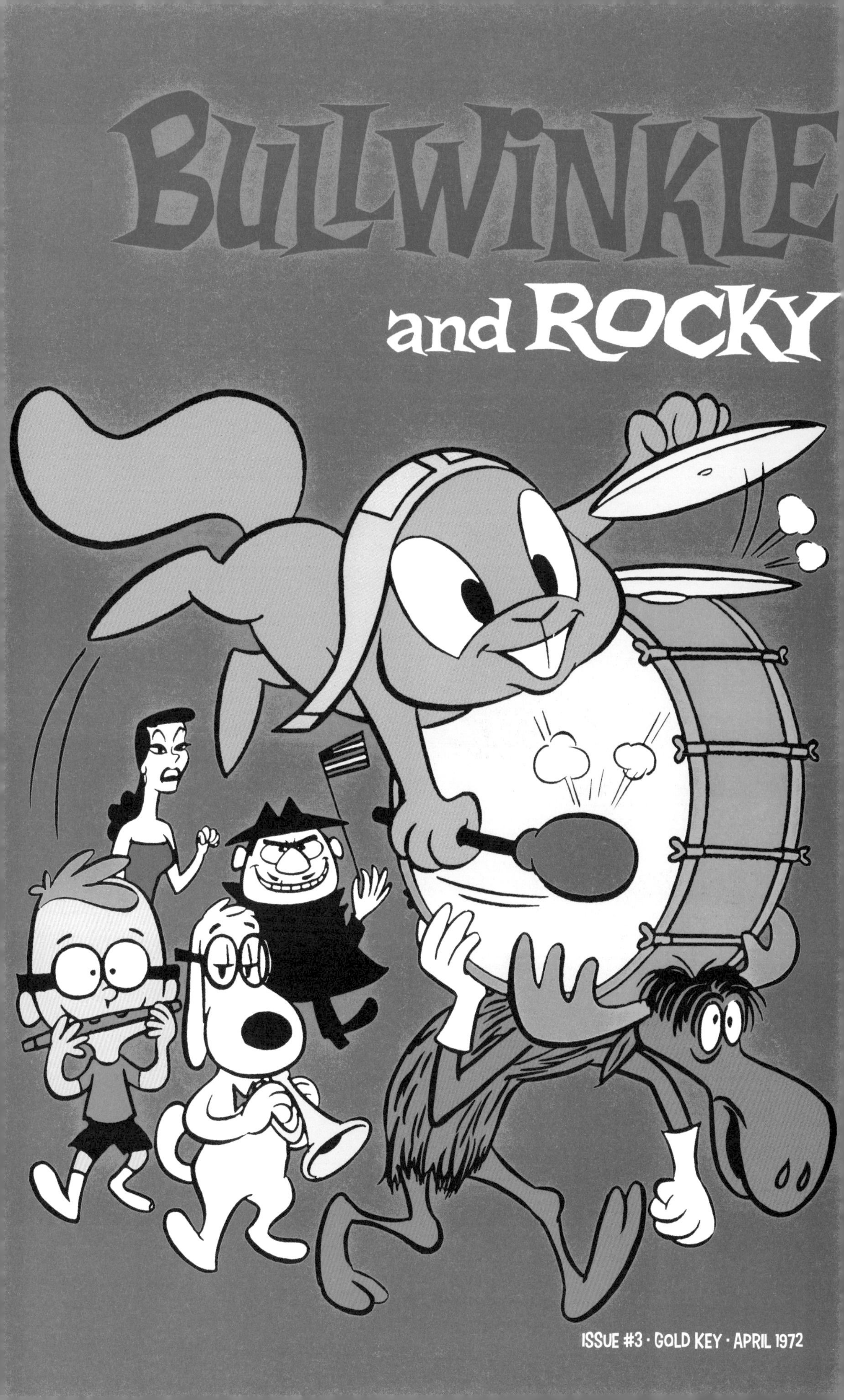
BULLWINKLE
and ROCKY
ISSUE #3 · GOLD KEY · APRIL 1972

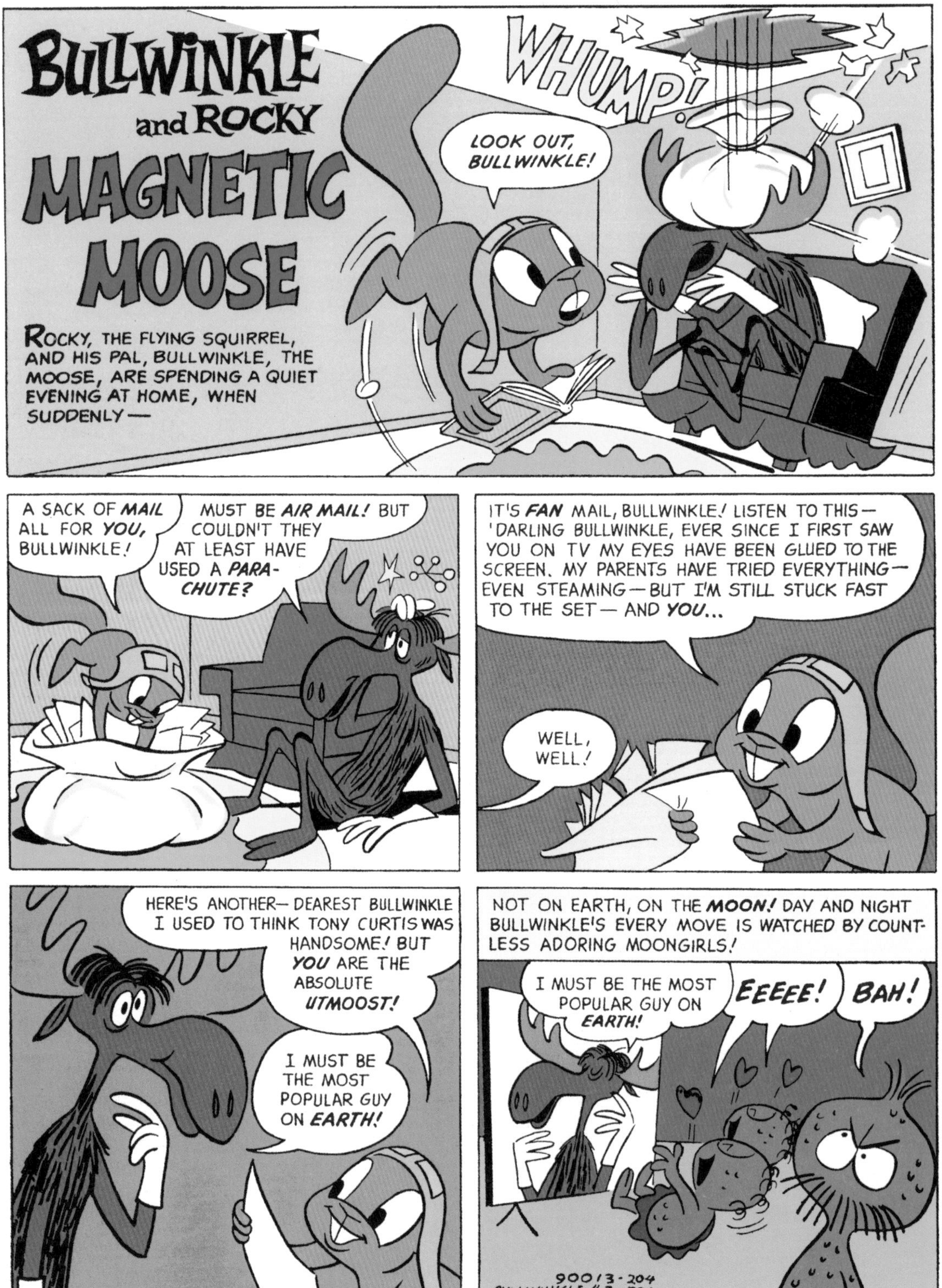
BULLWINKLE
and ROCKY
MAGNETIC
MOOSE
ROCKY, THE FLYING SQUIRREL, AND HIS PAL, BULLWINKLE, THE MOOSE, ARE SPENDING A QUIET EVENING AT HOME, WHEN SUDDENLY—
WHUMP!
LOOK OUT, BULLWINKLE!
A SACK OF MAIL ALL FOR YOU, BULLWINKLE!
MUST BE AIR MAIL! BUT COULDN'T THEY AT LEAST HAVE USED A PARA-CHUTE?
IT'S FAN MAIL, BULLWINKLE! LISTEN TO THIS— 'DARLING BULLWINKLE, EVER SINCE I FIRST SAW YOU ON TV MY EYES HAVE BEEN GLUED TO THE SCREEN. MY PARENTS HAVE TRIED EVERYTHING— EVEN STEAMING—BUT I'M STILL STUCK FAST TO THE SET— AND YOU...
WELL, WELL!
HERE'S ANOTHER— DEAREST BULLWINKLE I USED TO THINK TONY CURTIS WAS HANDSOME! BUT YOU ARE THE ABSOLUTE UTMOOST!
I MUST BE THE MOST POPULAR GUY ON EARTH!
NOT ON EARTH, ON THE MOON! DAY AND NIGHT BULLWINKLE'S EVERY MOVE IS WATCHED BY COUNT-LESS ADORING MOONGIRLS!
I MUST BE THE MOST POPULAR GUY ON EARTH!
EEEEE!
BAH!
90013-204
BULLWINKLE" 3-721

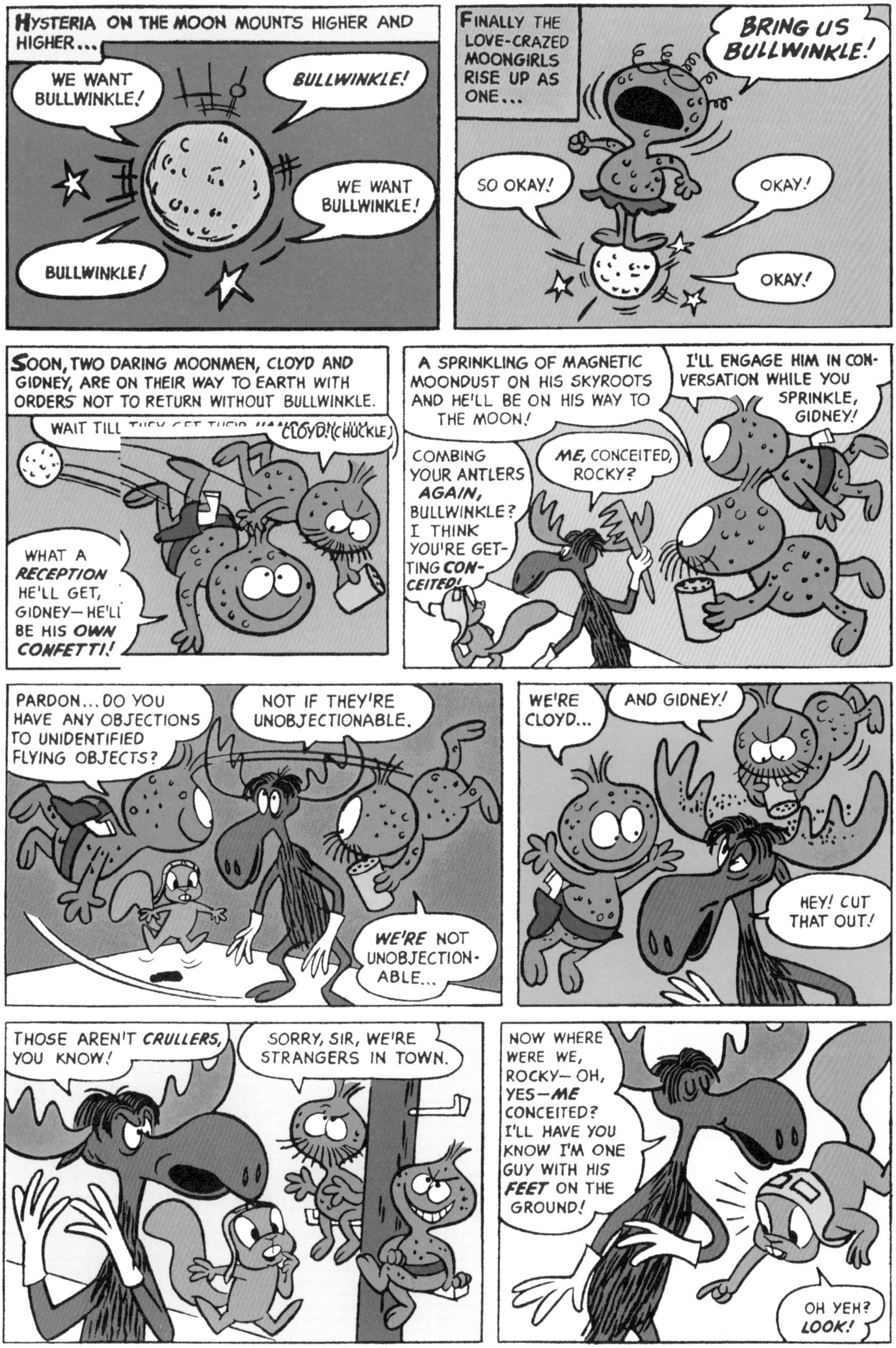
HYSTERIA ON THE MOON MOUNTS HIGHER AND HIGHER...
WE WANT BULLWINKLE!
BULLWINKLE!
WE WANT BULLWINKLE!
BULLWINKLE!
FINALLY THE LOVE-CRAZED MOONGIRLS RISE UP AS ONE...
BRING US BULLWINKLE!
SO OKAY!
OKAY!
OKAY!
SOON, TWO DARING MOONMEN, CLOYD AND GIDNEY, ARE ON THEIR WAY TO EARTH WITH ORDERS NOT TO RETURN WITHOUT BULLWINKLE.
WAIT TILL
CLOYD! (CHUCKLE)
WHAT A RECEPTION HE'LL GET, GIDNEY—HE'LL BE HIS OWN CONFETTI!
A SPRINKLING OF MAGNETIC MOONDUST ON HIS SKYROOTS AND HE'LL BE ON HIS WAY TO THE MOON!
I'LL ENGAGE HIM IN CONVERSATION WHILE YOU SPRINKLE, GIDNEY!
COMBING YOUR ANTLERS AGAIN, BULLWINKLE? I THINK YOU'RE GETTING CONCEITED!
ME, CONCEITED, ROCKY?
PARDON... DO YOU HAVE ANY OBJECTIONS TO UNIDENTIFIED FLYING OBJECTS?
NOT IF THEY'RE UNOBJECTIONABLE.
WE'RE NOT UNOBJECTIONABLE...
WE'RE CLOYD...
AND GIDNEY!
HEY! CUT THAT OUT!
THOSE AREN'T CRULLERS, YOU KNOW!
SORRY, SIR, WE'RE STRANGERS IN TOWN.
NOW WHERE WERE WE, ROCKY—OH, YES—ME CONCEITED? I'LL HAVE YOU KNOW I'M ONE GUY WITH HIS FEET ON THE GROUND!
OH YEH? LOOK!

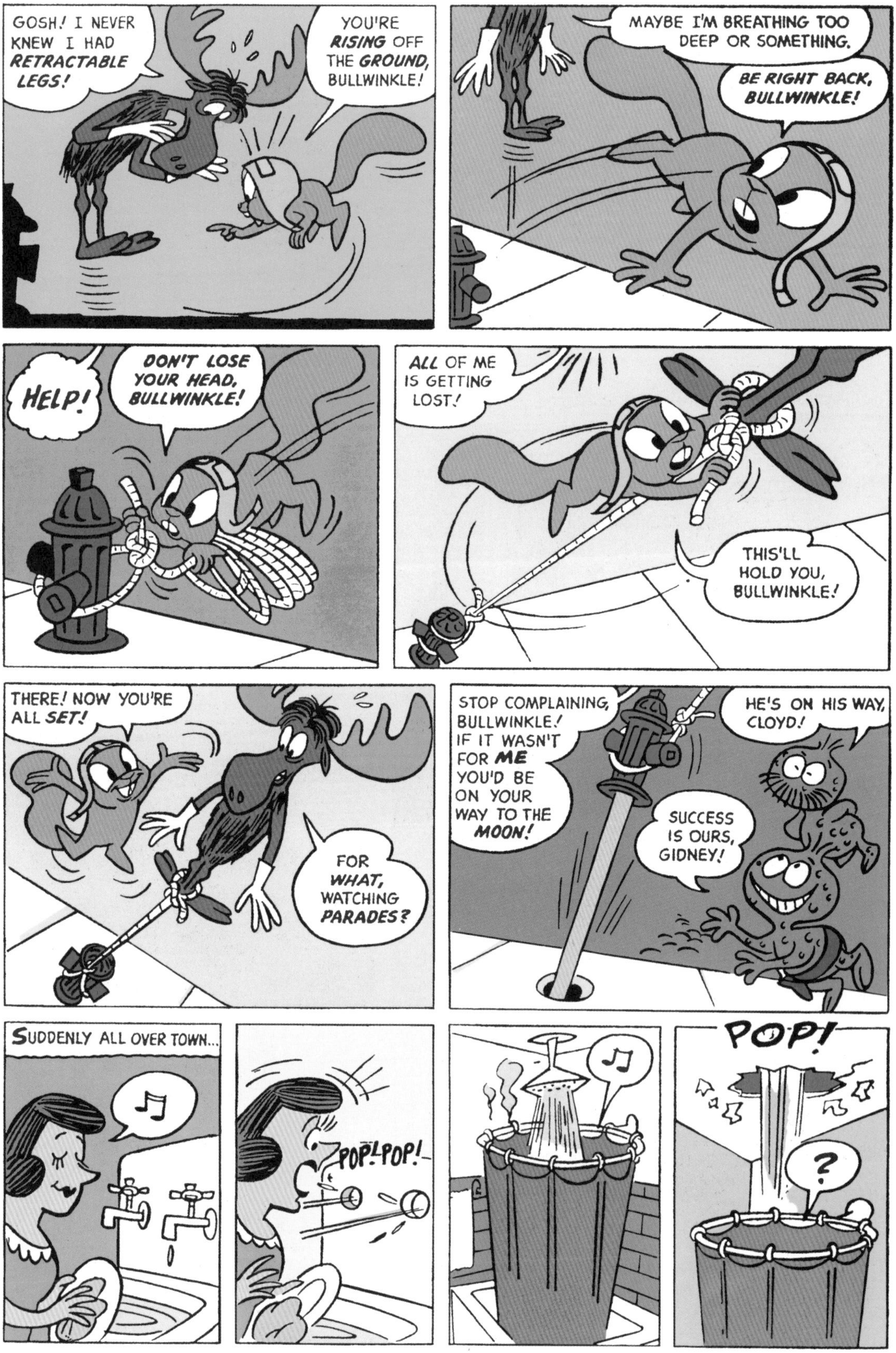
GOSH! I NEVER KNEW I HAD RETRACTABLE LEGS!
YOU'RE RISING OFF THE GROUND, BULLWINKLE!
MAYBE I'M BREATHING TOO DEEP OR SOMETHING.
BE RIGHT BACK, BULLWINKLE!
HELP!
DON'T LOSE YOUR HEAD, BULLWINKLE!
ALL OF ME IS GETTING LOST!
THIS'LL HOLD YOU, BULLWINKLE!
THERE! NOW YOU'RE ALL SET!
FOR WHAT, WATCHING PARADES?
STOP COMPLAINING, BULLWINKLE! IF IT WASN'T FOR ME YOU'D BE ON YOUR WAY TO THE MOON!
HE'S ON HIS WAY, CLOYD!
SUCCESS IS OURS, GIDNEY!
SUDDENLY ALL OVER TOWN...
♫
POP! POP!
♫
POP!
?

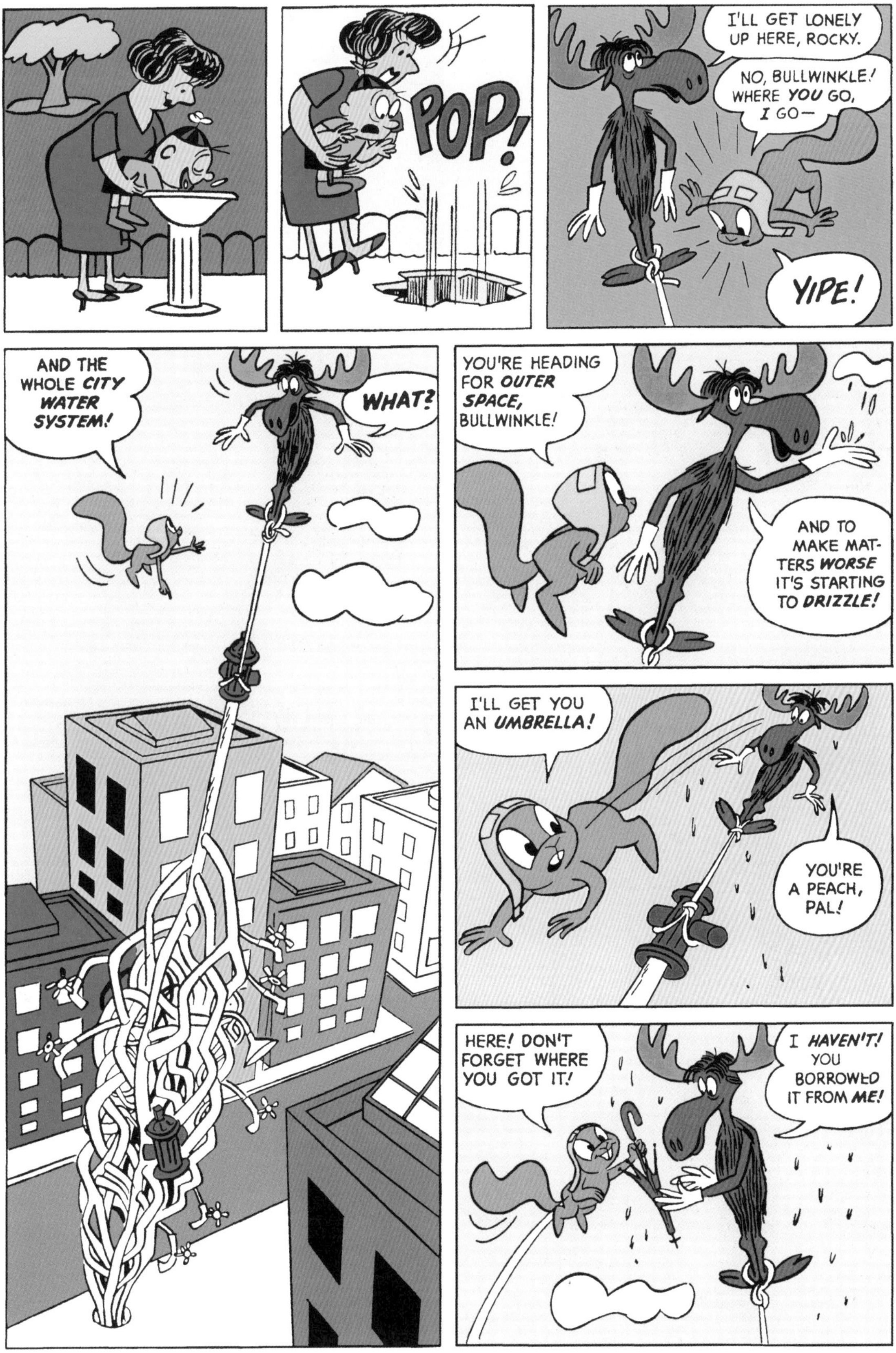

POP!
I'LL GET LONELY UP HERE, ROCKY.
NO, BULLWINKLE! WHERE YOU GO, I GO—
YIPE!
AND THE WHOLE CITY WATER SYSTEM!
WHAT?
YOU'RE HEADING FOR OUTER SPACE, BULLWINKLE!
AND TO MAKE MATTERS WORSE IT'S STARTING TO DRIZZLE!
I'LL GET YOU AN UMBRELLA!
YOU'RE A PEACH, PAL!
HERE! DON'T FORGET WHERE YOU GOT IT!
I HAVEN'T! YOU BORROWED IT FROM ME!

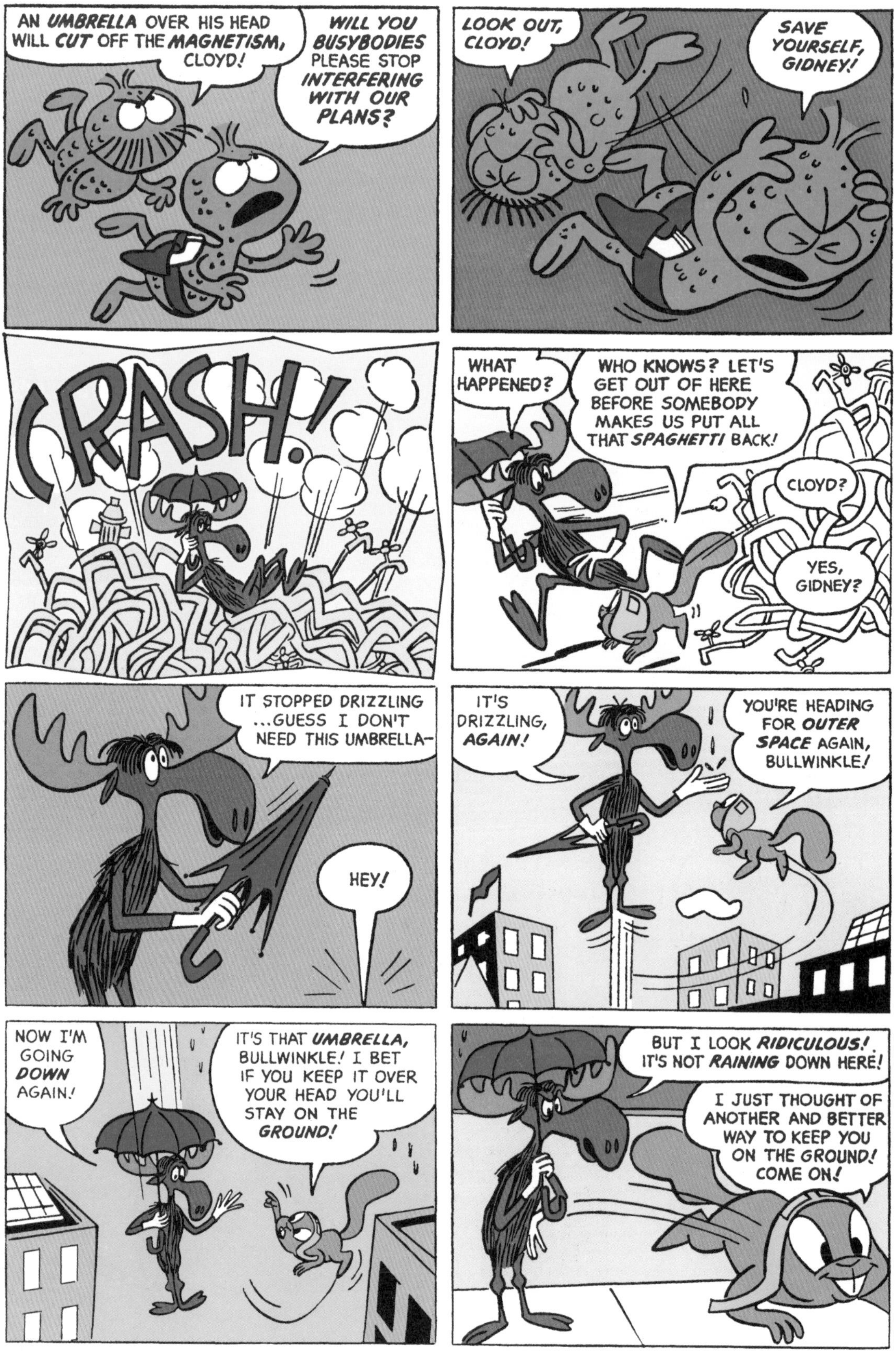
AN *UMBRELLA* OVER HIS HEAD WILL *CUT* OFF THE *MAGNETISM,* CLOYD!
WILL YOU BUSYBODIES PLEASE STOP *INTERFERING WITH OUR PLANS?*
LOOK OUT, CLOYD!
SAVE YOURSELF, GIDNEY!
CRASH!
WHAT HAPPENED?
WHO KNOWS? LET'S GET OUT OF HERE BEFORE SOMEBODY MAKES US PUT ALL THAT *SPAGHETTI* BACK!
CLOYD?
YES, GIDNEY?
IT STOPPED DRIZZLING ...GUESS I DON'T NEED THIS UMBRELLA-
HEY!
IT'S DRIZZLING, *AGAIN!*
YOU'RE HEADING FOR *OUTER SPACE* AGAIN, BULLWINKLE!
NOW I'M GOING *DOWN* AGAIN!
IT'S THAT *UMBRELLA,* BULLWINKLE! I BET IF YOU KEEP IT OVER YOUR HEAD YOU'LL STAY ON THE *GROUND!*
BUT I LOOK *RIDICULOUS!* IT'S NOT *RAINING* DOWN HERE!
I JUST THOUGHT OF ANOTHER AND BETTER WAY TO KEEP YOU ON THE GROUND! COME ON!

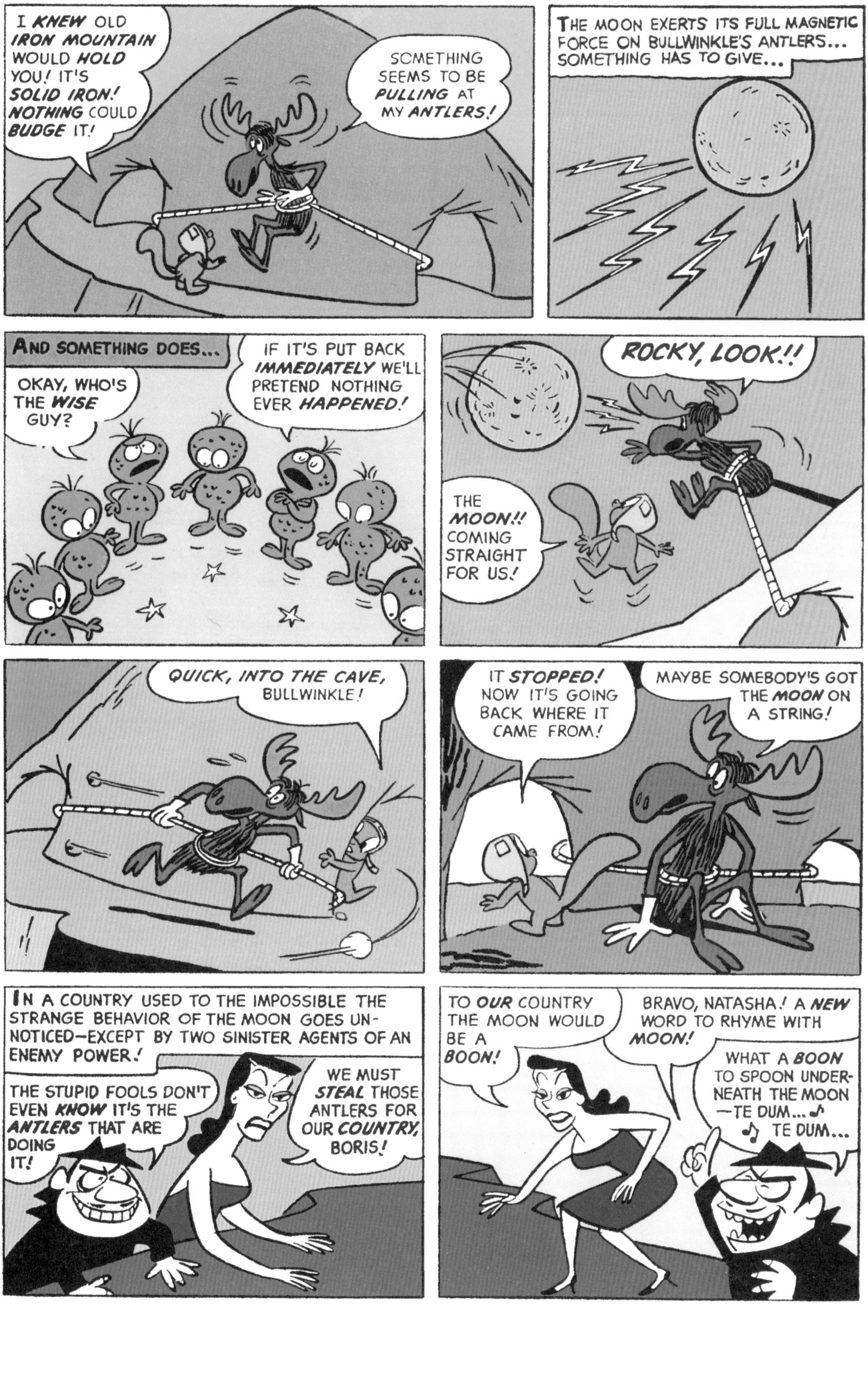
I KNEW OLD IRON MOUNTAIN WOULD HOLD YOU! IT'S SOLID IRON! NOTHING COULD BUDGE IT!
SOMETHING SEEMS TO BE PULLING AT MY ANTLERS!
THE MOON EXERTS ITS FULL MAGNETIC FORCE ON BULLWINKLE'S ANTLERS... SOMETHING HAS TO GIVE...
AND SOMETHING DOES...
OKAY, WHO'S THE WISE GUY?
IF IT'S PUT BACK IMMEDIATELY WE'LL PRETEND NOTHING EVER HAPPENED!
ROCKY, LOOK!!
THE MOON!! COMING STRAIGHT FOR US!
QUICK, INTO THE CAVE, BULLWINKLE!
IT STOPPED! NOW IT'S GOING BACK WHERE IT CAME FROM!
MAYBE SOMEBODY'S GOT THE MOON ON A STRING!
IN A COUNTRY USED TO THE IMPOSSIBLE THE STRANGE BEHAVIOR OF THE MOON GOES UN-NOTICED—EXCEPT BY TWO SINISTER AGENTS OF AN ENEMY POWER!
THE STUPID FOOLS DON'T EVEN KNOW IT'S THE ANTLERS THAT ARE DOING IT!
WE MUST STEAL THOSE ANTLERS FOR OUR COUNTRY, BORIS!
TO OUR COUNTRY THE MOON WOULD BE A BOON!
BRAVO, NATASHA! A NEW WORD TO RHYME WITH MOON!
WHAT A BOON TO SPOON UNDER-NEATH THE MOON —TE DUM... ♪ ♫ TE DUM...

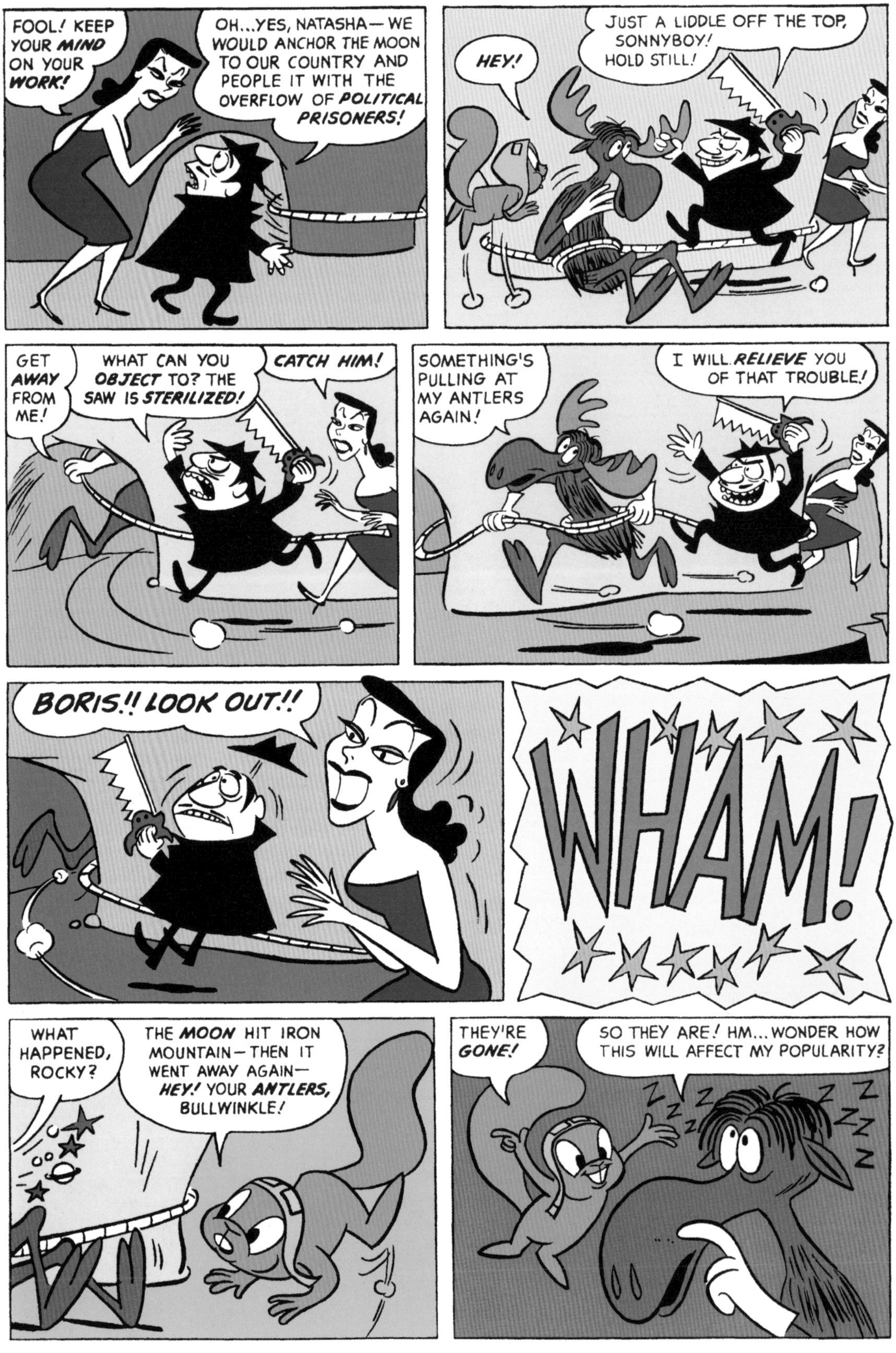
FOOL! KEEP YOUR MIND ON YOUR WORK!
OH...YES, NATASHA—WE WOULD ANCHOR THE MOON TO OUR COUNTRY AND PEOPLE IT WITH THE OVERFLOW OF POLITICAL PRISONERS!
HEY!
JUST A LIDDLE OFF THE TOP, SONNYBOY! HOLD STILL!
GET AWAY FROM ME!
WHAT CAN YOU OBJECT TO? THE SAW IS STERILIZED!
CATCH HIM!
SOMETHING'S PULLING AT MY ANTLERS AGAIN!
I WILL RELIEVE YOU OF THAT TROUBLE!
BORIS!! LOOK OUT!!
WHAM!
WHAT HAPPENED, ROCKY?
THE MOON HIT IRON MOUNTAIN—THEN IT WENT AWAY AGAIN—HEY! YOUR ANTLERS, BULLWINKLE!
THEY'RE GONE!
SO THEY ARE! HM...WONDER HOW THIS WILL AFFECT MY POPULARITY?

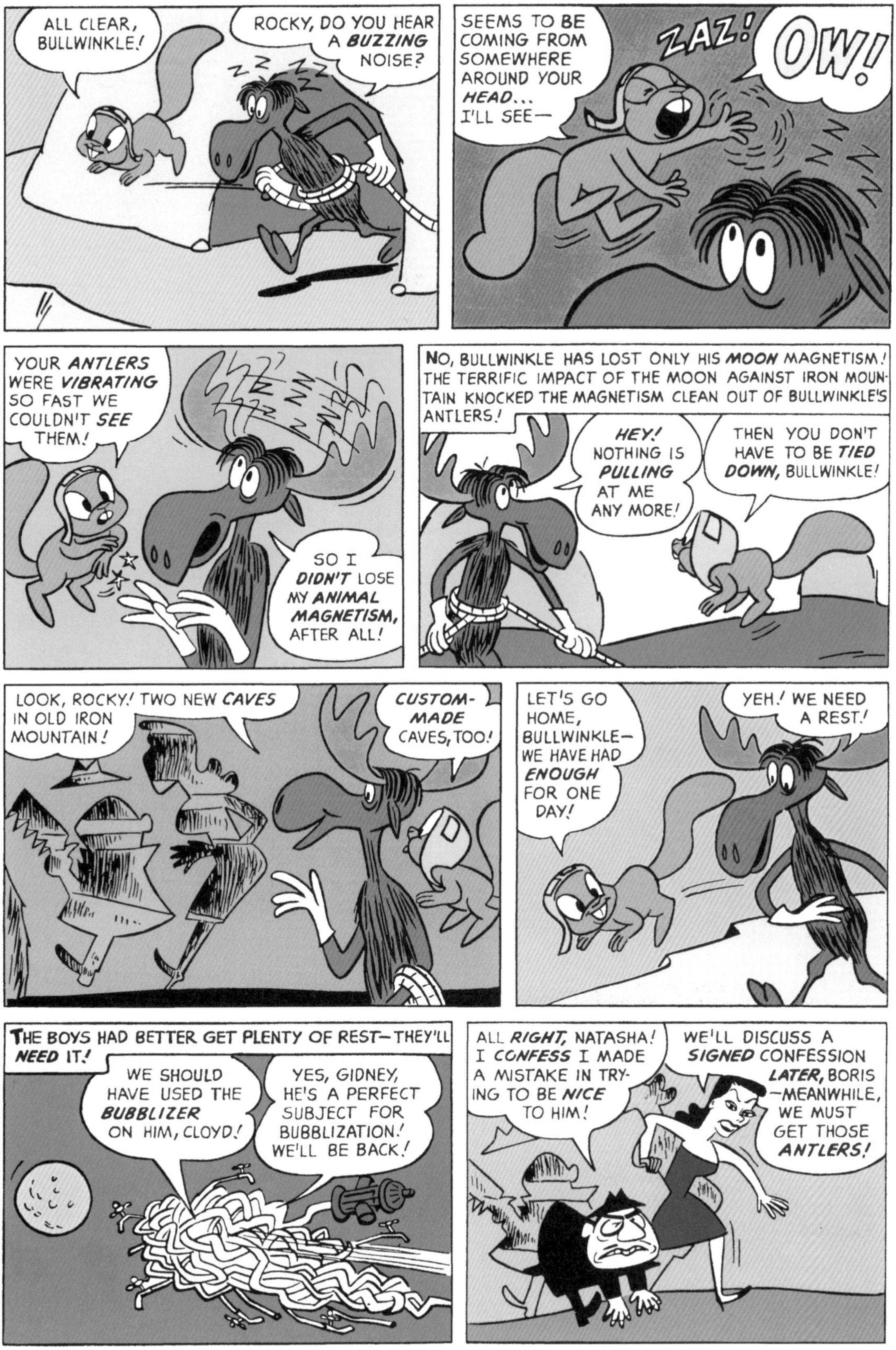

ALL CLEAR, BULLWINKLE!
ROCKY, DO YOU HEAR A BUZZING NOISE?
SEEMS TO BE COMING FROM SOMEWHERE AROUND YOUR HEAD... I'LL SEE—
ZAZ!
OW!
YOUR ANTLERS WERE VIBRATING SO FAST WE COULDN'T SEE THEM!
SO I DIDN'T LOSE MY ANIMAL MAGNETISM, AFTER ALL!
NO, BULLWINKLE HAS LOST ONLY HIS MOON MAGNETISM! THE TERRIFIC IMPACT OF THE MOON AGAINST IRON MOUNTAIN KNOCKED THE MAGNETISM CLEAN OUT OF BULLWINKLE'S ANTLERS!
HEY! NOTHING IS PULLING AT ME ANY MORE!
THEN YOU DON'T HAVE TO BE TIED DOWN, BULLWINKLE!
LOOK, ROCKY! TWO NEW CAVES IN OLD IRON MOUNTAIN!
CUSTOM-MADE CAVES, TOO!
LET'S GO HOME, BULLWINKLE— WE HAVE HAD ENOUGH FOR ONE DAY!
YEH! WE NEED A REST!
THE BOYS HAD BETTER GET PLENTY OF REST—THEY'LL NEED IT!
WE SHOULD HAVE USED THE BUBBLIZER ON HIM, CLOYD!
YES, GIDNEY, HE'S A PERFECT SUBJECT FOR BUBBLIZATION! WE'LL BE BACK!
ALL RIGHT, NATASHA! I CONFESS I MADE A MISTAKE IN TRYING TO BE NICE TO HIM!
WE'LL DISCUSS A SIGNED CONFESSION LATER, BORIS —MEANWHILE, WE MUST GET THOSE ANTLERS!

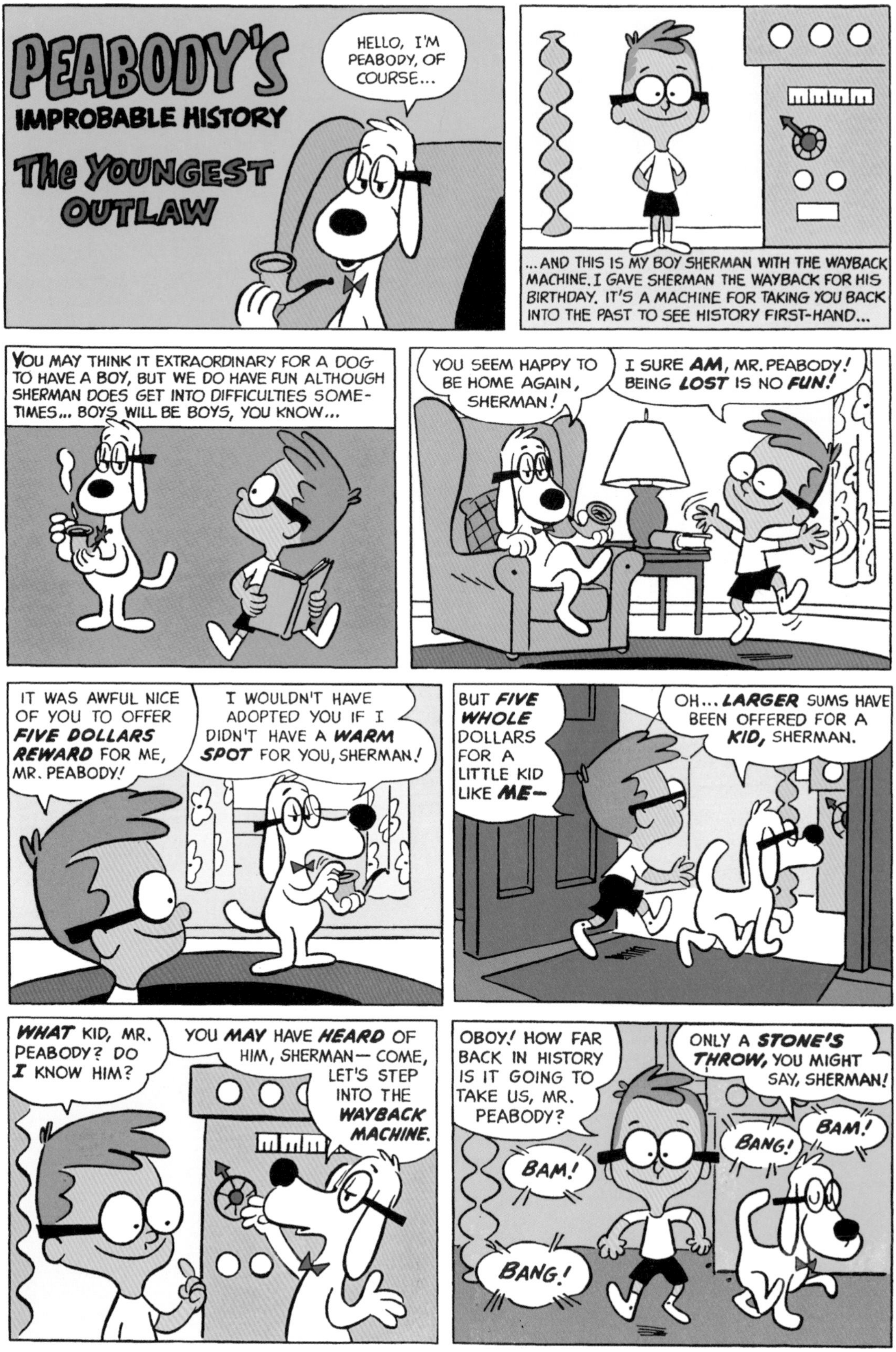
PEABODY'S
IMPROBABLE HISTORY
The YOUNGEST OUTLAW
HELLO, I'M PEABODY, OF COURSE...
...AND THIS IS MY BOY SHERMAN WITH THE WAYBACK MACHINE. I GAVE SHERMAN THE WAYBACK FOR HIS BIRTHDAY. IT'S A MACHINE FOR TAKING YOU BACK INTO THE PAST TO SEE HISTORY FIRST-HAND...
YOU MAY THINK IT EXTRAORDINARY FOR A DOG TO HAVE A BOY, BUT WE DO HAVE FUN ALTHOUGH SHERMAN DOES GET INTO DIFFICULTIES SOMETIMES... BOYS WILL BE BOYS, YOU KNOW...
YOU SEEM HAPPY TO BE HOME AGAIN, SHERMAN!
I SURE AM, MR. PEABODY! BEING LOST IS NO FUN!
IT WAS AWFUL NICE OF YOU TO OFFER FIVE DOLLARS REWARD FOR ME, MR. PEABODY!
I WOULDN'T HAVE ADOPTED YOU IF I DIDN'T HAVE A WARM SPOT FOR YOU, SHERMAN!
BUT FIVE WHOLE DOLLARS FOR A LITTLE KID LIKE ME—
OH... LARGER SUMS HAVE BEEN OFFERED FOR A KID, SHERMAN.
WHAT KID, MR. PEABODY? DO I KNOW HIM?
YOU MAY HAVE HEARD OF HIM, SHERMAN— COME, LET'S STEP INTO THE WAYBACK MACHINE.
OBOY! HOW FAR BACK IN HISTORY IS IT GOING TO TAKE US, MR. PEABODY?
ONLY A STONE'S THROW, YOU MIGHT SAY, SHERMAN!
BAM!
BANG!
BAM!
BANG!

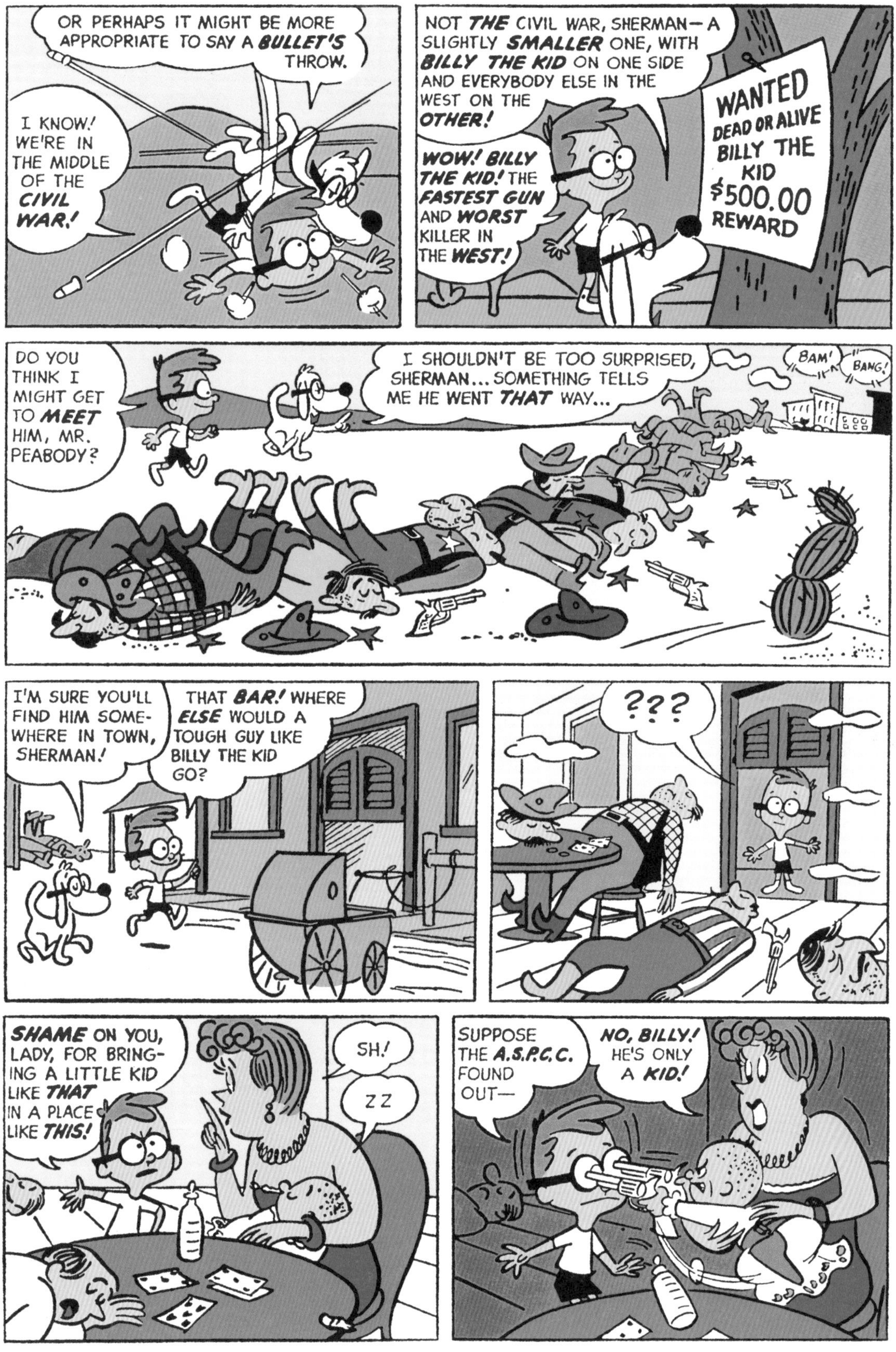
OR PERHAPS IT MIGHT BE MORE APPROPRIATE TO SAY A BULLET'S THROW.
I KNOW! WE'RE IN THE MIDDLE OF THE CIVIL WAR!
NOT THE CIVIL WAR, SHERMAN— A SLIGHTLY SMALLER ONE, WITH BILLY THE KID ON ONE SIDE AND EVERYBODY ELSE IN THE WEST ON THE OTHER!
WOW! BILLY THE KID! THE FASTEST GUN AND WORST KILLER IN THE WEST!
WANTED DEAD OR ALIVE BILLY THE KID $500.00 REWARD
DO YOU THINK I MIGHT GET TO MEET HIM, MR. PEABODY?
I SHOULDN'T BE TOO SURPRISED, SHERMAN... SOMETHING TELLS ME HE WENT THAT WAY...
BAM!
BANG!
I'M SURE YOU'LL FIND HIM SOMEWHERE IN TOWN, SHERMAN!
THAT BAR! WHERE ELSE WOULD A TOUGH GUY LIKE BILLY THE KID GO?
???
SHAME ON YOU, LADY, FOR BRINGING A LITTLE KID LIKE THAT IN A PLACE LIKE THIS!
SH!
Z Z
SUPPOSE THE A.S.P.C.C. FOUND OUT—
NO, BILLY! HE'S ONLY A KID!

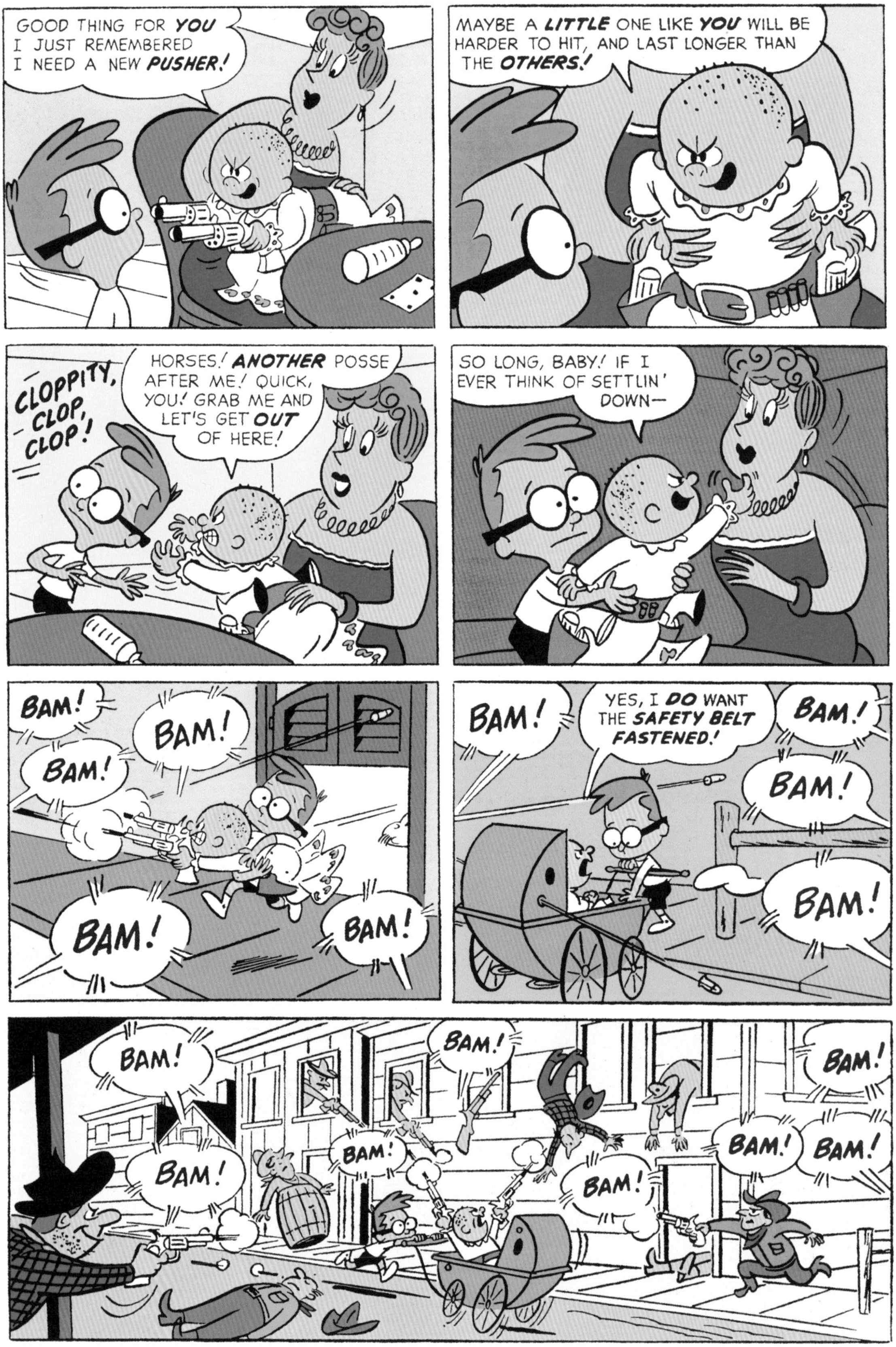
GOOD THING FOR YOU I JUST REMEMBERED I NEED A NEW PUSHER!
MAYBE A LITTLE ONE LIKE YOU WILL BE HARDER TO HIT, AND LAST LONGER THAN THE OTHERS!
CLOPPITY, CLOP, CLOP!
HORSES! ANOTHER POSSE AFTER ME! QUICK, YOU! GRAB ME AND LET'S GET OUT OF HERE!
SO LONG, BABY! IF I EVER THINK OF SETTLIN' DOWN—
BAM!
BAM!
BAM!
BAM!
BAM!
BAM!
YES, I DO WANT THE SAFETY BELT FASTENED!
BAM!
BAM!
BAM!
BAM!
BAM!
BAM!
BAM!
BAM!
BAM!
BAM!
BAM!
BAM!

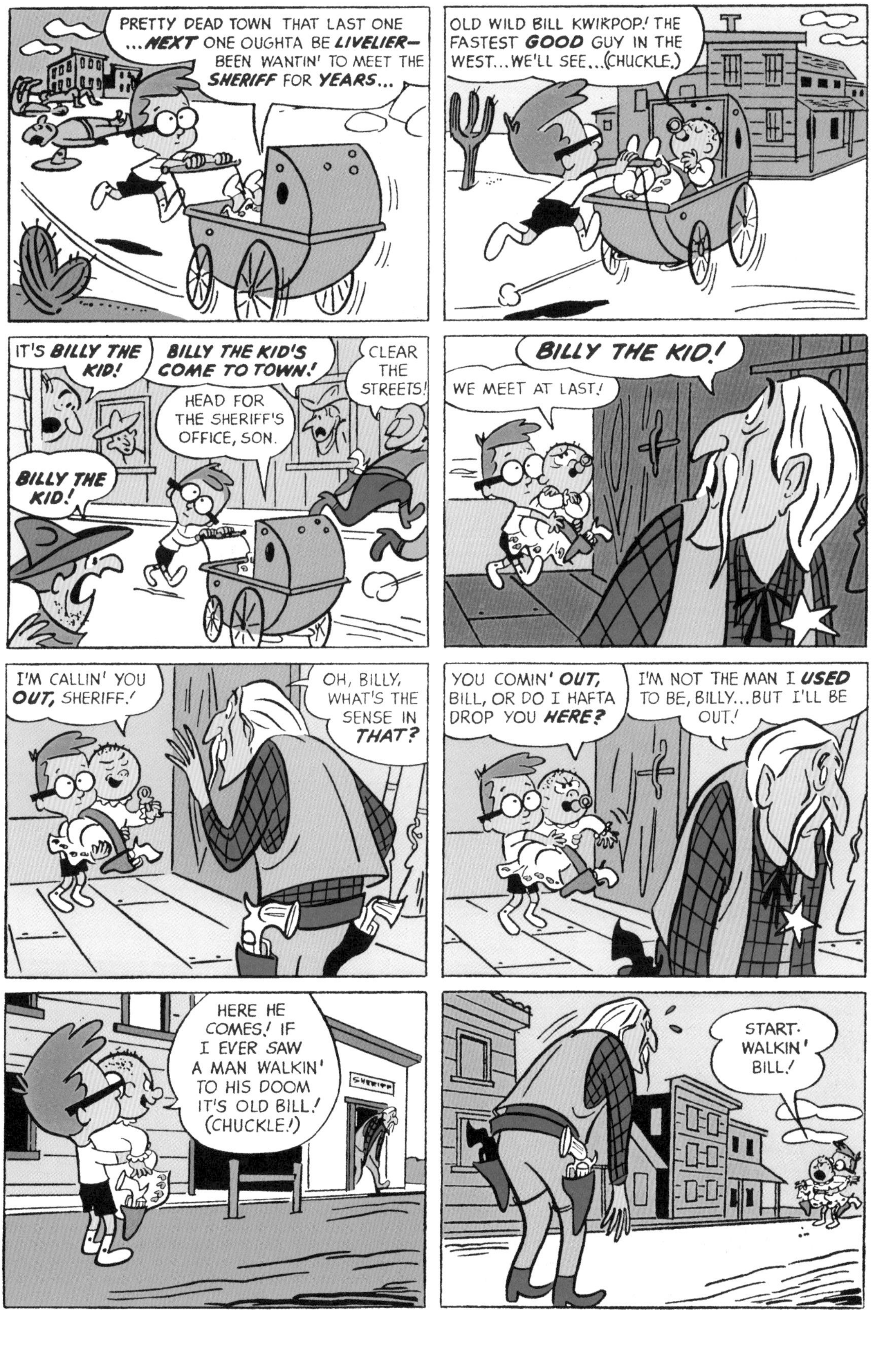
PRETTY DEAD TOWN THAT LAST ONE ...NEXT ONE OUGHTA BE LIVELIER— BEEN WANTIN' TO MEET THE SHERIFF FOR YEARS...
OLD WILD BILL KWIKPOP! THE FASTEST GOOD GUY IN THE WEST...WE'LL SEE...(CHUCKLE.)
IT'S BILLY THE KID!
BILLY THE KID'S COME TO TOWN!
CLEAR THE STREETS!
HEAD FOR THE SHERIFF'S OFFICE, SON.
BILLY THE KID!
BILLY THE KID!
WE MEET AT LAST!
I'M CALLIN' YOU OUT, SHERIFF!
OH, BILLY, WHAT'S THE SENSE IN THAT?
YOU COMIN' OUT, BILL, OR DO I HAFTA DROP YOU HERE?
I'M NOT THE MAN I USED TO BE, BILLY...BUT I'LL BE OUT!
HERE HE COMES! IF I EVER SAW A MAN WALKIN' TO HIS DOOM IT'S OLD BILL! (CHUCKLE!)
SHERIFF
START WALKIN' BILL!

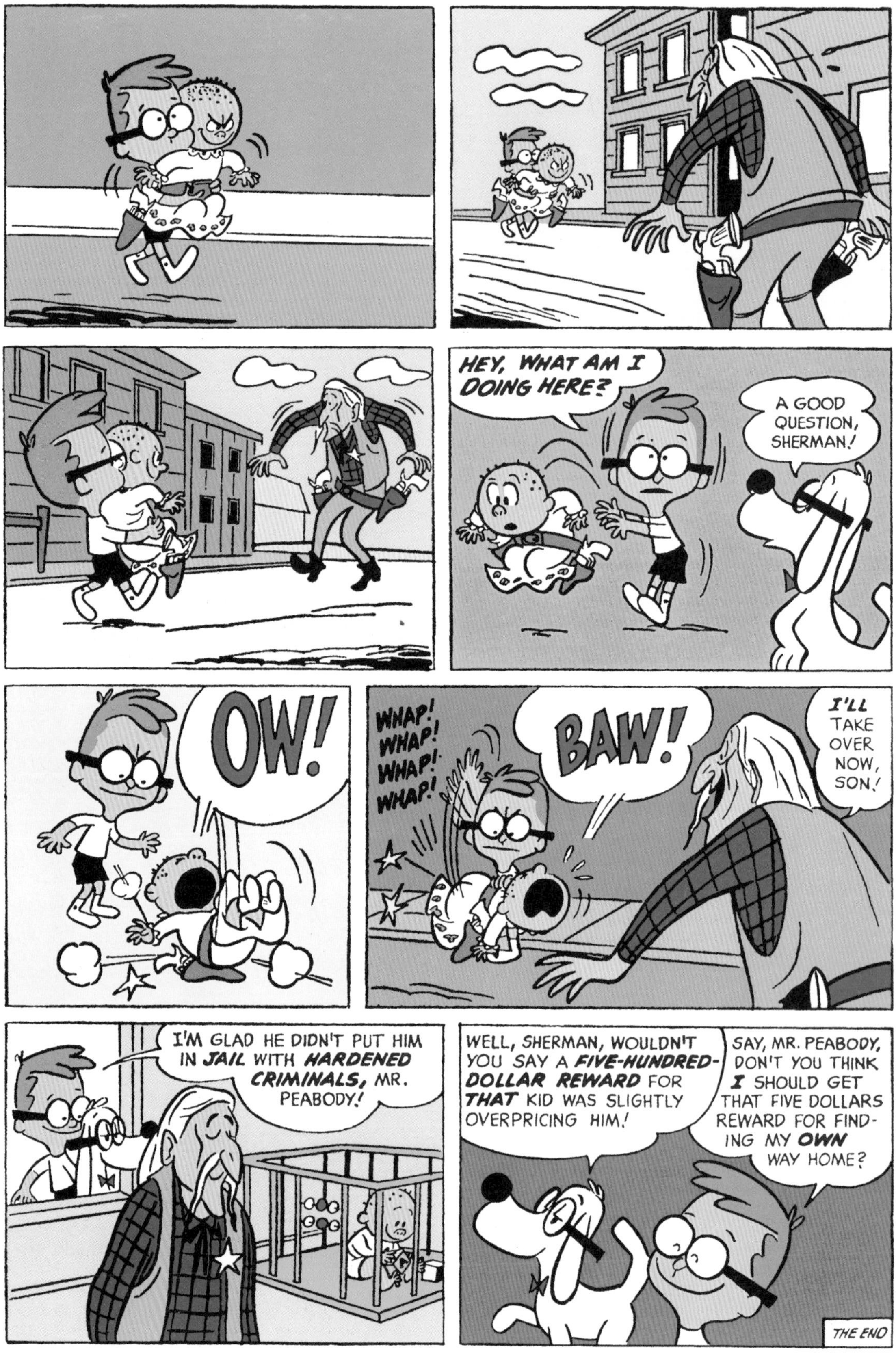
HEY, WHAT AM I DOING HERE?
A GOOD QUESTION, SHERMAN!
OW!
WHAP! WHAP! WHAP! WHAP!
BAW!
I'LL TAKE OVER NOW, SON!
I'M GLAD HE DIDN'T PUT HIM IN JAIL WITH HARDENED CRIMINALS, MR. PEABODY!
WELL, SHERMAN, WOULDN'T YOU SAY A FIVE-HUNDRED-DOLLAR REWARD FOR THAT KID WAS SLIGHTLY OVERPRICING HIM!
SAY, MR. PEABODY, DON'T YOU THINK I SHOULD GET THAT FIVE DOLLARS REWARD FOR FINDING MY OWN WAY HOME?
THE END

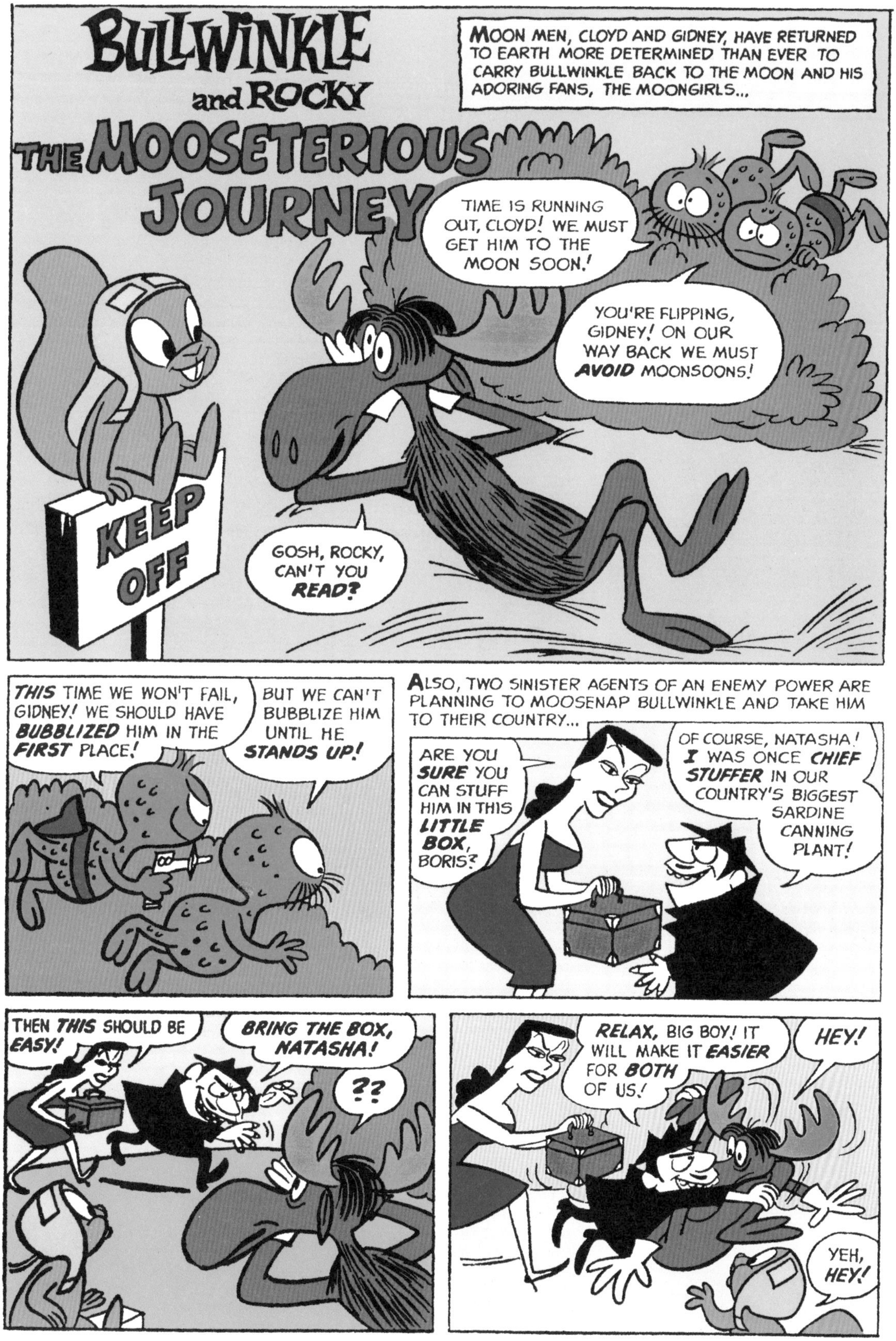
BULLWINKLE and ROCKY
THE MOOSETERIOUS JOURNEY
MOON MEN, CLOYD AND GIDNEY, HAVE RETURNED TO EARTH MORE DETERMINED THAN EVER TO CARRY BULLWINKLE BACK TO THE MOON AND HIS ADORING FANS, THE MOONGIRLS...
TIME IS RUNNING OUT, CLOYD! WE MUST GET HIM TO THE MOON SOON!
YOU'RE FLIPPING, GIDNEY! ON OUR WAY BACK WE MUST AVOID MOONSOONS!
KEEP OFF
GOSH, ROCKY, CAN'T YOU READ?
THIS TIME WE WON'T FAIL, GIDNEY! WE SHOULD HAVE BUBBLIZED HIM IN THE FIRST PLACE!
BUT WE CAN'T BUBBLIZE HIM UNTIL HE STANDS UP!
ALSO, TWO SINISTER AGENTS OF AN ENEMY POWER ARE PLANNING TO MOOSENAP BULLWINKLE AND TAKE HIM TO THEIR COUNTRY...
ARE YOU SURE YOU CAN STUFF HIM IN THIS LITTLE BOX, BORIS?
OF COURSE, NATASHA! I WAS ONCE CHIEF STUFFER IN OUR COUNTRY'S BIGGEST SARDINE CANNING PLANT!
THEN THIS SHOULD BE EASY!
BRING THE BOX, NATASHA!
??
RELAX, BIG BOY! IT WILL MAKE IT EASIER FOR BOTH OF US!
HEY!
YEH, HEY!

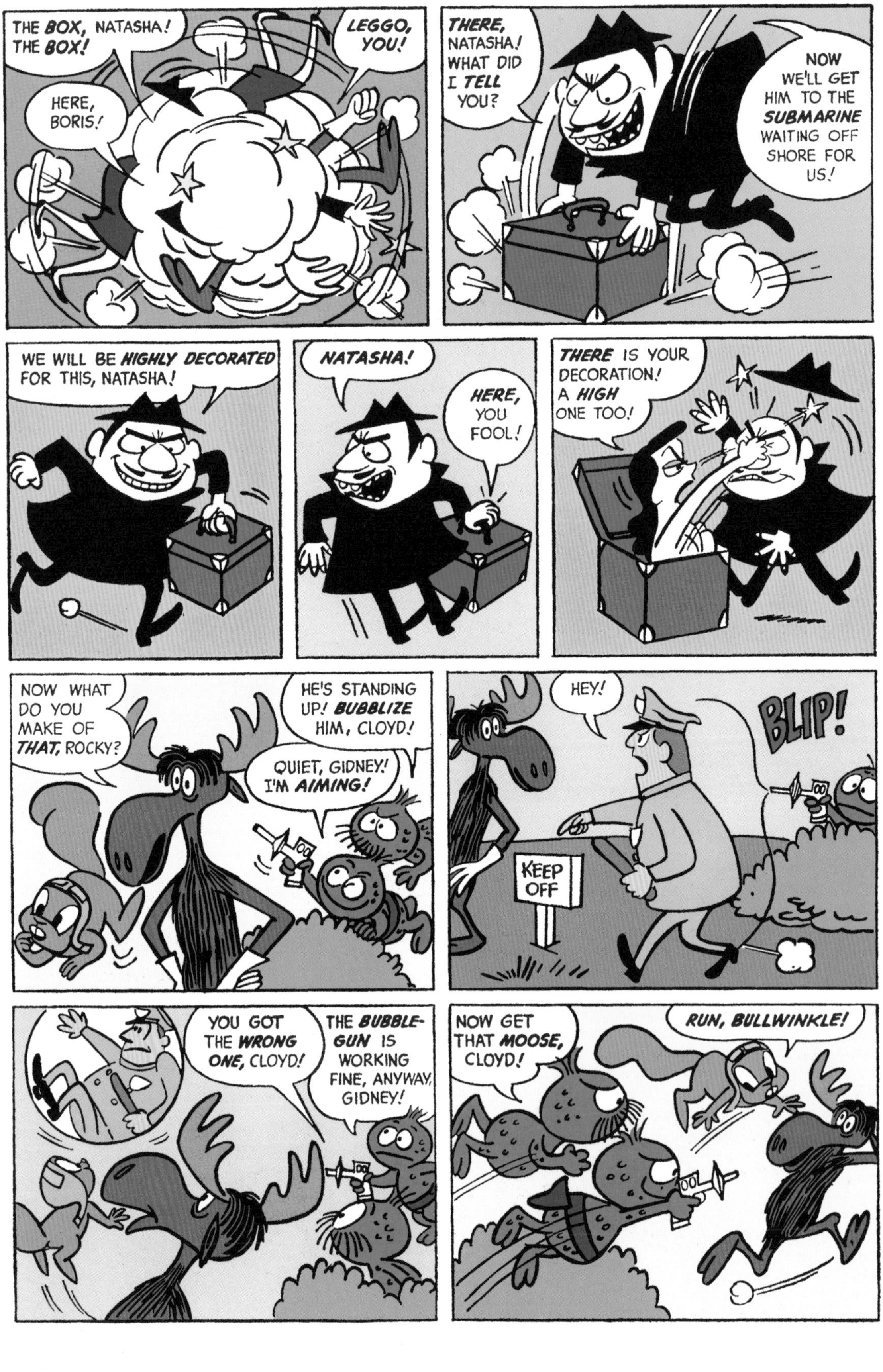

THE BOX, NATASHA! THE BOX!
LEGGO, YOU!
HERE, BORIS!
THERE, NATASHA! WHAT DID I TELL YOU?
NOW WE'LL GET HIM TO THE SUBMARINE WAITING OFF SHORE FOR US!
WE WILL BE HIGHLY DECORATED FOR THIS, NATASHA!
NATASHA!
HERE, YOU FOOL!
THERE IS YOUR DECORATION! A HIGH ONE TOO!
NOW WHAT DO YOU MAKE OF THAT, ROCKY?
HE'S STANDING UP! BUBBLIZE HIM, CLOYD!
QUIET, GIDNEY! I'M AIMING!
HEY!
BLIP!
KEEP OFF
YOU GOT THE WRONG ONE, CLOYD!
THE BUBBLE-GUN IS WORKING FINE, ANYWAY, GIDNEY!
NOW GET THAT MOOSE, CLOYD!
RUN, BULLWINKLE!

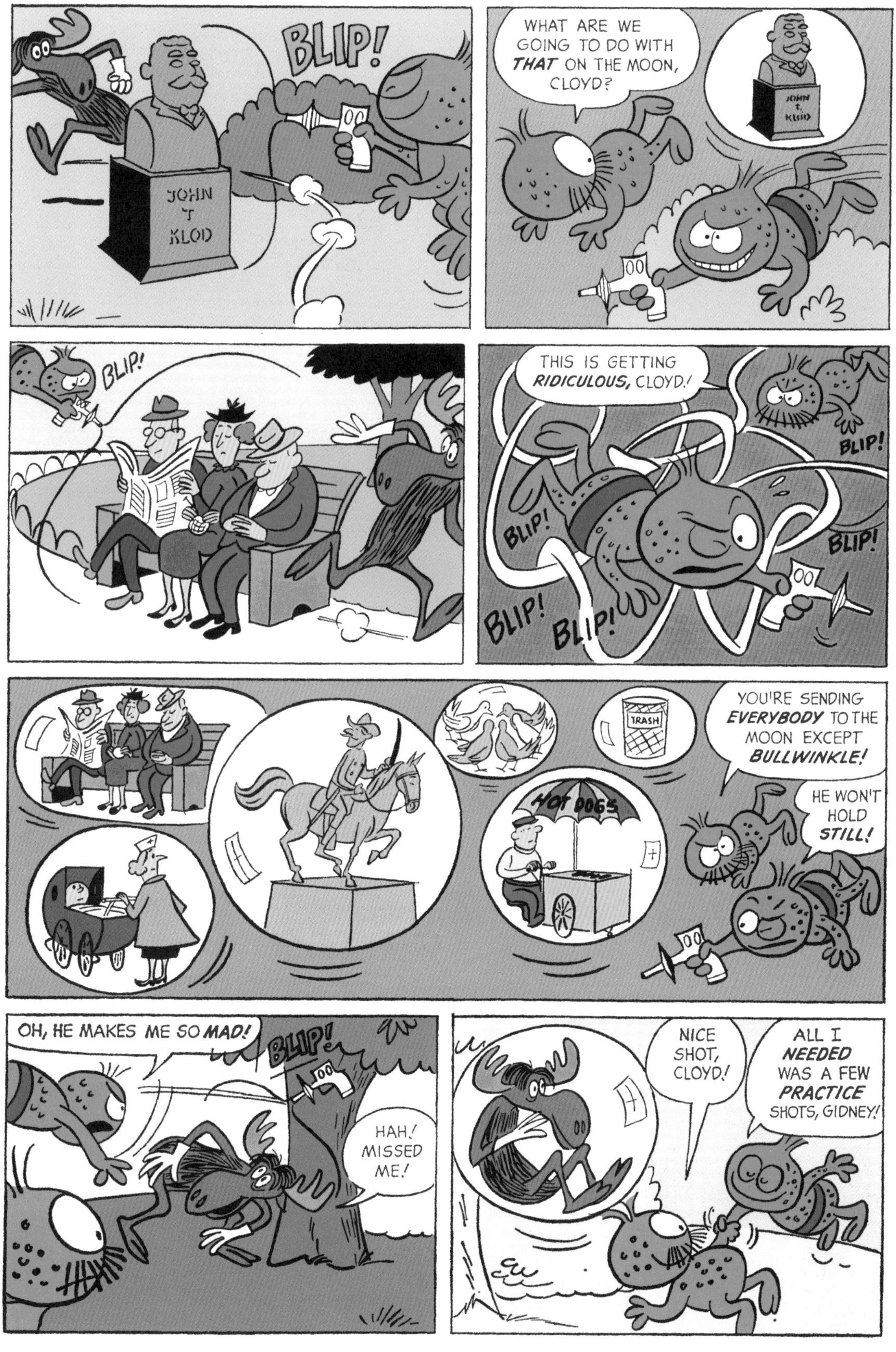

BLIP!
JOHN T KLOD
WHAT ARE WE GOING TO DO WITH THAT ON THE MOON, CLOYD?
JOHN T. KLOD
BLIP!
THIS IS GETTING RIDICULOUS, CLOYD!
BLIP!
BLIP!
BLIP!
BLIP!
BLIP!
TRASH
HOT DOGS
YOU'RE SENDING EVERYBODY TO THE MOON EXCEPT BULLWINKLE!
HE WON'T HOLD STILL!
OH, HE MAKES ME SO MAD!
BLIP!
HAH! MISSED ME!
NICE SHOT, CLOYD!
ALL I NEEDED WAS A FEW PRACTICE SHOTS, GIDNEY!

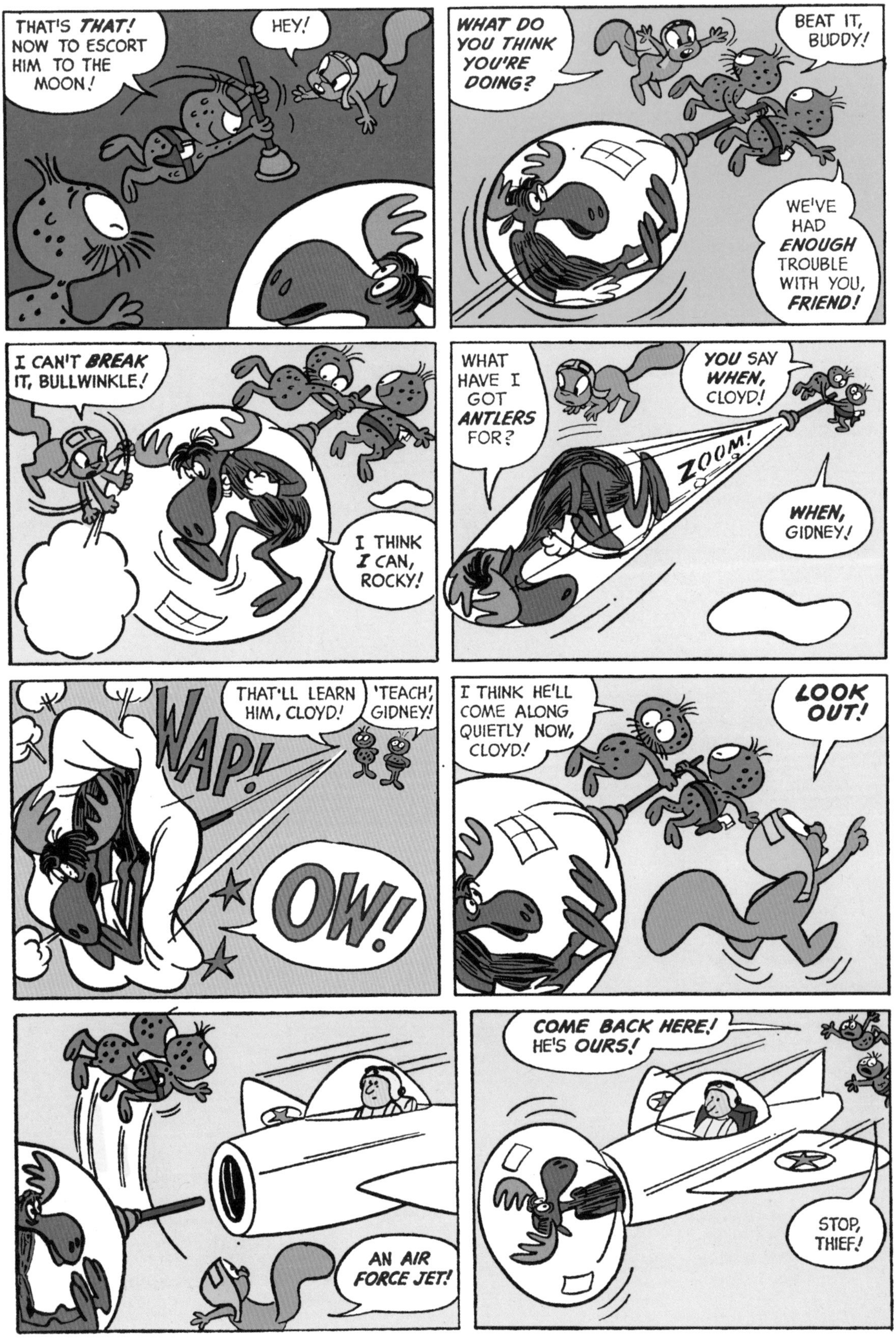
THAT'S THAT! NOW TO ESCORT HIM TO THE MOON!
HEY!
WHAT DO YOU THINK YOU'RE DOING?
BEAT IT, BUDDY!
WE'VE HAD ENOUGH TROUBLE WITH YOU, FRIEND!
I CAN'T BREAK IT, BULLWINKLE!
I THINK I CAN, ROCKY!
WHAT HAVE I GOT ANTLERS FOR?
YOU SAY WHEN, CLOYD!
ZOOM!
WHEN, GIDNEY!
WAP!
THAT'LL LEARN HIM, CLOYD!
'TEACH,' GIDNEY!
OW!
I THINK HE'LL COME ALONG QUIETLY NOW, CLOYD!
LOOK OUT!
AN AIR FORCE JET!
COME BACK HERE! HE'S OURS!
STOP, THIEF!

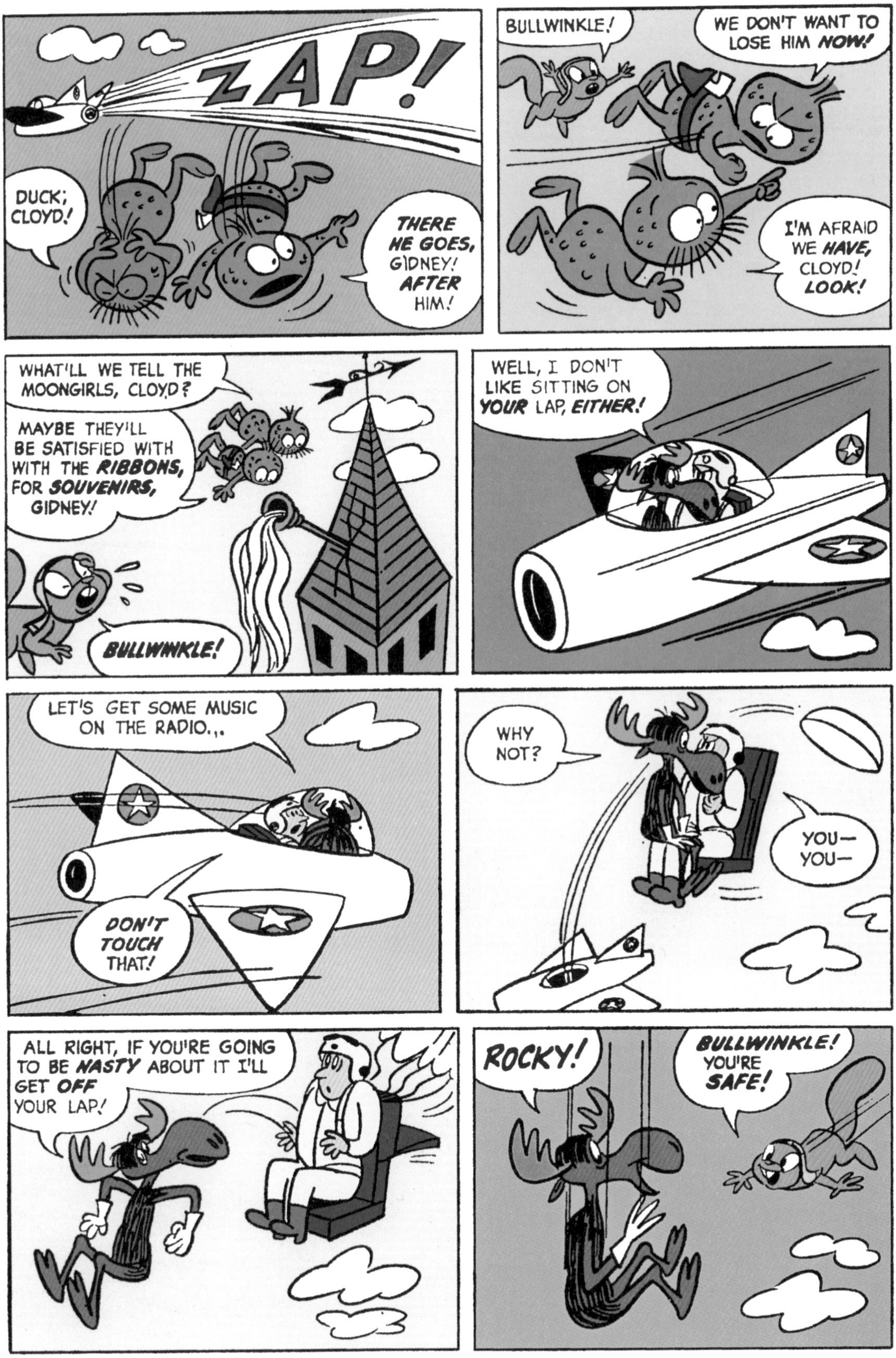
ZAP!
DUCK; CLOYD!
THERE HE GOES, GIDNEY! AFTER HIM!
BULLWINKLE!
WE DON'T WANT TO LOSE HIM NOW!
I'M AFRAID WE HAVE, CLOYD! LOOK!
WHAT'LL WE TELL THE MOONGIRLS, CLOYD?
MAYBE THEY'LL BE SATISFIED WITH WITH THE RIBBONS, FOR SOUVENIRS, GIDNEY!
BULLWINKLE!
WELL, I DON'T LIKE SITTING ON YOUR LAP, EITHER!
LET'S GET SOME MUSIC ON THE RADIO...
DON'T TOUCH THAT!
WHY NOT?
YOU— YOU—
ALL RIGHT, IF YOU'RE GOING TO BE NASTY ABOUT IT I'LL GET OFF YOUR LAP!
ROCKY!
BULLWINKLE! YOU'RE SAFE!

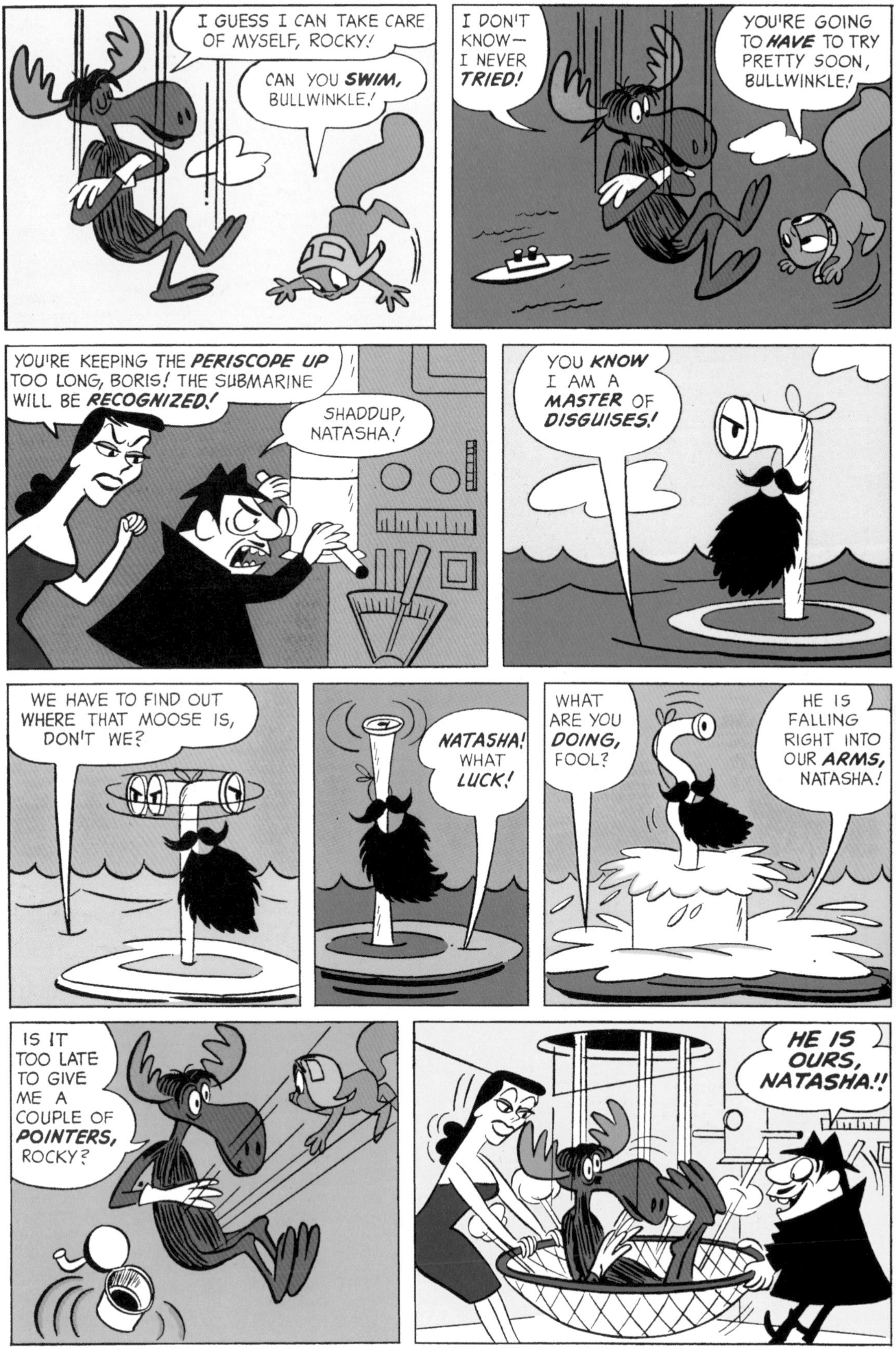
I GUESS I CAN TAKE CARE OF MYSELF, ROCKY!
CAN YOU SWIM, BULLWINKLE!
I DON'T KNOW— I NEVER TRIED!
YOU'RE GOING TO HAVE TO TRY PRETTY SOON, BULLWINKLE!
YOU'RE KEEPING THE PERISCOPE UP TOO LONG, BORIS! THE SUBMARINE WILL BE RECOGNIZED!
SHADDUP, NATASHA!
YOU KNOW I AM A MASTER OF DISGUISES!
WE HAVE TO FIND OUT WHERE THAT MOOSE IS, DON'T WE?
NATASHA! WHAT LUCK!
WHAT ARE YOU DOING, FOOL?
HE IS FALLING RIGHT INTO OUR ARMS, NATASHA!
IS IT TOO LATE TO GIVE ME A COUPLE OF POINTERS, ROCKY?
HE IS OURS, NATASHA!!

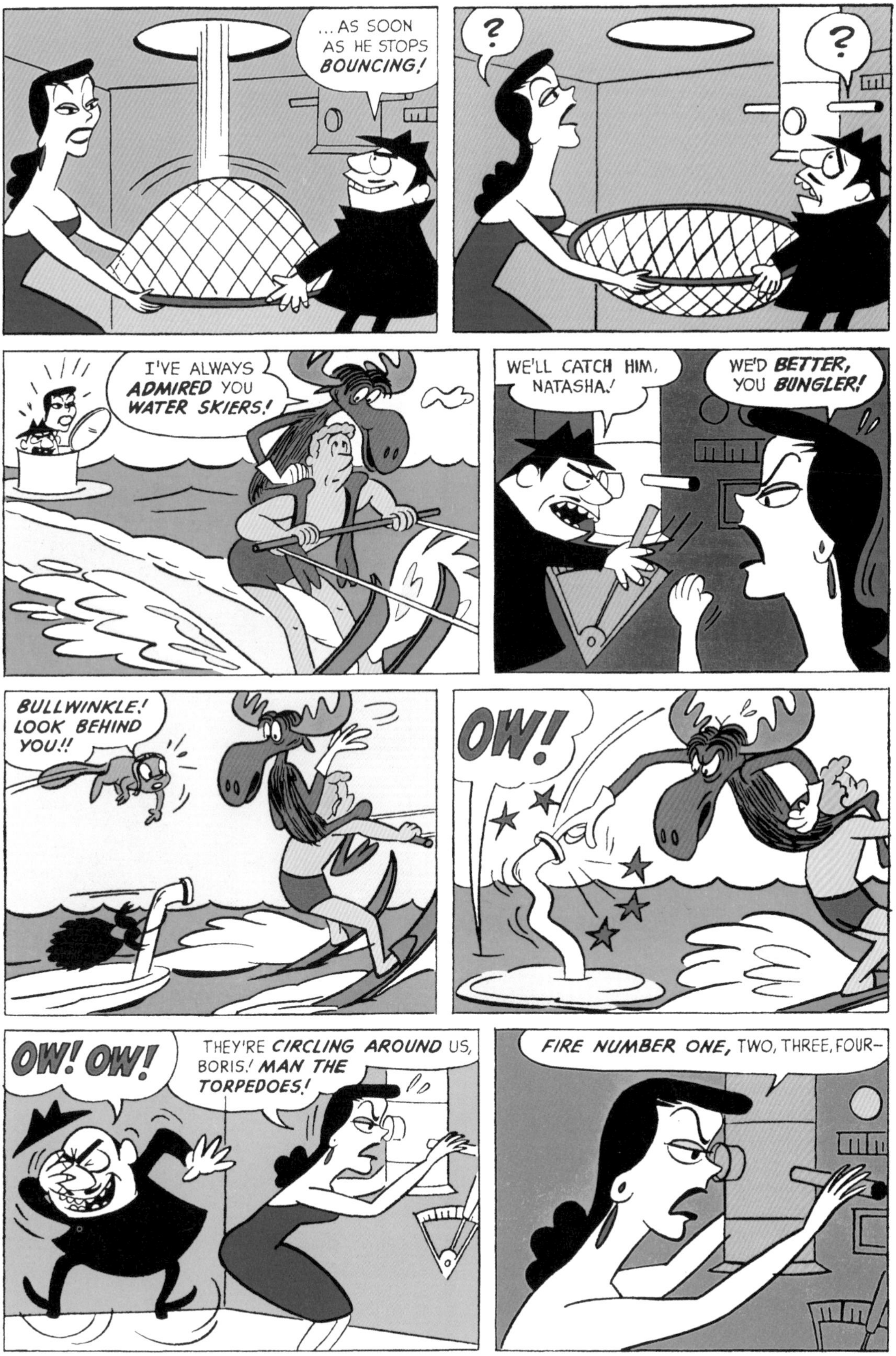
...AS SOON AS HE STOPS BOUNCING!
?
?
I'VE ALWAYS ADMIRED YOU WATER SKIERS!
WE'LL CATCH HIM, NATASHA!
WE'D BETTER, YOU BUNGLER!
BULLWINKLE! LOOK BEHIND YOU!!
OW!
OW! OW!
THEY'RE CIRCLING AROUND US, BORIS! MAN THE TORPEDOES!
FIRE NUMBER ONE, TWO, THREE, FOUR—

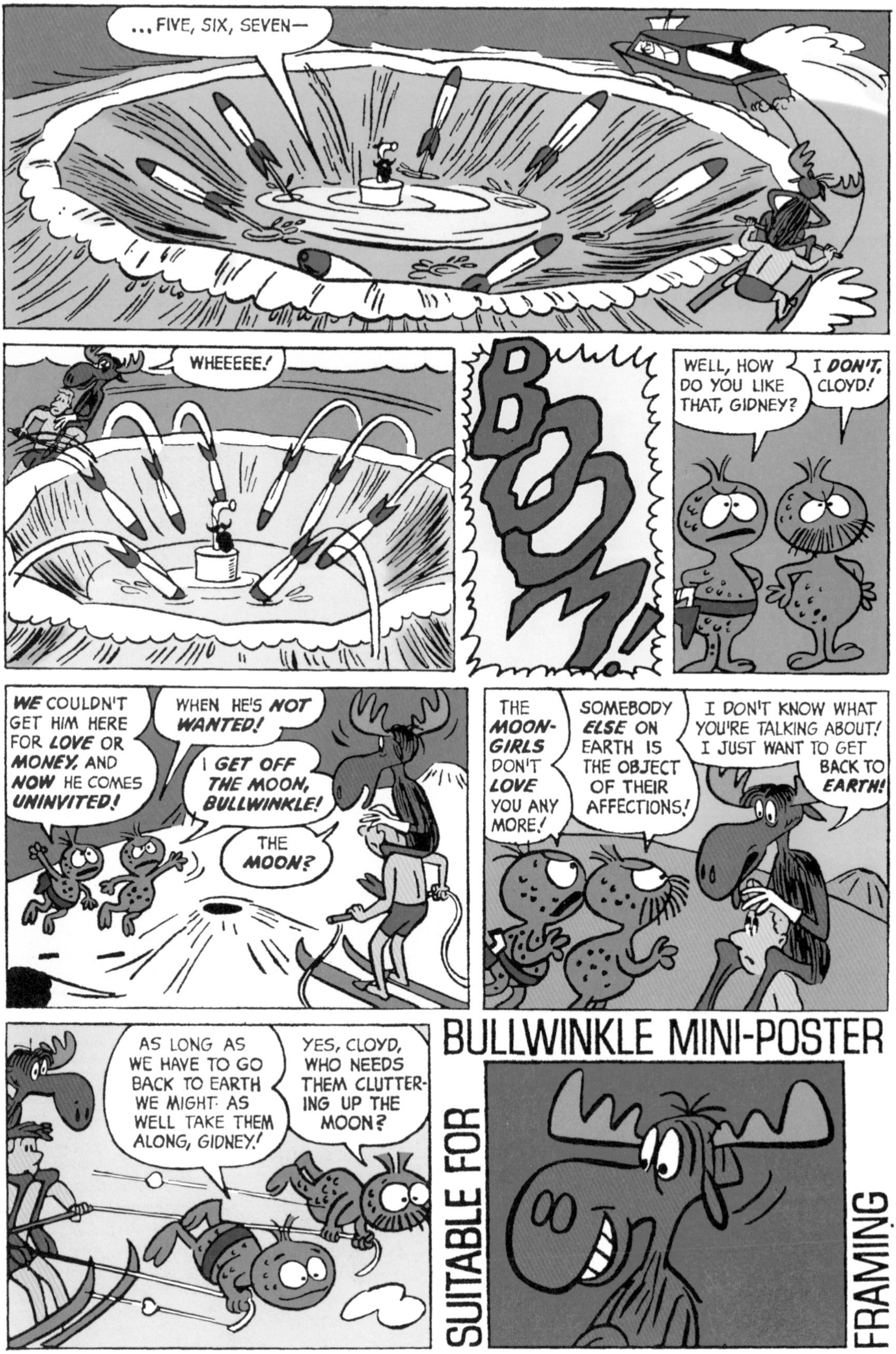
...FIVE, SIX, SEVEN—
WHEEEEEE!
BOOM!
WELL, HOW DO YOU LIKE THAT, GIDNEY?
I DON'T, CLOYD!
WE COULDN'T GET HIM HERE FOR LOVE OR MONEY, AND NOW HE COMES UNINVITED!
WHEN HE'S NOT WANTED!
I GET OFF THE MOON, BULLWINKLE!
THE MOON?
THE MOON-GIRLS DON'T LOVE YOU ANY MORE!
SOMEBODY ELSE ON EARTH IS THE OBJECT OF THEIR AFFECTIONS!
I DON'T KNOW WHAT YOU'RE TALKING ABOUT! I JUST WANT TO GET BACK TO EARTH!
AS LONG AS WE HAVE TO GO BACK TO EARTH WE MIGHT AS WELL TAKE THEM ALONG, GIDNEY!
YES, CLOYD, WHO NEEDS THEM CLUTTERING UP THE MOON?
BULLWINKLE MINI-POSTER
SUITABLE FOR
FRAMING

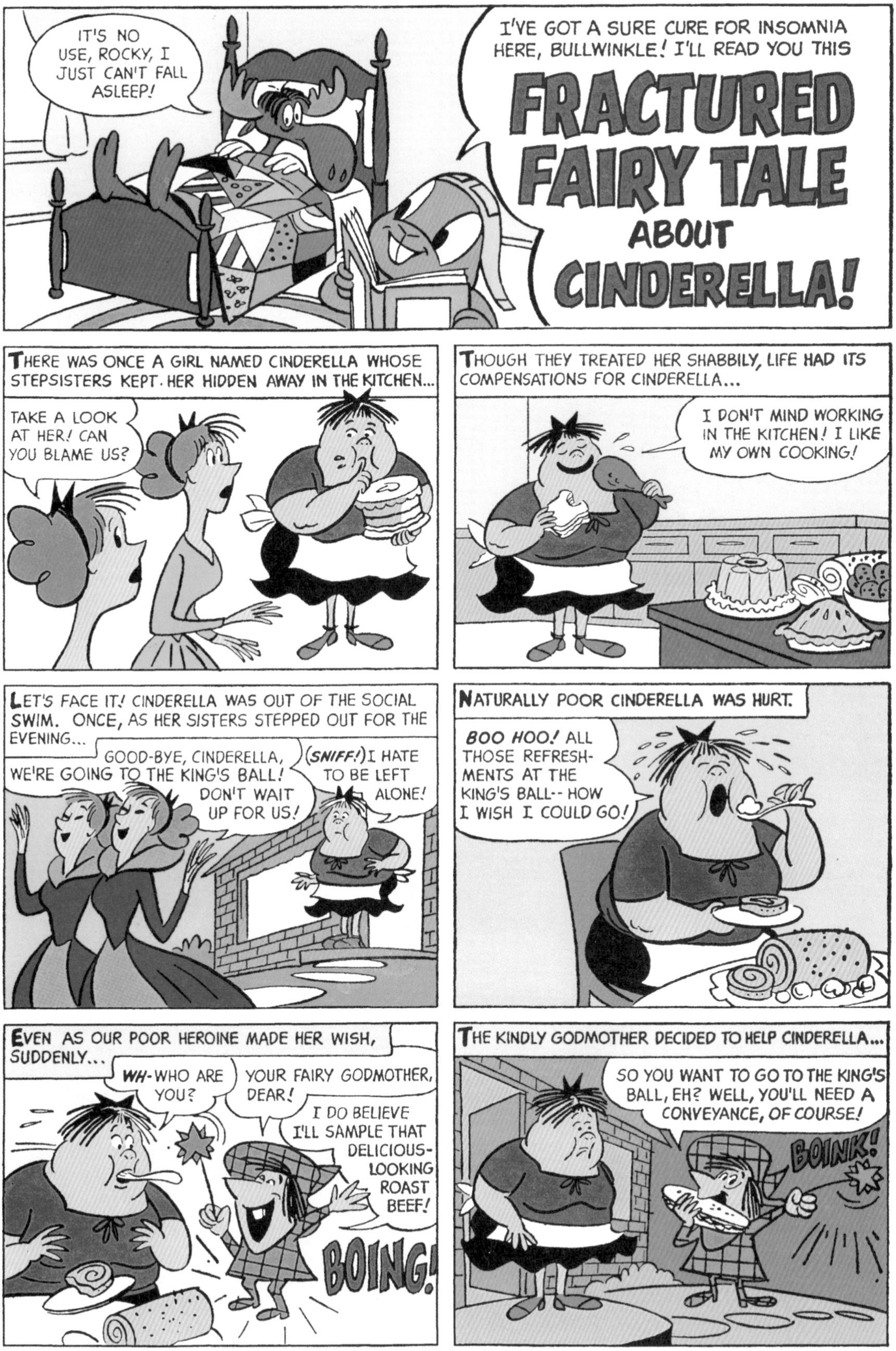

IT'S NO USE, ROCKY, I JUST CAN'T FALL ASLEEP!
I'VE GOT A SURE CURE FOR INSOMNIA HERE, BULLWINKLE! I'LL READ YOU THIS
FRACTURED FAIRY TALE ABOUT CINDERELLA!
THERE WAS ONCE A GIRL NAMED CINDERELLA WHOSE STEPSISTERS KEPT HER HIDDEN AWAY IN THE KITCHEN...
TAKE A LOOK AT HER! CAN YOU BLAME US?
THOUGH THEY TREATED HER SHABBILY, LIFE HAD ITS COMPENSATIONS FOR CINDERELLA...
I DON'T MIND WORKING IN THE KITCHEN! I LIKE MY OWN COOKING!
LET'S FACE IT! CINDERELLA WAS OUT OF THE SOCIAL SWIM. ONCE, AS HER SISTERS STEPPED OUT FOR THE EVENING...
GOOD-BYE, CINDERELLA, WE'RE GOING TO THE KING'S BALL! DON'T WAIT UP FOR US!
(SNIFF!) I HATE TO BE LEFT ALONE!
NATURALLY POOR CINDERELLA WAS HURT.
BOO HOO! ALL THOSE REFRESH-MENTS AT THE KING'S BALL-- HOW I WISH I COULD GO!
EVEN AS OUR POOR HEROINE MADE HER WISH, SUDDENLY...
WH-WHO ARE YOU?
YOUR FAIRY GODMOTHER, DEAR!
I DO BELIEVE I'LL SAMPLE THAT DELICIOUS-LOOKING ROAST BEEF!
BOING!
THE KINDLY GODMOTHER DECIDED TO HELP CINDERELLA...
SO YOU WANT TO GO TO THE KING'S BALL, EH? WELL, YOU'LL NEED A CONVEYANCE, OF COURSE!
BOINK!

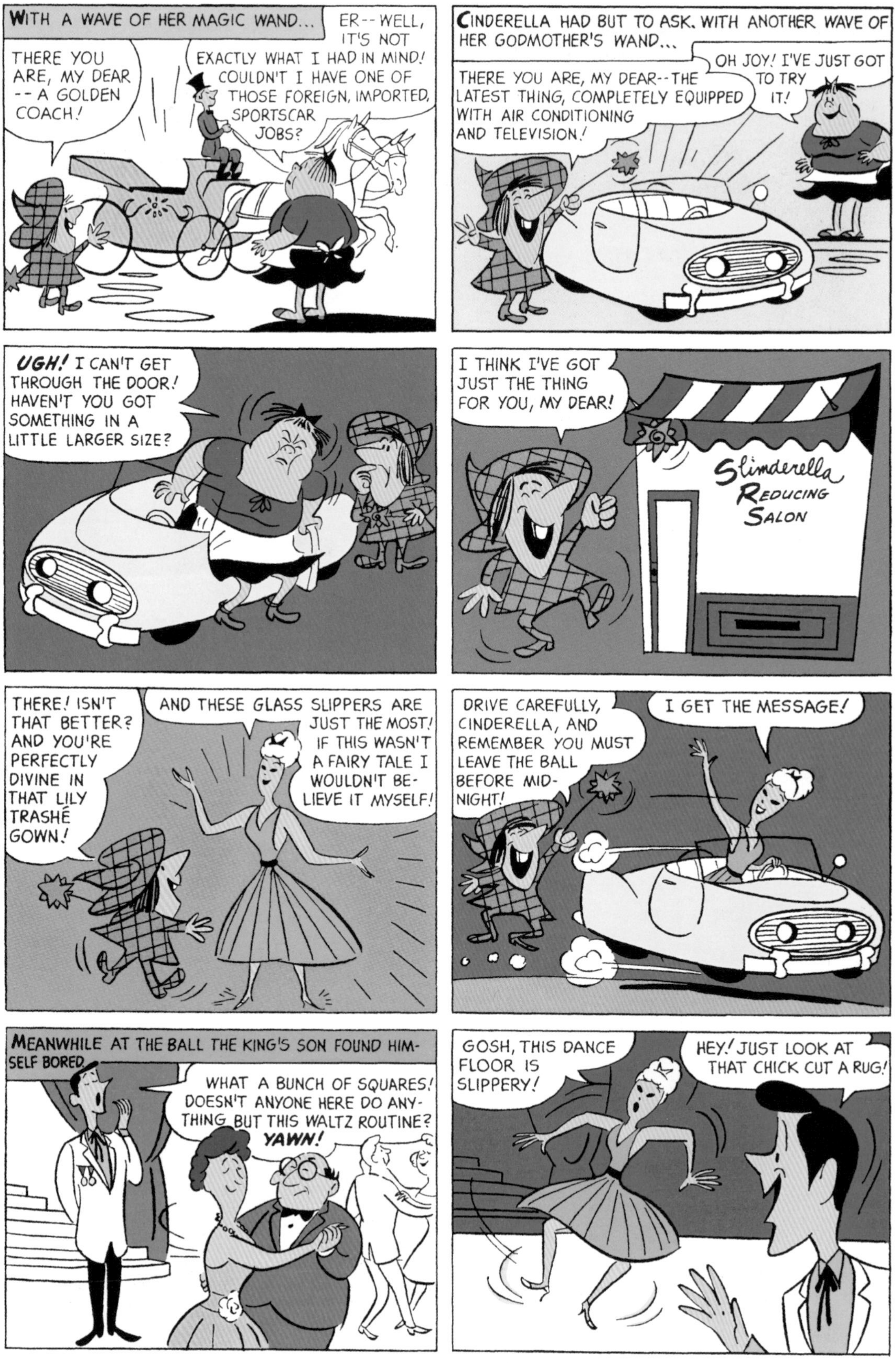
WITH A WAVE OF HER MAGIC WAND...
THERE YOU ARE, MY DEAR -- A GOLDEN COACH!
ER--WELL, IT'S NOT EXACTLY WHAT I HAD IN MIND! COULDN'T I HAVE ONE OF THOSE FOREIGN, IMPORTED, SPORTSCAR JOBS?
CINDERELLA HAD BUT TO ASK. WITH ANOTHER WAVE OF HER GODMOTHER'S WAND...
THERE YOU ARE, MY DEAR--THE LATEST THING, COMPLETELY EQUIPPED WITH AIR CONDITIONING AND TELEVISION!
OH JOY! I'VE JUST GOT TO TRY IT!
UGH! I CAN'T GET THROUGH THE DOOR! HAVEN'T YOU GOT SOMETHING IN A LITTLE LARGER SIZE?
I THINK I'VE GOT JUST THE THING FOR YOU, MY DEAR!
Slimderella Reducing Salon
THERE! ISN'T THAT BETTER? AND YOU'RE PERFECTLY DIVINE IN THAT LILY TRASHÉ GOWN!
AND THESE GLASS SLIPPERS ARE JUST THE MOST! IF THIS WASN'T A FAIRY TALE I WOULDN'T BELIEVE IT MYSELF!
DRIVE CAREFULLY, CINDERELLA, AND REMEMBER YOU MUST LEAVE THE BALL BEFORE MIDNIGHT!
I GET THE MESSAGE!
MEANWHILE AT THE BALL THE KING'S SON FOUND HIMSELF BORED.
WHAT A BUNCH OF SQUARES! DOESN'T ANYONE HERE DO ANYTHING BUT THIS WALTZ ROUTINE? YAWN!
GOSH, THIS DANCE FLOOR IS SLIPPERY!
HEY! JUST LOOK AT THAT CHICK CUT A RUG!

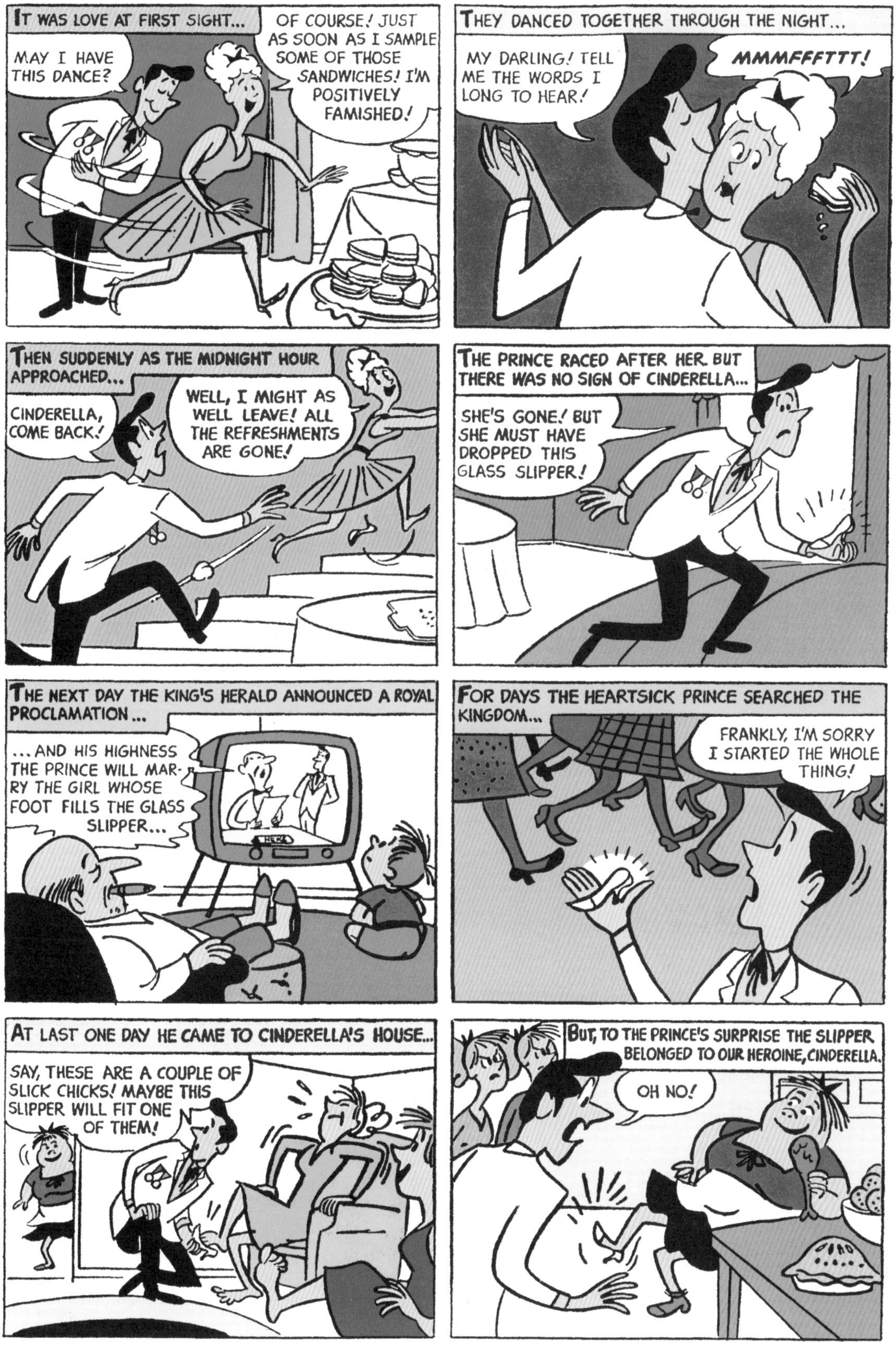
IT WAS LOVE AT FIRST SIGHT...
MAY I HAVE THIS DANCE?
OF COURSE! JUST AS SOON AS I SAMPLE SOME OF THOSE SANDWICHES! I'M POSITIVELY FAMISHED!
THEY DANCED TOGETHER THROUGH THE NIGHT...
MY DARLING! TELL ME THE WORDS I LONG TO HEAR!
MMMFFFTTT!
THEN SUDDENLY AS THE MIDNIGHT HOUR APPROACHED...
CINDERELLA, COME BACK!
WELL, I MIGHT AS WELL LEAVE! ALL THE REFRESHMENTS ARE GONE!
THE PRINCE RACED AFTER HER BUT THERE WAS NO SIGN OF CINDERELLA...
SHE'S GONE! BUT SHE MUST HAVE DROPPED THIS GLASS SLIPPER!
THE NEXT DAY THE KING'S HERALD ANNOUNCED A ROYAL PROCLAMATION...
...AND HIS HIGHNESS THE PRINCE WILL MARRY THE GIRL WHOSE FOOT FILLS THE GLASS SLIPPER...
FOR DAYS THE HEARTSICK PRINCE SEARCHED THE KINGDOM...
FRANKLY, I'M SORRY I STARTED THE WHOLE THING!
AT LAST ONE DAY HE CAME TO CINDERELLA'S HOUSE...
SAY, THESE ARE A COUPLE OF SLICK CHICKS! MAYBE THIS SLIPPER WILL FIT ONE OF THEM!
BUT, TO THE PRINCE'S SURPRISE THE SLIPPER BELONGED TO OUR HEROINE, CINDERELLA.
OH NO!

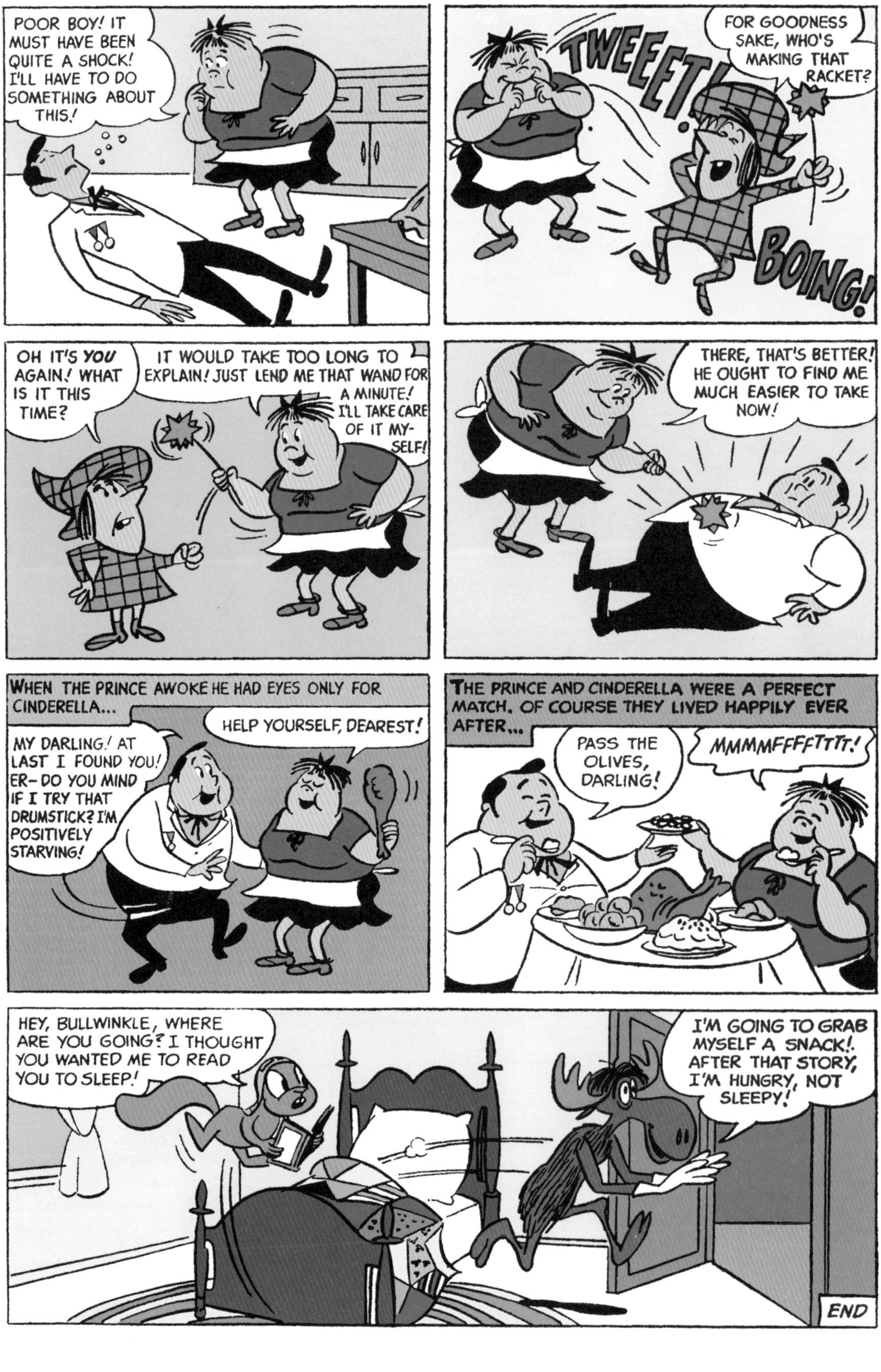
POOR BOY! IT MUST HAVE BEEN QUITE A SHOCK! I'LL HAVE TO DO SOMETHING ABOUT THIS!
TWEEET!
FOR GOODNESS SAKE, WHO'S MAKING THAT RACKET?
BOING!
OH IT'S *YOU* AGAIN! WHAT IS IT THIS TIME?
IT WOULD TAKE TOO LONG TO EXPLAIN! JUST LEND ME THAT WAND FOR A MINUTE! I'LL TAKE CARE OF IT MY-SELF!
THERE, THAT'S BETTER! HE OUGHT TO FIND ME MUCH EASIER TO TAKE NOW!
WHEN THE PRINCE AWOKE HE HAD EYES ONLY FOR CINDERELLA...
MY DARLING! AT LAST I FOUND YOU! ER- DO YOU MIND IF I TRY THAT DRUMSTICK? I'M POSITIVELY STARVING!
HELP YOURSELF, DEAREST!
THE PRINCE AND CINDERELLA WERE A PERFECT MATCH. OF COURSE THEY LIVED HAPPILY EVER AFTER...
PASS THE OLIVES, DARLING!
MMMMFFFFTTTT!
HEY, BULLWINKLE, WHERE ARE YOU GOING? I THOUGHT YOU WANTED ME TO READ YOU TO SLEEP!
I'M GOING TO GRAB MYSELF A SNACK!. AFTER THAT STORY, I'M HUNGRY, NOT SLEEPY!
END

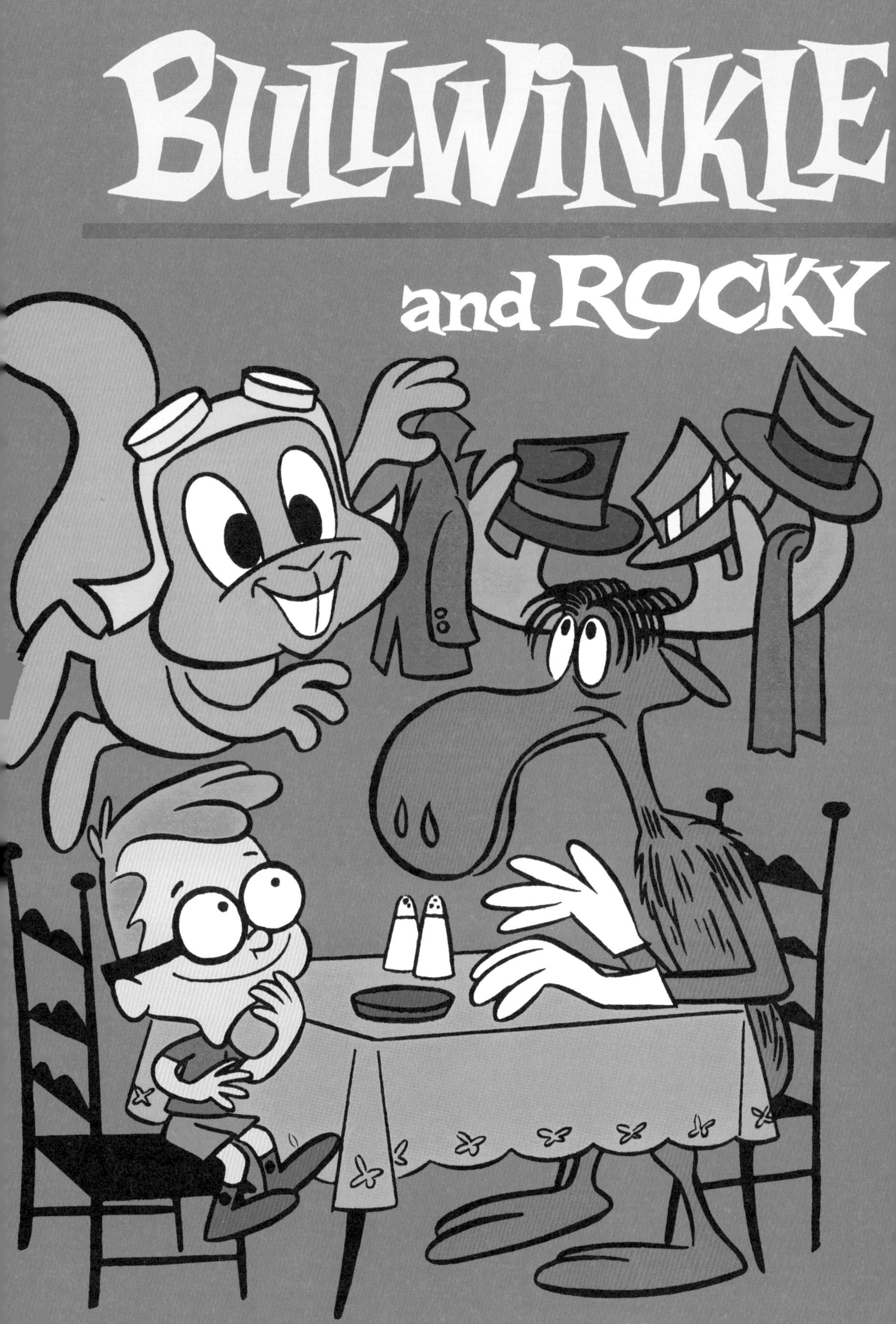
BULLWINKLE
and ROCKY

ISSUE #4 · GOLD KEY · JULY 1972

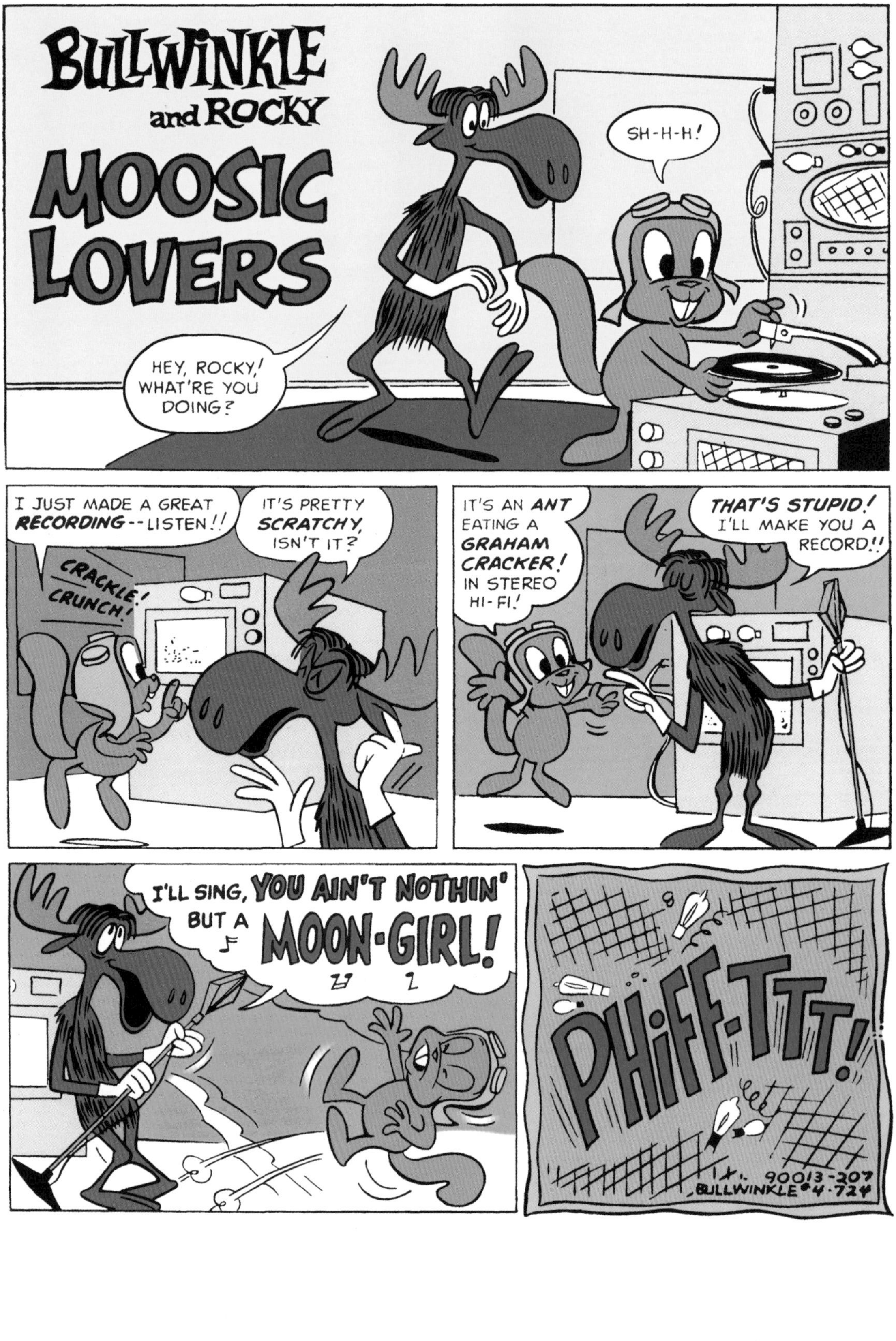
BULLWINKLE and ROCKY
MOOSIC LOVERS
HEY, ROCKY! WHAT'RE YOU DOING?
SH-H-H!
I JUST MADE A GREAT RECORDING--LISTEN!!
IT'S PRETTY SCRATCHY, ISN'T IT?
CRACKLE! CRUNCH!
IT'S AN ANT EATING A GRAHAM CRACKER! IN STEREO HI-FI!
THAT'S STUPID! I'LL MAKE YOU A RECORD!!
I'LL SING, YOU AIN'T NOTHIN' BUT A MOON-GIRL!
PHiFF-TTTT!
90013-207
BULLWINKLE #4-724

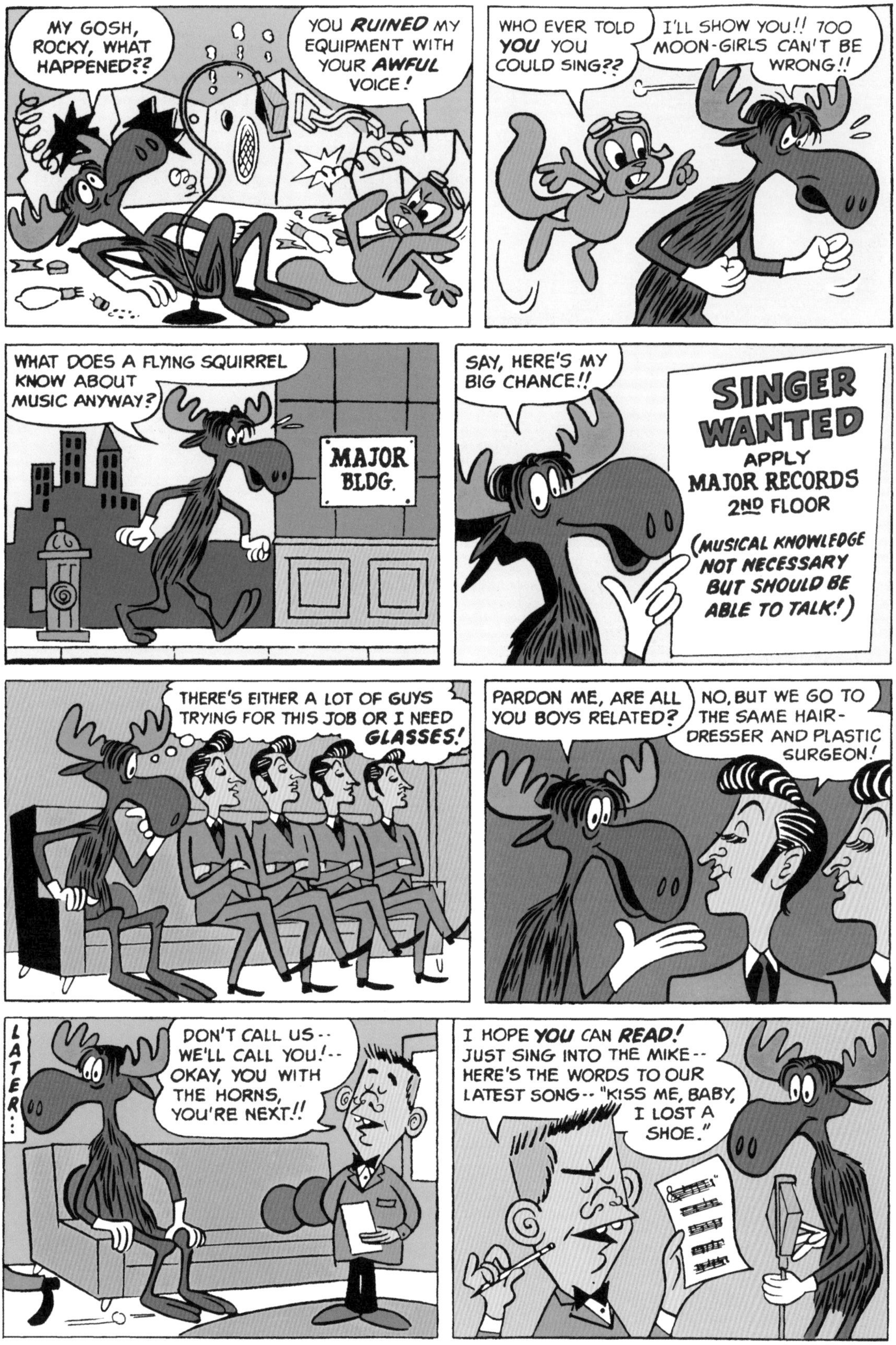
MY GOSH, ROCKY, WHAT HAPPENED??
YOU RUINED MY EQUIPMENT WITH YOUR AWFUL VOICE!
WHO EVER TOLD YOU YOU COULD SING??
I'LL SHOW YOU!! 700 MOON-GIRLS CAN'T BE WRONG!!
WHAT DOES A FLYING SQUIRREL KNOW ABOUT MUSIC ANYWAY?
MAJOR BLDG.
SAY, HERE'S MY BIG CHANCE!!
SINGER WANTED
APPLY MAJOR RECORDS 2ND FLOOR
(MUSICAL KNOWLEDGE NOT NECESSARY BUT SHOULD BE ABLE TO TALK!)
THERE'S EITHER A LOT OF GUYS TRYING FOR THIS JOB OR I NEED GLASSES!
PARDON ME, ARE ALL YOU BOYS RELATED?
NO, BUT WE GO TO THE SAME HAIR-DRESSER AND PLASTIC SURGEON!
LATER...
DON'T CALL US-- WE'LL CALL YOU!-- OKAY, YOU WITH THE HORNS, YOU'RE NEXT!!
I HOPE YOU CAN READ! JUST SING INTO THE MIKE-- HERE'S THE WORDS TO OUR LATEST SONG-- "KISS ME, BABY, I LOST A SHOE."

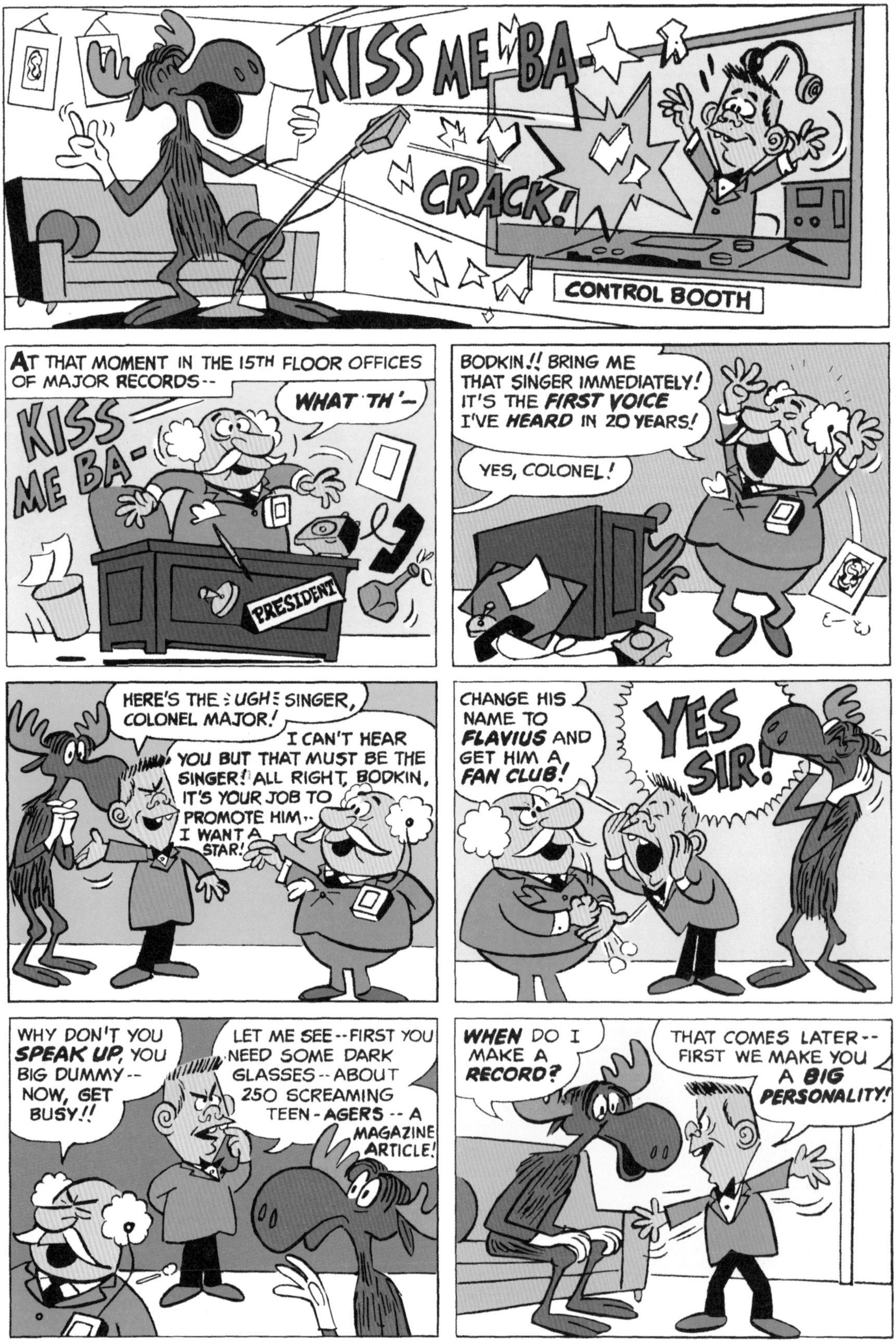
KISS ME BA-
CRACK!
CONTROL BOOTH
AT THAT MOMENT IN THE 15TH FLOOR OFFICES OF MAJOR RECORDS--
KISS ME BA-
WHAT TH'--
PRESIDENT
BODKIN!! BRING ME THAT SINGER IMMEDIATELY! IT'S THE FIRST VOICE I'VE HEARD IN 20 YEARS!
YES, COLONEL!
HERE'S THE :UGH: SINGER, COLONEL MAJOR!
I CAN'T HEAR YOU BUT THAT MUST BE THE SINGER! ALL RIGHT, BODKIN, IT'S YOUR JOB TO PROMOTE HIM-- I WANT A STAR!
CHANGE HIS NAME TO FLAVIUS AND GET HIM A FAN CLUB!
YES SIR!
WHY DON'T YOU SPEAK UP, YOU BIG DUMMY-- NOW, GET BUSY!!
LET ME SEE--FIRST YOU NEED SOME DARK GLASSES--ABOUT 250 SCREAMING TEEN-AGERS--A MAGAZINE ARTICLE!
WHEN DO I MAKE A RECORD?
THAT COMES LATER-- FIRST WE MAKE YOU A BIG PERSONALITY!

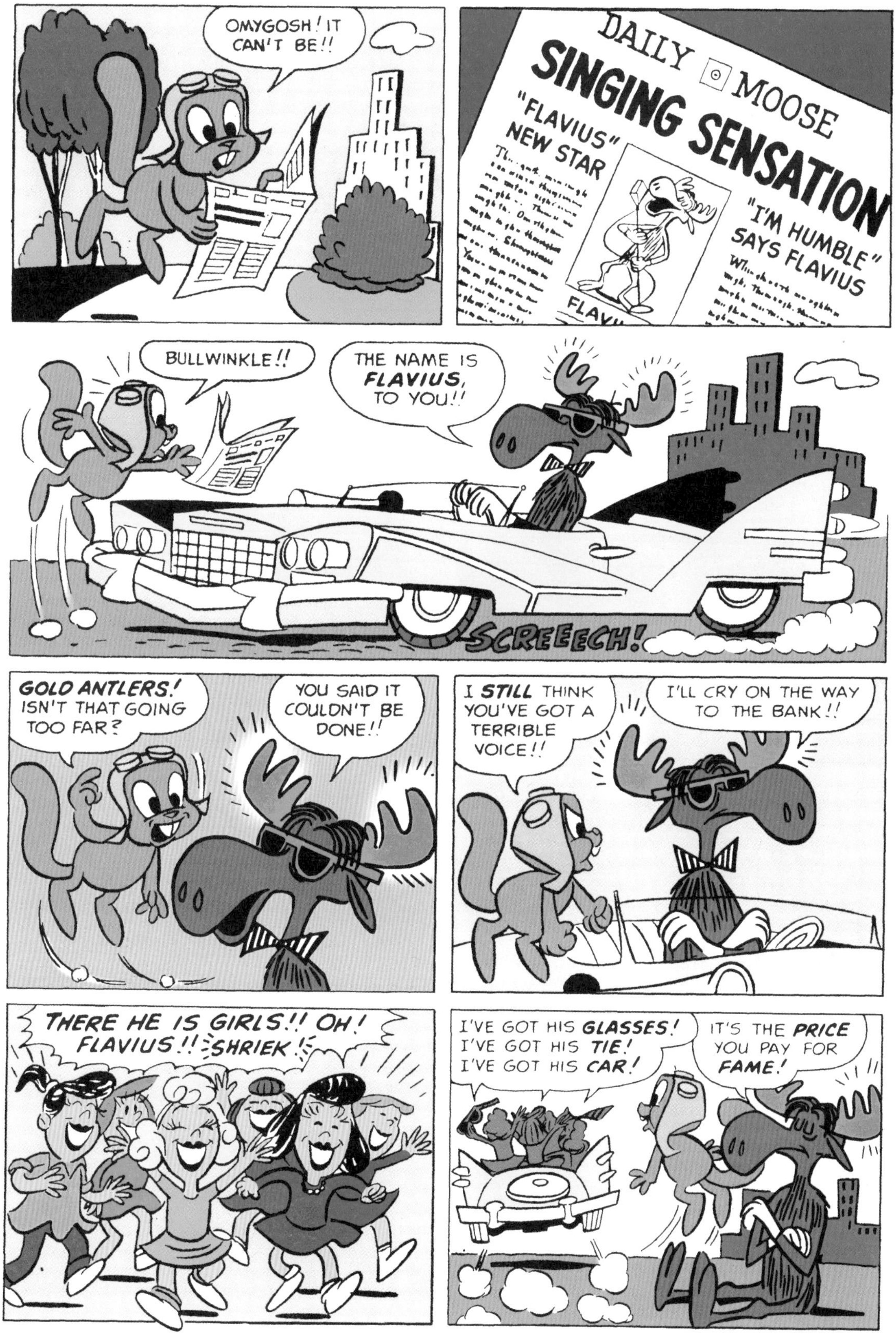
OMYGOSH! IT CAN'T BE!!
DAILY MOOSE
SINGING SENSATION
"FLAVIUS" NEW STAR
"I'M HUMBLE" SAYS FLAVIUS
BULLWINKLE!!
THE NAME IS FLAVIUS, TO YOU!!
SCREEECH!
GOLD ANTLERS! ISN'T THAT GOING TOO FAR?
YOU SAID IT COULDN'T BE DONE!!
I STILL THINK YOU'VE GOT A TERRIBLE VOICE!!
I'LL CRY ON THE WAY TO THE BANK!!
THERE HE IS GIRLS!! OH! FLAVIUS!! SHRIEK!
I'VE GOT HIS GLASSES! I'VE GOT HIS TIE! I'VE GOT HIS CAR!
IT'S THE PRICE YOU PAY FOR FAME!

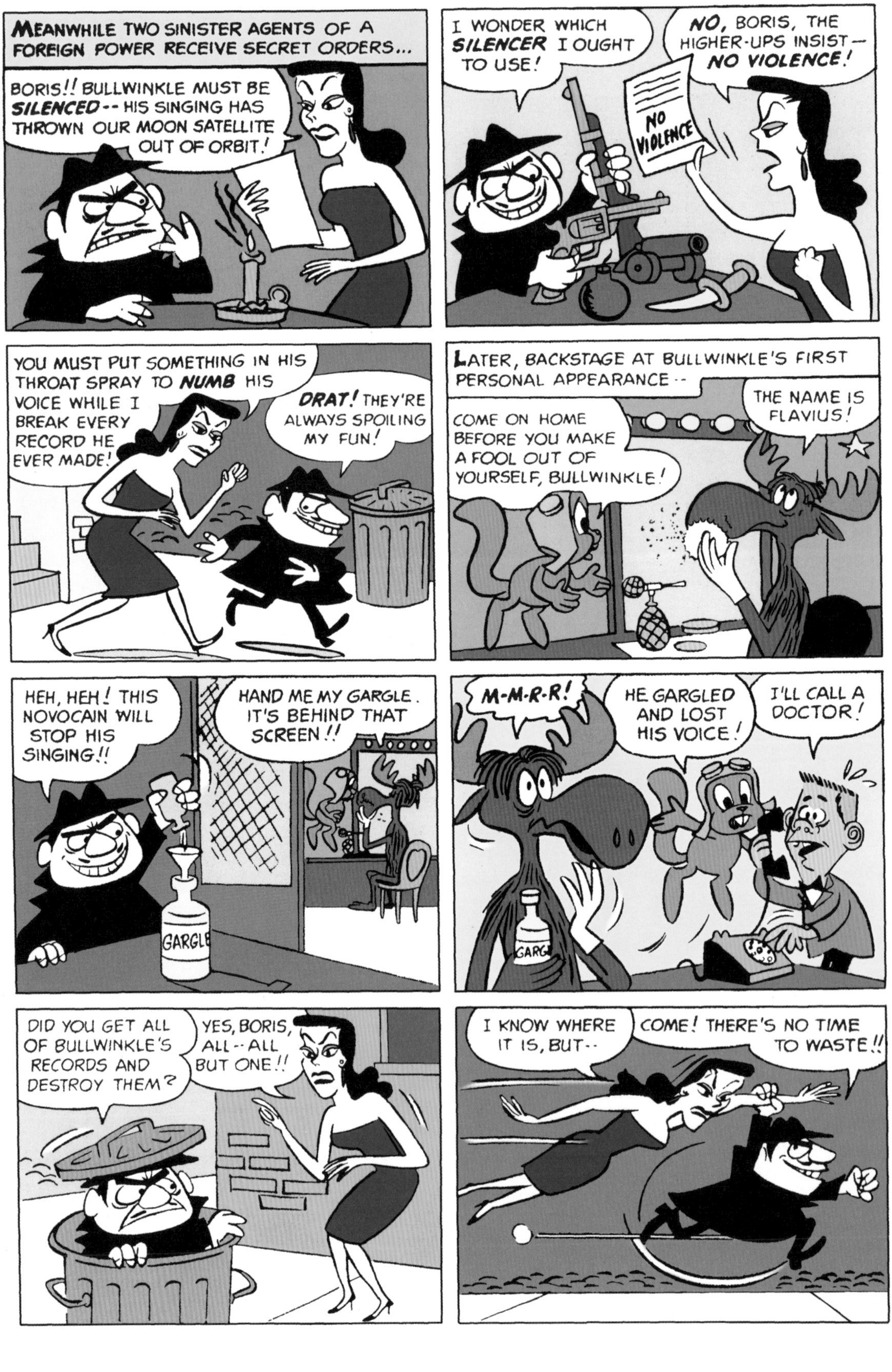
MEANWHILE TWO SINISTER AGENTS OF A FOREIGN POWER RECEIVE SECRET ORDERS...
BORIS!! BULLWINKLE MUST BE SILENCED -- HIS SINGING HAS THROWN OUR MOON SATELLITE OUT OF ORBIT!
I WONDER WHICH SILENCER I OUGHT TO USE!
NO, BORIS, THE HIGHER-UPS INSIST — NO VIOLENCE!
NO VIOLENCE
YOU MUST PUT SOMETHING IN HIS THROAT SPRAY TO NUMB HIS VOICE WHILE I BREAK EVERY RECORD HE EVER MADE!
DRAT! THEY'RE ALWAYS SPOILING MY FUN!
LATER, BACKSTAGE AT BULLWINKLE'S FIRST PERSONAL APPEARANCE --
COME ON HOME BEFORE YOU MAKE A FOOL OUT OF YOURSELF, BULLWINKLE!
THE NAME IS FLAVIUS!
HEH, HEH! THIS NOVOCAIN WILL STOP HIS SINGING!!
HAND ME MY GARGLE. IT'S BEHIND THAT SCREEN!!
GARGLE
M-M-R-R!
HE GARGLED AND LOST HIS VOICE!
I'LL CALL A DOCTOR!
DID YOU GET ALL OF BULLWINKLE'S RECORDS AND DESTROY THEM?
YES, BORIS, ALL -- ALL BUT ONE!!
I KNOW WHERE IT IS, BUT --
COME! THERE'S NO TIME TO WASTE!!

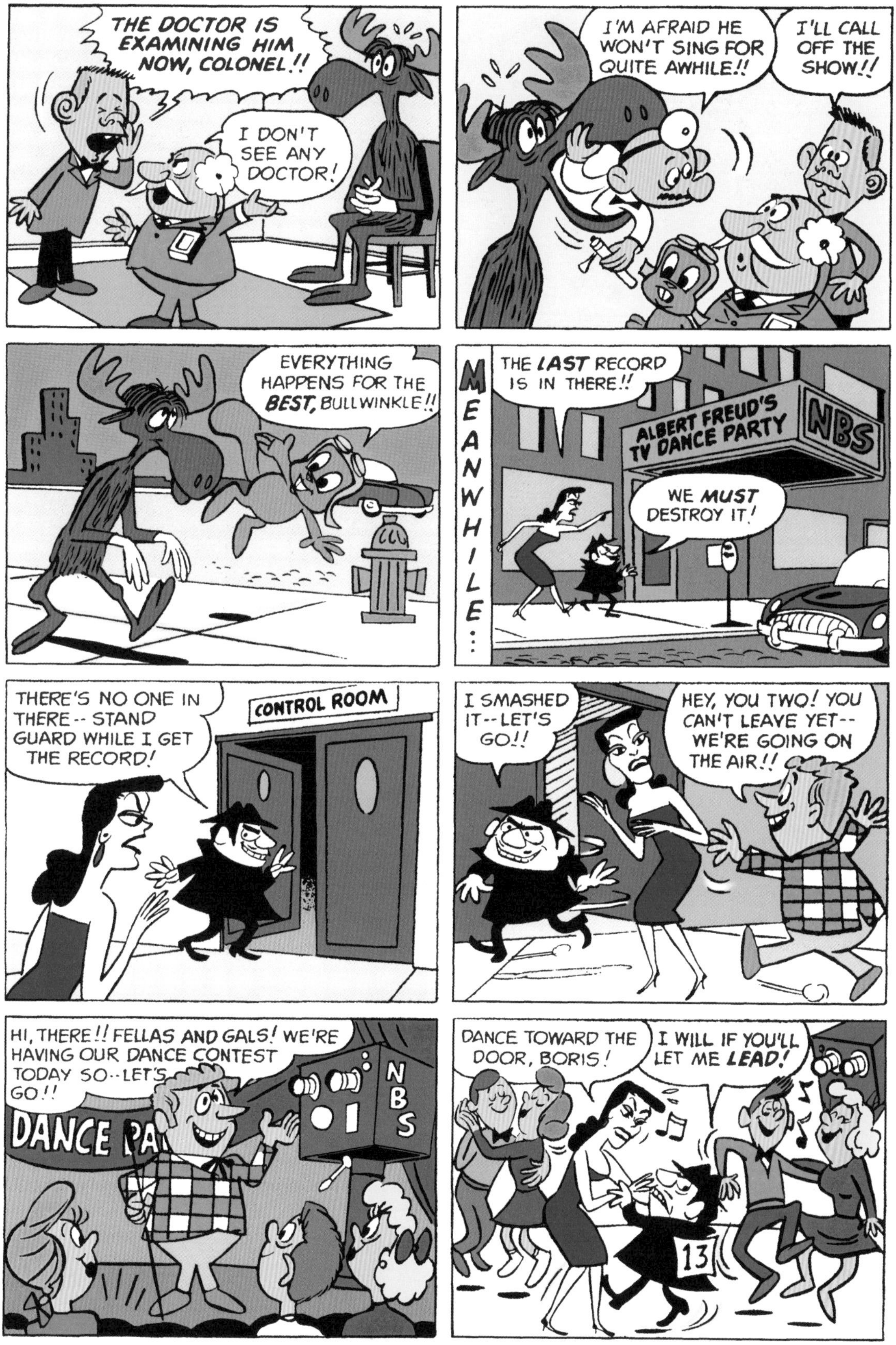
THE DOCTOR IS EXAMINING HIM NOW, COLONEL!!
I DON'T SEE ANY DOCTOR!
I'M AFRAID HE WON'T SING FOR QUITE AWHILE!!
I'LL CALL OFF THE SHOW!!
EVERYTHING HAPPENS FOR THE BEST, BULLWINKLE!!
MEANWHILE...
THE LAST RECORD IS IN THERE!!
ALBERT FREUD'S TV DANCE PARTY
NBS
WE MUST DESTROY IT!
THERE'S NO ONE IN THERE -- STAND GUARD WHILE I GET THE RECORD!
CONTROL ROOM
I SMASHED IT -- LET'S GO!!
HEY, YOU TWO! YOU CAN'T LEAVE YET -- WE'RE GOING ON THE AIR!!
HI, THERE!! FELLAS AND GALS! WE'RE HAVING OUR DANCE CONTEST TODAY SO -- LET'S GO!!
DANCE PA
NBS
DANCE TOWARD THE DOOR, BORIS!
I WILL IF YOU'LL LET ME LEAD!
13

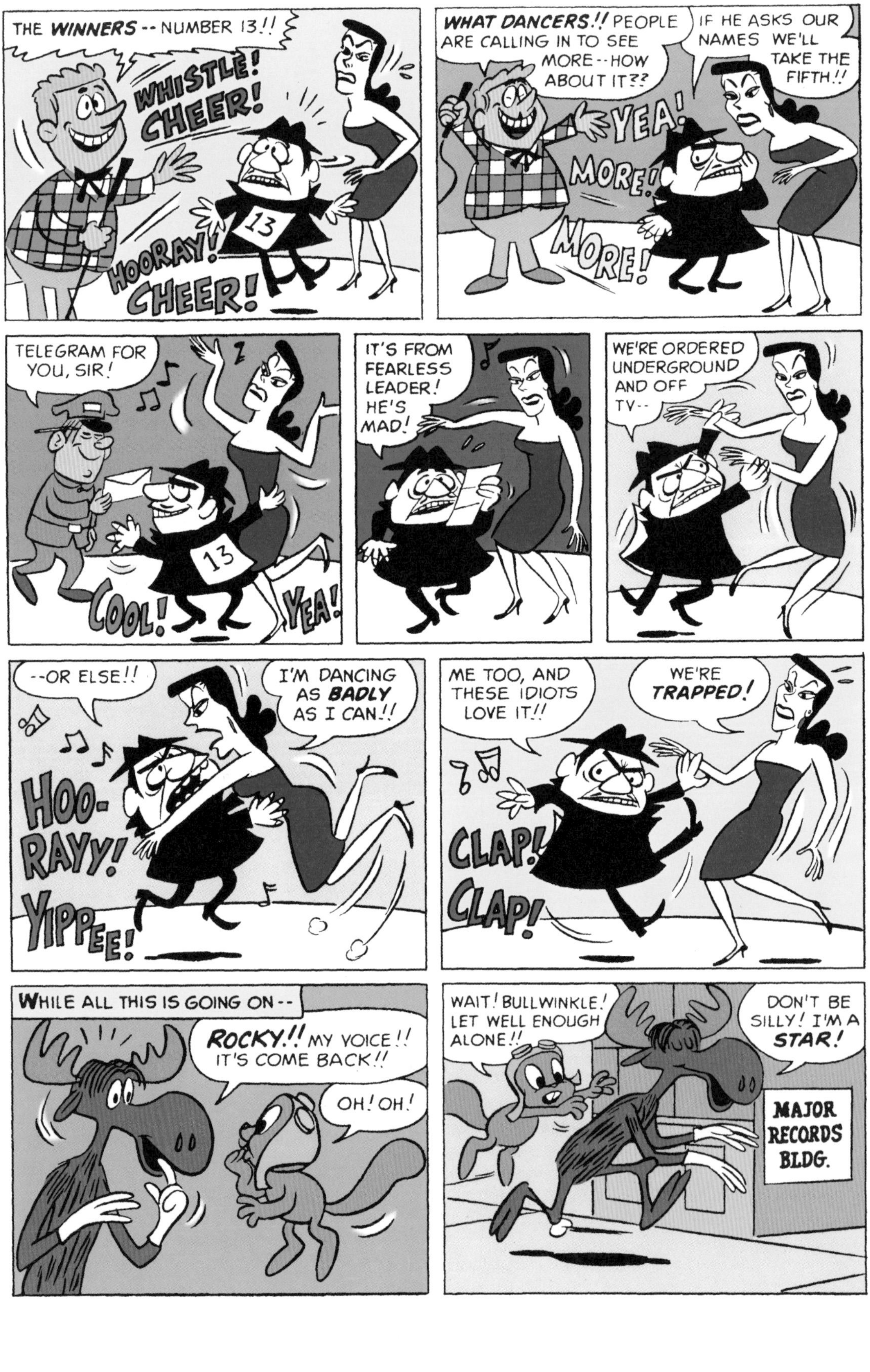
THE WINNERS -- NUMBER 13!!
WHISTLE! CHEER!
HOORAY! CHEER!
WHAT DANCERS!! PEOPLE ARE CALLING IN TO SEE MORE -- HOW ABOUT IT??
IF HE ASKS OUR NAMES WE'LL TAKE THE FIFTH!!
YEA! MORE! MORE!
TELEGRAM FOR YOU, SIR!
COOL! YEA!
IT'S FROM FEARLESS LEADER! HE'S MAD!
WE'RE ORDERED UNDERGROUND AND OFF TV--
--OR ELSE!!
I'M DANCING AS BADLY AS I CAN!!
HOO-RAYY! YIPPEE!
ME TOO, AND THESE IDIOTS LOVE IT!!
WE'RE TRAPPED!
CLAP! CLAP!
WHILE ALL THIS IS GOING ON --
ROCKY!! MY VOICE!! IT'S COME BACK!!
OH! OH!
WAIT! BULLWINKLE! LET WELL ENOUGH ALONE!!
DON'T BE SILLY! I'M A STAR!
MAJOR RECORDS BLDG.

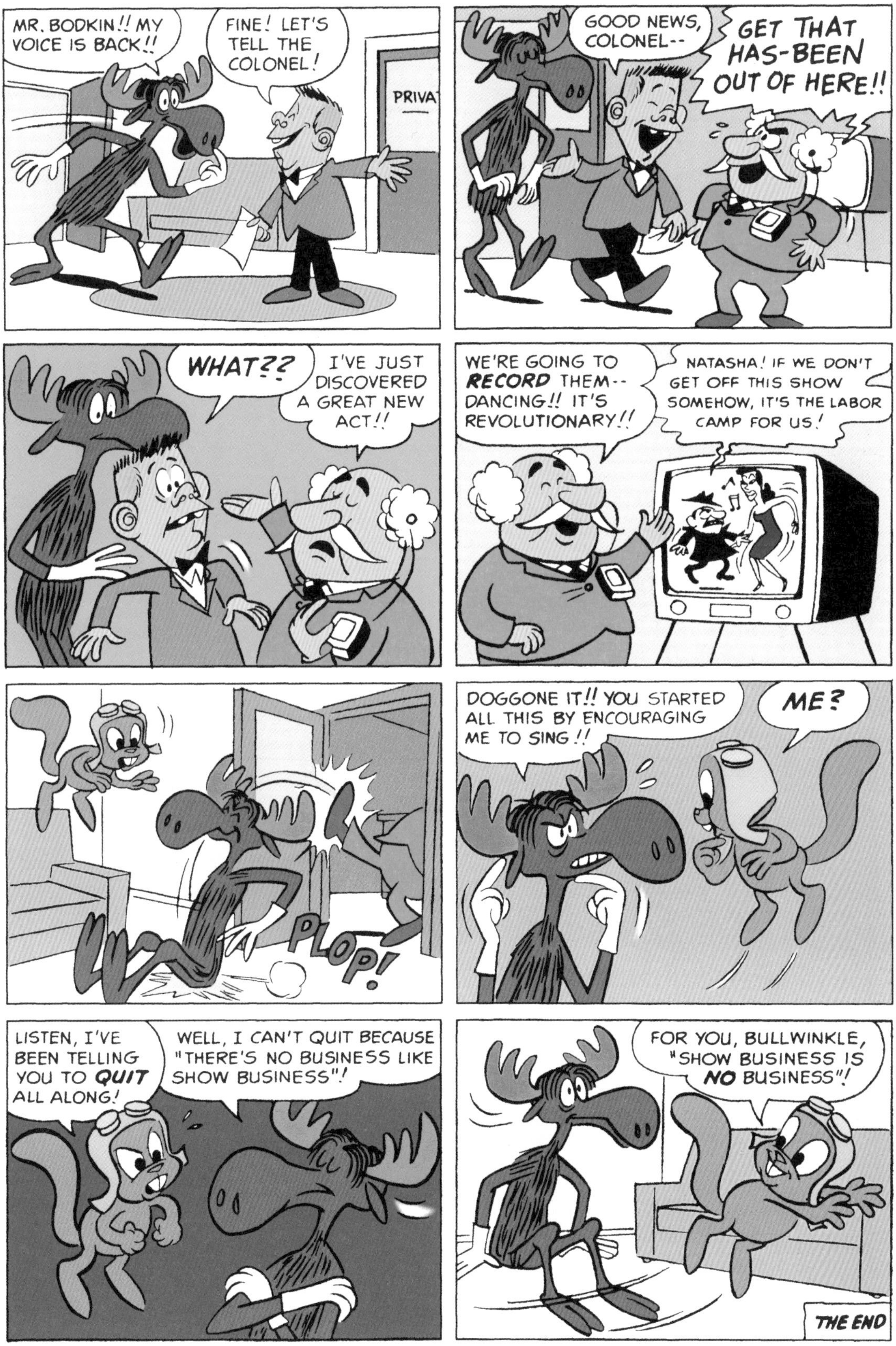
MR. BODKIN!! MY VOICE IS BACK!!
FINE! LET'S TELL THE COLONEL!
PRIVA
GOOD NEWS, COLONEL--
GET THAT HAS-BEEN OUT OF HERE!!
WHAT??
I'VE JUST DISCOVERED A GREAT NEW ACT!!
WE'RE GOING TO RECORD THEM--DANCING!! IT'S REVOLUTIONARY!!
NATASHA! IF WE DON'T GET OFF THIS SHOW SOMEHOW, IT'S THE LABOR CAMP FOR US!
PLOP!
DOGGONE IT!! YOU STARTED ALL THIS BY ENCOURAGING ME TO SING!!
ME?
LISTEN, I'VE BEEN TELLING YOU TO QUIT ALL ALONG!
WELL, I CAN'T QUIT BECAUSE "THERE'S NO BUSINESS LIKE SHOW BUSINESS"!
FOR YOU, BULLWINKLE, "SHOW BUSINESS IS NO BUSINESS"!
THE END

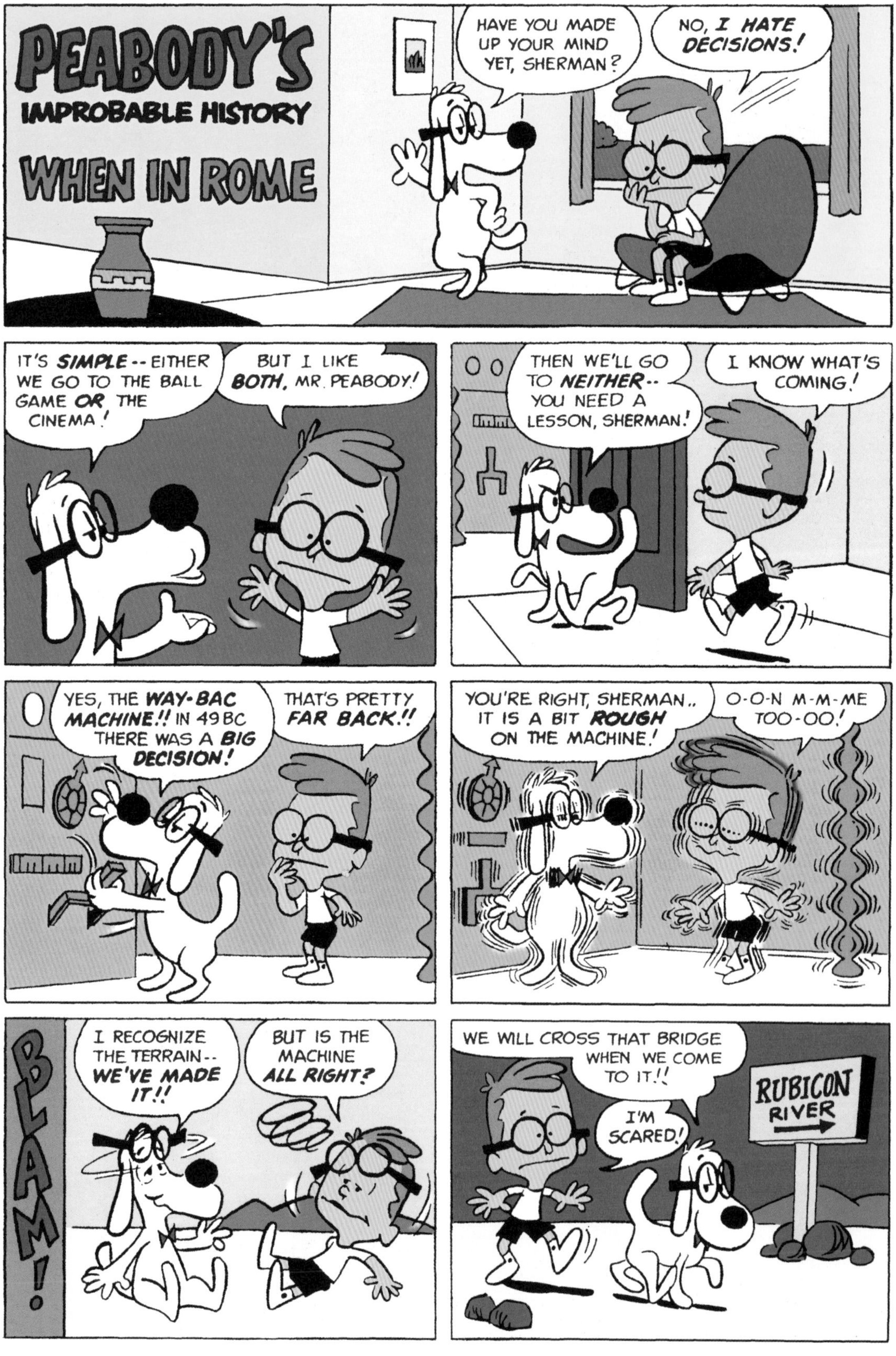
PEABODY'S
IMPROBABLE HISTORY
WHEN IN ROME
HAVE YOU MADE UP YOUR MIND YET, SHERMAN?
NO, I HATE DECISIONS!
IT'S SIMPLE -- EITHER WE GO TO THE BALL GAME OR THE CINEMA!
BUT I LIKE BOTH, MR. PEABODY!
THEN WE'LL GO TO NEITHER -- YOU NEED A LESSON, SHERMAN!
I KNOW WHAT'S COMING!
YES, THE WAY-BAC MACHINE!! IN 49 BC THERE WAS A BIG DECISION!
THAT'S PRETTY FAR BACK!!
YOU'RE RIGHT, SHERMAN.. IT IS A BIT ROUGH ON THE MACHINE!
O-O-N M-M-ME TOO-OO!
BLAM!
I RECOGNIZE THE TERRAIN -- WE'VE MADE IT!!
BUT IS THE MACHINE ALL RIGHT?
WE WILL CROSS THAT BRIDGE WHEN WE COME TO IT!!
I'M SCARED!
RUBICON RIVER

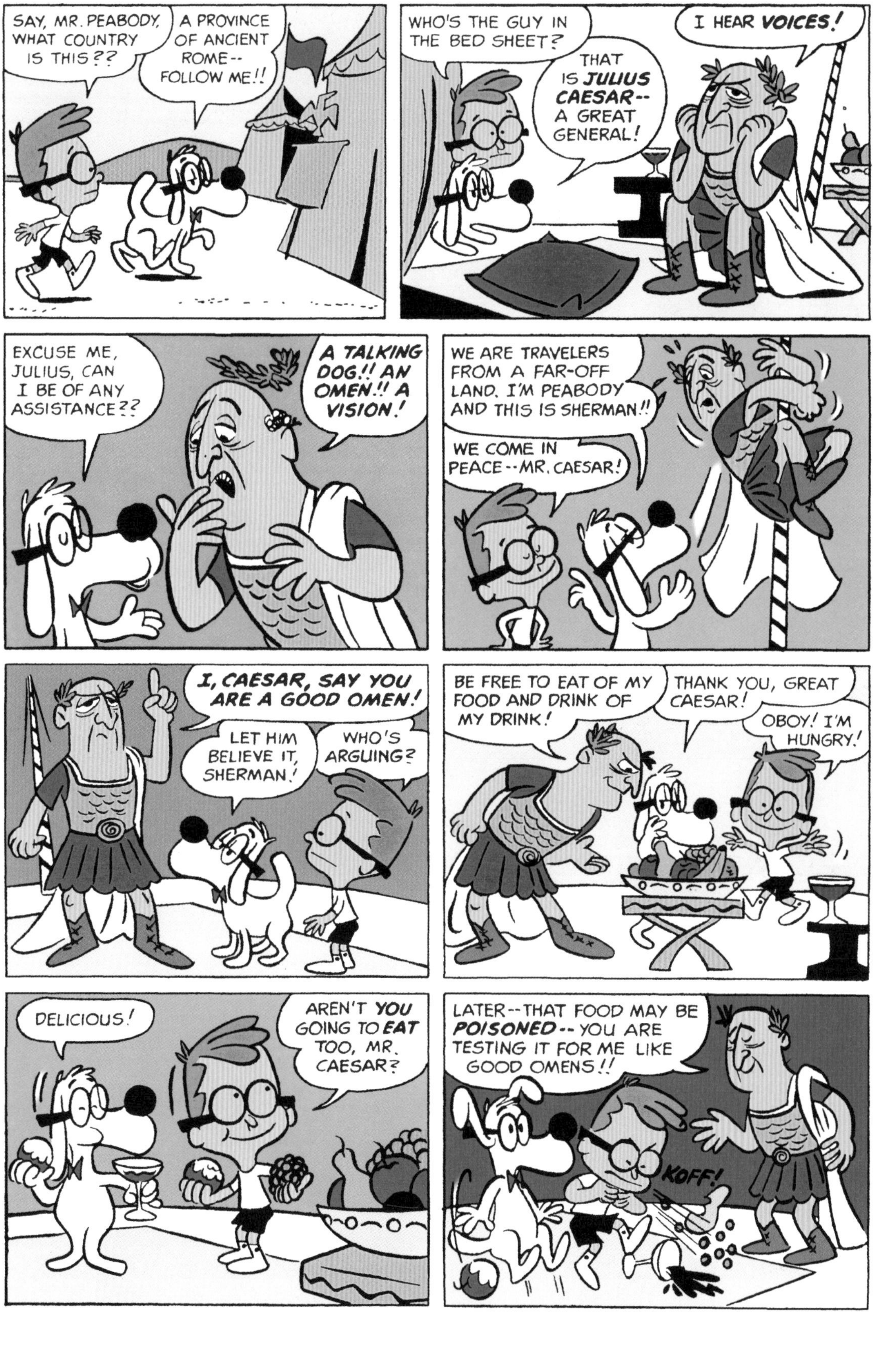
SAY, MR. PEABODY, WHAT COUNTRY IS THIS??
A PROVINCE OF ANCIENT ROME-- FOLLOW ME!!
WHO'S THE GUY IN THE BED SHEET?
THAT IS JULIUS CAESAR-- A GREAT GENERAL!
I HEAR VOICES!
EXCUSE ME, JULIUS, CAN I BE OF ANY ASSISTANCE??
A TALKING DOG!! AN OMEN!! A VISION!
WE ARE TRAVELERS FROM A FAR-OFF LAND. I'M PEABODY AND THIS IS SHERMAN!!
WE COME IN PEACE--MR. CAESAR!
I, CAESAR, SAY YOU ARE A GOOD OMEN!
LET HIM BELIEVE IT, SHERMAN!
WHO'S ARGUING?
BE FREE TO EAT OF MY FOOD AND DRINK OF MY DRINK!
THANK YOU, GREAT CAESAR!
OBOY! I'M HUNGRY!
DELICIOUS!
AREN'T YOU GOING TO EAT TOO, MR. CAESAR?
LATER--THAT FOOD MAY BE POISONED--YOU ARE TESTING IT FOR ME LIKE GOOD OMENS!!
KOFF!

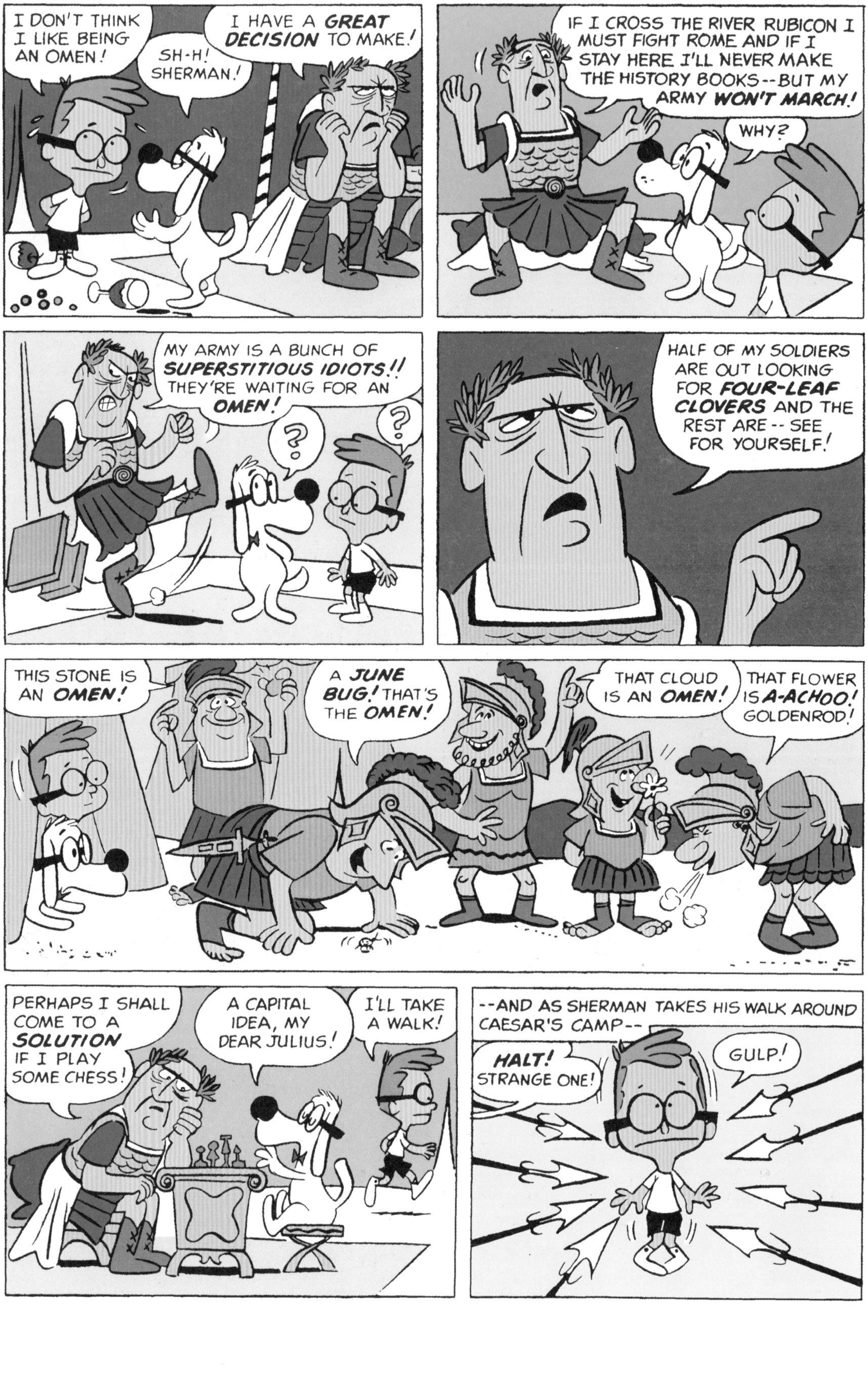

I DON'T THINK I LIKE BEING AN OMEN!
SH-H! SHERMAN!
I HAVE A **GREAT DECISION** TO MAKE!
IF I CROSS THE RIVER RUBICON I MUST FIGHT ROME AND IF I STAY HERE I'LL NEVER MAKE THE HISTORY BOOKS--BUT MY ARMY **WON'T MARCH!**
WHY?
MY ARMY IS A BUNCH OF **SUPERSTITIOUS IDIOTS!!** THEY'RE WAITING FOR AN **OMEN!**
?
?
HALF OF MY SOLDIERS ARE OUT LOOKING FOR **FOUR-LEAF CLOVERS** AND THE REST ARE -- SEE FOR YOURSELF!
THIS STONE IS AN **OMEN!**
A **JUNE BUG!** THAT'S THE **OMEN!**
THAT CLOUD IS AN **OMEN!**
THAT FLOWER IS **A-ACHOO!** GOLDENROD!
PERHAPS I SHALL COME TO A **SOLUTION** IF I PLAY SOME CHESS!
A CAPITAL IDEA, MY DEAR JULIUS!
I'LL TAKE A WALK!
--AND AS SHERMAN TAKES HIS WALK AROUND CAESAR'S CAMP--
HALT! STRANGE ONE!
GULP!

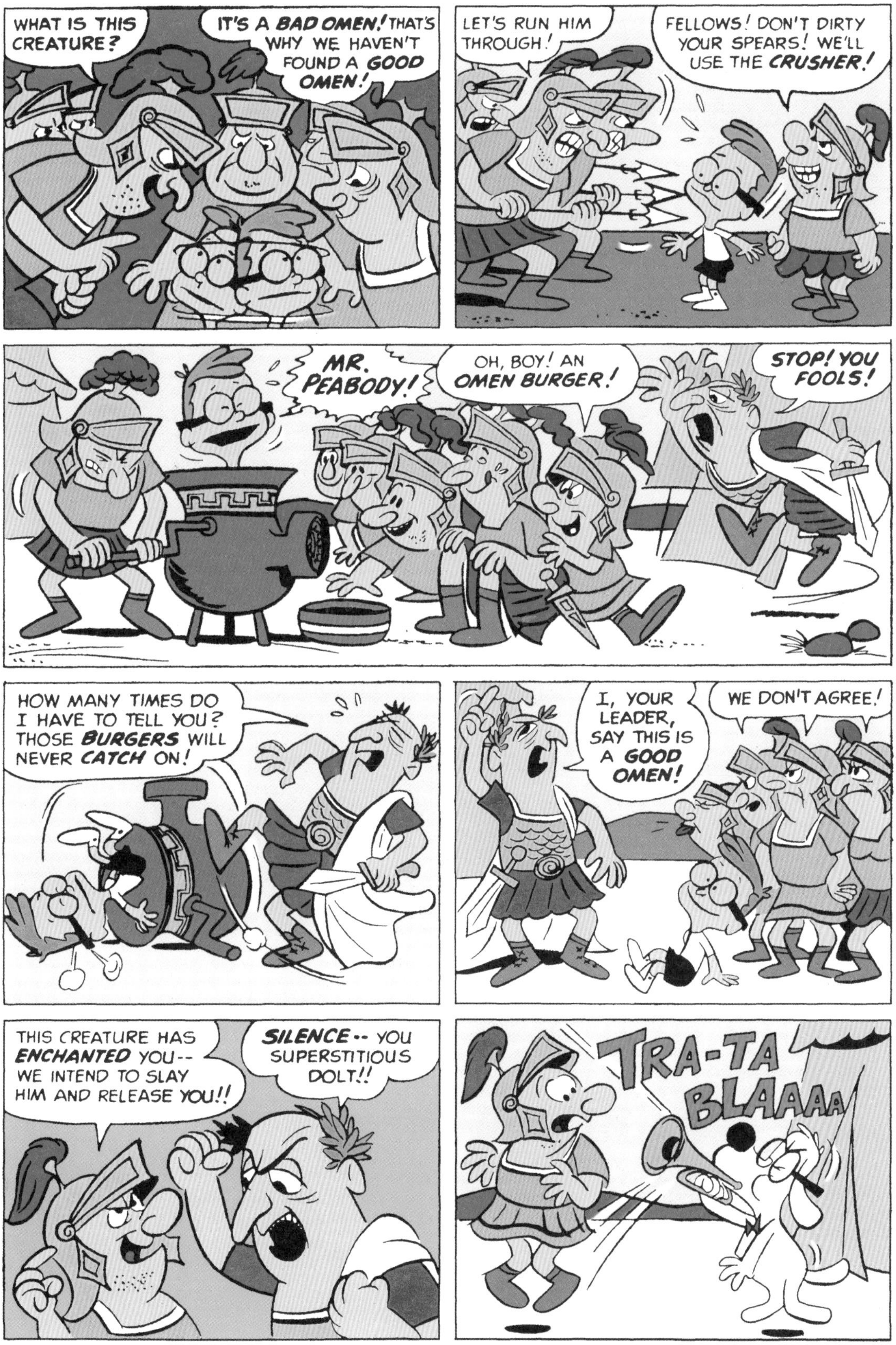
WHAT IS THIS CREATURE?
IT'S A BAD OMEN! THAT'S WHY WE HAVEN'T FOUND A GOOD OMEN!
LET'S RUN HIM THROUGH!
FELLOWS! DON'T DIRTY YOUR SPEARS! WE'LL USE THE CRUSHER!
MR. PEABODY!
OH, BOY! AN OMEN BURGER!
STOP! YOU FOOLS!
HOW MANY TIMES DO I HAVE TO TELL YOU? THOSE BURGERS WILL NEVER CATCH ON!
I, YOUR LEADER, SAY THIS IS A GOOD OMEN!
WE DON'T AGREE!
THIS CREATURE HAS ENCHANTED YOU-- WE INTEND TO SLAY HIM AND RELEASE YOU!!
SILENCE-- YOU SUPERSTITIOUS DOLT!!
TRA-TA BLAAAA

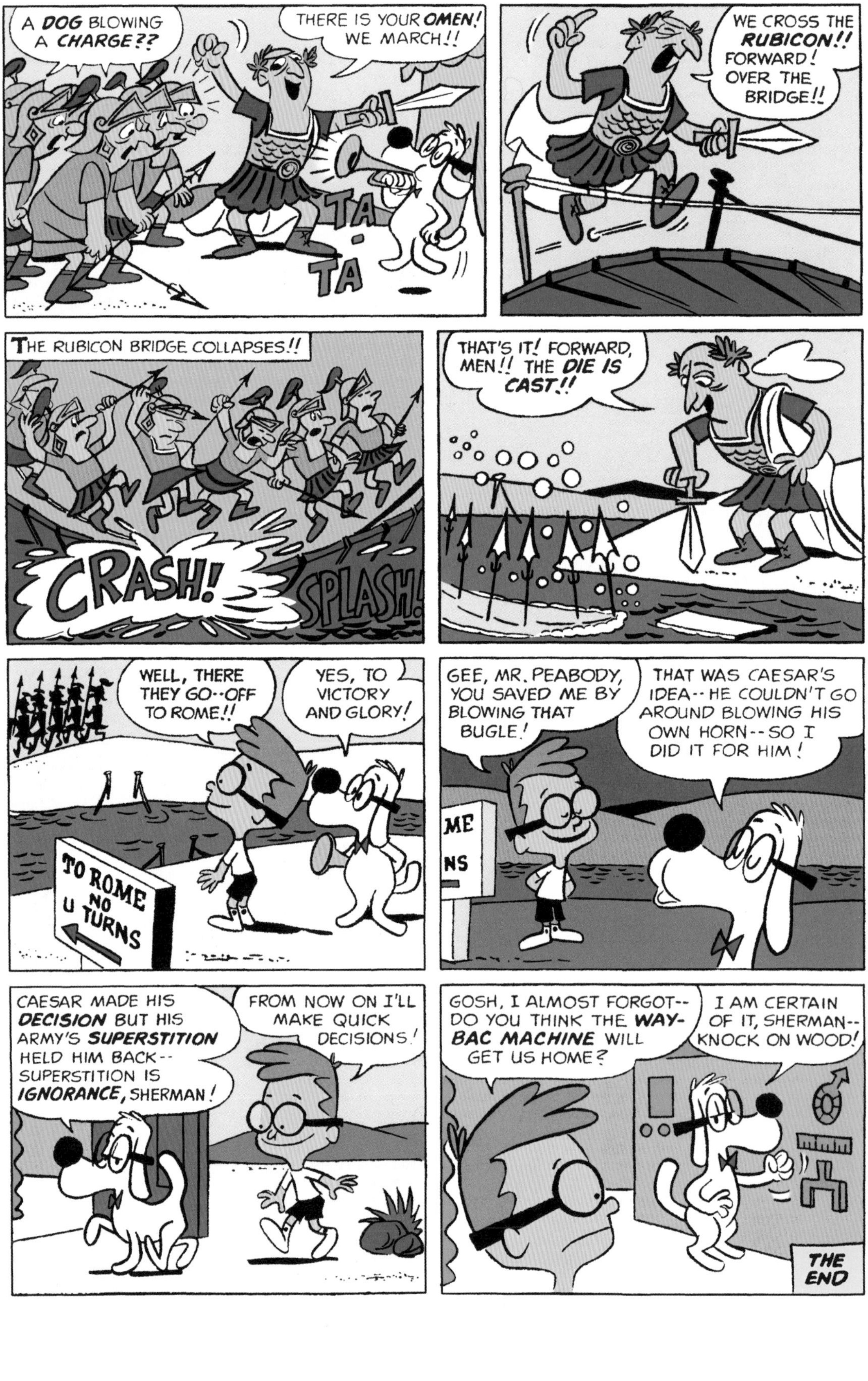
A DOG BLOWING A CHARGE??
THERE IS YOUR OMEN! WE MARCH!!
TA - TA
WE CROSS THE RUBICON!! FORWARD! OVER THE BRIDGE!!
THE RUBICON BRIDGE COLLAPSES!!
CRASH!
SPLASH!
THAT'S IT! FORWARD, MEN!! THE DIE IS CAST!!
WELL, THERE THEY GO--OFF TO ROME!!
YES, TO VICTORY AND GLORY!
TO ROME NO U TURNS
GEE, MR. PEABODY, YOU SAVED ME BY BLOWING THAT BUGLE!
THAT WAS CAESAR'S IDEA--HE COULDN'T GO AROUND BLOWING HIS OWN HORN--SO I DID IT FOR HIM!
CAESAR MADE HIS DECISION BUT HIS ARMY'S SUPERSTITION HELD HIM BACK--SUPERSTITION IS IGNORANCE, SHERMAN!
FROM NOW ON I'LL MAKE QUICK DECISIONS!
GOSH, I ALMOST FORGOT--DO YOU THINK THE WAY-BAC MACHINE WILL GET US HOME?
I AM CERTAIN OF IT, SHERMAN--KNOCK ON WOOD!
THE END

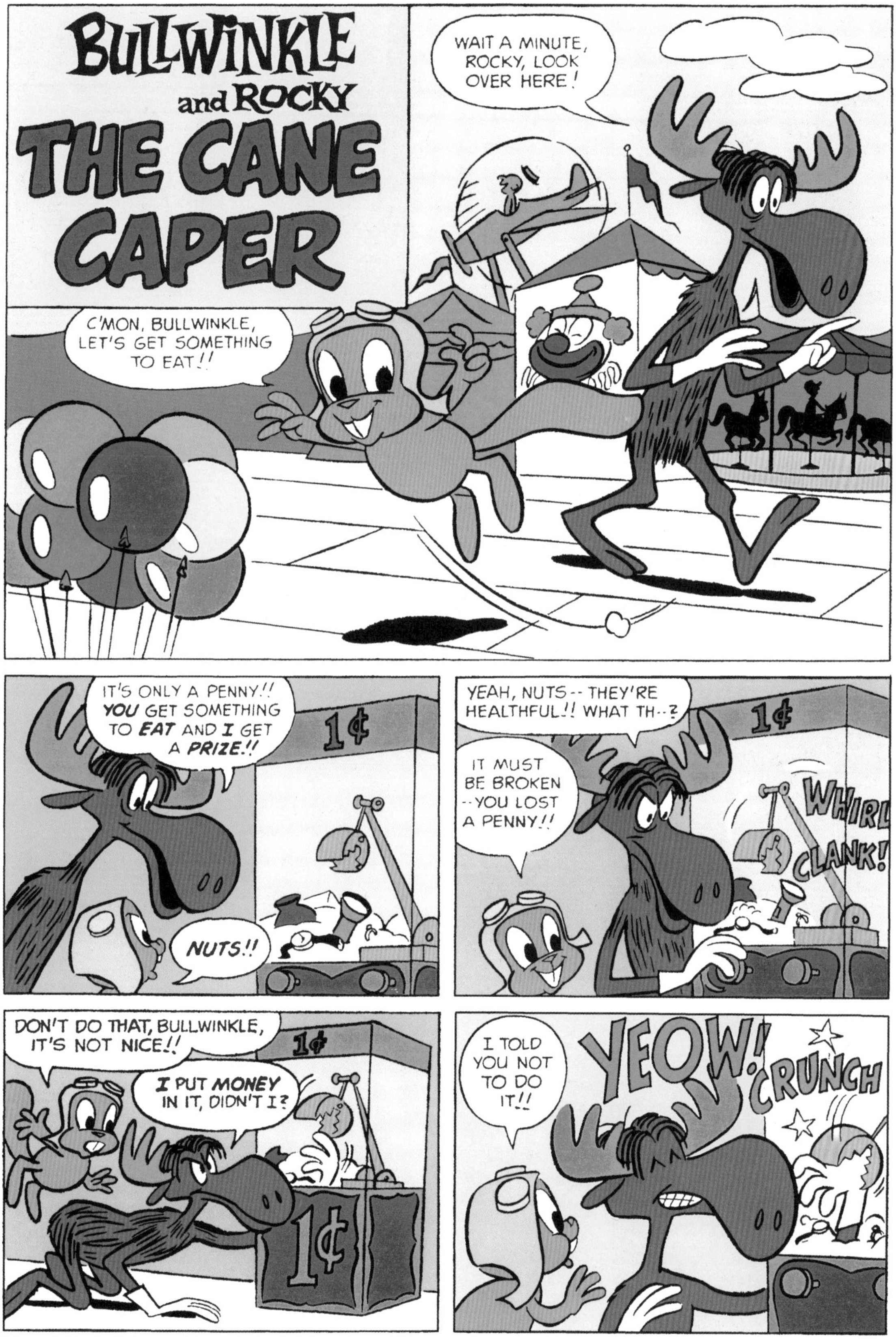
BULLWINKLE
and ROCKY
THE CANE CAPER
WAIT A MINUTE, ROCKY, LOOK OVER HERE!
C'MON, BULLWINKLE, LET'S GET SOMETHING TO EAT!!
IT'S ONLY A PENNY!! YOU GET SOMETHING TO EAT AND I GET A PRIZE!!
1¢
NUTS!!
YEAH, NUTS-- THEY'RE HEALTHFUL!! WHAT TH--?
IT MUST BE BROKEN --YOU LOST A PENNY!!
1¢
WHIRL
CLANK!
DON'T DO THAT, BULLWINKLE, IT'S NOT NICE!!
I PUT MONEY IN IT, DIDN'T I?
1¢
1¢
I TOLD YOU NOT TO DO IT!!
YEOW!
CRUNCH

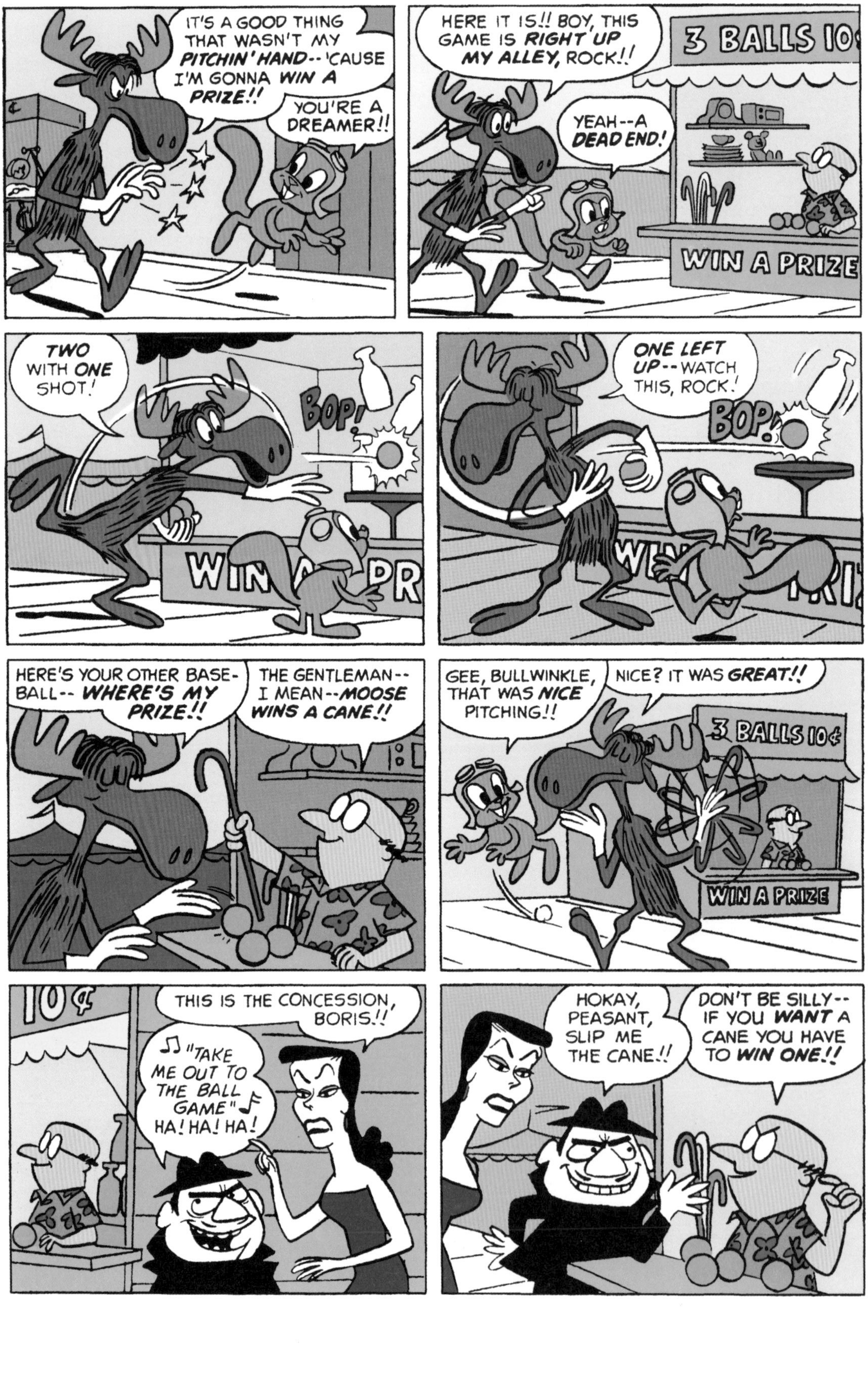
IT'S A GOOD THING THAT WASN'T MY PITCHIN' HAND--'CAUSE I'M GONNA WIN A PRIZE!!
YOU'RE A DREAMER!!
HERE IT IS!! BOY, THIS GAME IS RIGHT UP MY ALLEY, ROCK!!
YEAH--A DEAD END!
3 BALLS 10¢
WIN A PRIZE
TWO WITH ONE SHOT!
BOP!
ONE LEFT UP--WATCH THIS, ROCK!
BOP!
HERE'S YOUR OTHER BASE-BALL-- WHERE'S MY PRIZE!!
THE GENTLEMAN--I MEAN--MOOSE WINS A CANE!!
GEE, BULLWINKLE, THAT WAS NICE PITCHING!!
NICE? IT WAS GREAT!!
3 BALLS 10¢
WIN A PRIZE
THIS IS THE CONCESSION, BORIS!!
"TAKE ME OUT TO THE BALL GAME" HA! HA! HA!
HOKAY, PEASANT, SLIP ME THE CANE!!
DON'T BE SILLY--IF YOU WANT A CANE YOU HAVE TO WIN ONE!!

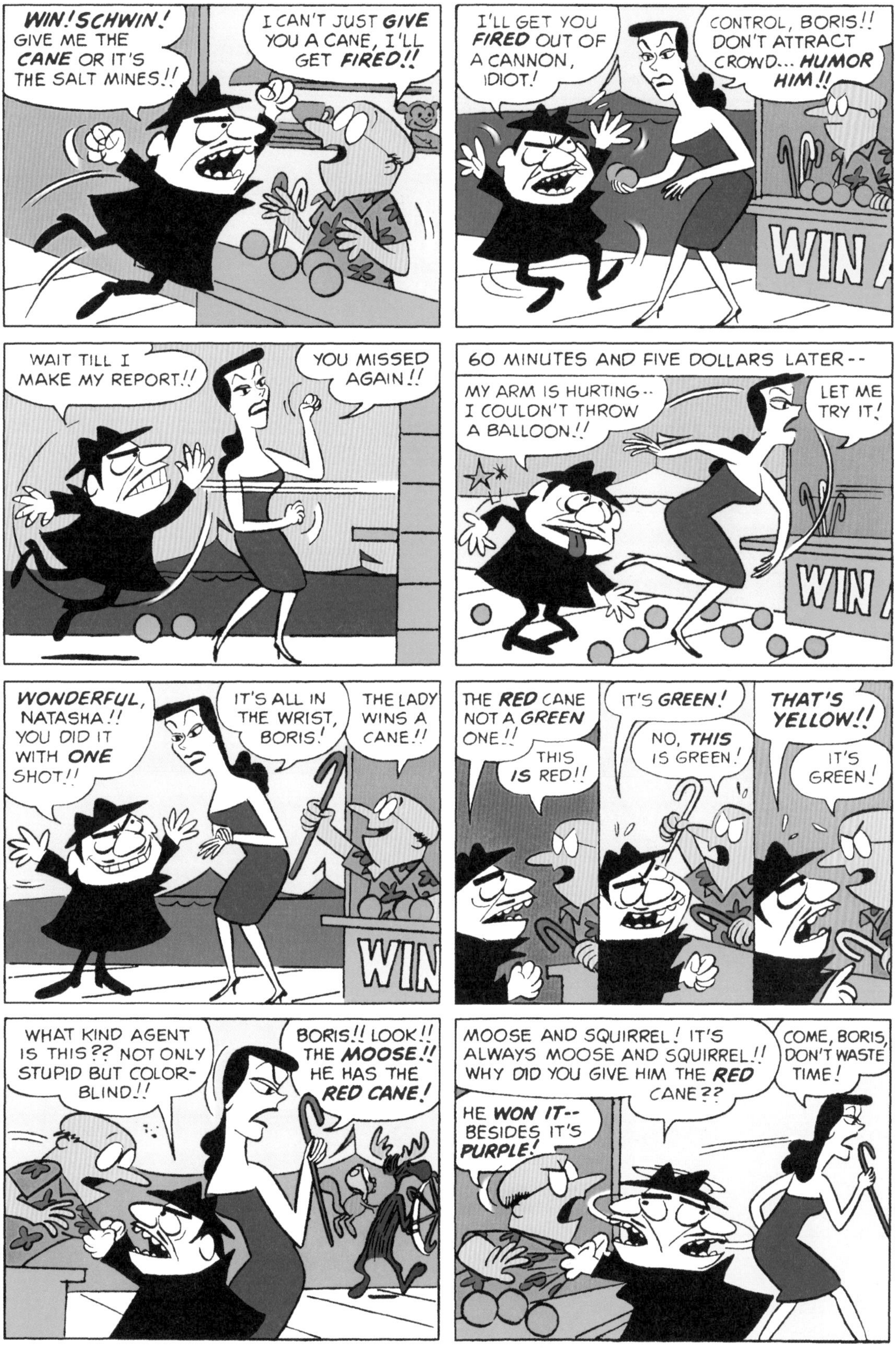
WIN! SCHWIN! GIVE ME THE CANE OR IT'S THE SALT MINES!!
I CAN'T JUST GIVE YOU A CANE, I'LL GET FIRED!!
I'LL GET YOU FIRED OUT OF A CANNON, IDIOT!
CONTROL, BORIS!! DON'T ATTRACT CROWD... HUMOR HIM!!
WIN
WAIT TILL I MAKE MY REPORT!!
YOU MISSED AGAIN!!
60 MINUTES AND FIVE DOLLARS LATER--
MY ARM IS HURTING-- I COULDN'T THROW A BALLOON!!
LET ME TRY IT!
WIN
WONDERFUL, NATASHA!! YOU DID IT WITH ONE SHOT!!
IT'S ALL IN THE WRIST, BORIS!
THE LADY WINS A CANE!!
WIN
THE RED CANE NOT A GREEN ONE!!
THIS IS RED!!
IT'S GREEN!
NO, THIS IS GREEN!
THAT'S YELLOW!!
IT'S GREEN!
WHAT KIND AGENT IS THIS?? NOT ONLY STUPID BUT COLOR-BLIND!!
BORIS!! LOOK!! THE MOOSE!! HE HAS THE RED CANE!
MOOSE AND SQUIRREL! IT'S ALWAYS MOOSE AND SQUIRREL!! WHY DID YOU GIVE HIM THE RED CANE??
COME, BORIS, DON'T WASTE TIME!
HE WON IT-- BESIDES IT'S PURPLE!

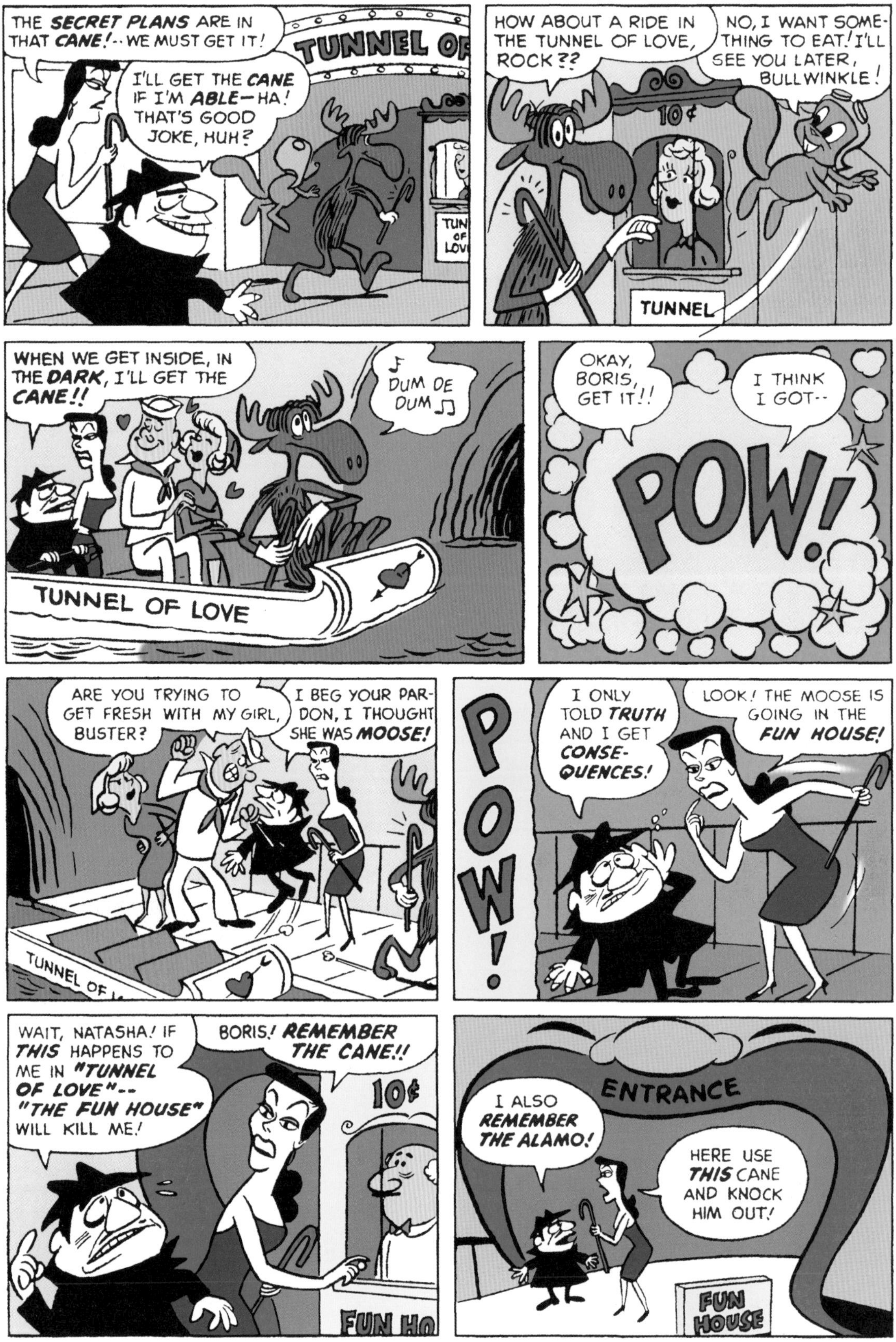
THE SECRET PLANS ARE IN THAT CANE!.. WE MUST GET IT!
TUNNEL OF
I'LL GET THE CANE IF I'M ABLE—HA! THAT'S GOOD JOKE, HUH?
HOW ABOUT A RIDE IN THE TUNNEL OF LOVE, ROCK??
NO, I WANT SOMETHING TO EAT! I'LL SEE YOU LATER, BULLWINKLE!
10¢
TUNNEL
WHEN WE GET INSIDE, IN THE DARK, I'LL GET THE CANE!!
DUM DE DUM
TUNNEL OF LOVE
OKAY, BORIS, GET IT!!
I THINK I GOT--
POW!
ARE YOU TRYING TO GET FRESH WITH MY GIRL, BUSTER?
I BEG YOUR PARDON, I THOUGHT SHE WAS MOOSE!
POW!
I ONLY TOLD TRUTH AND I GET CONSEQUENCES!
LOOK! THE MOOSE IS GOING IN THE FUN HOUSE!
WAIT, NATASHA! IF THIS HAPPENS TO ME IN "TUNNEL OF LOVE"-- "THE FUN HOUSE" WILL KILL ME!
BORIS! REMEMBER THE CANE!!
10¢
ENTRANCE
I ALSO REMEMBER THE ALAMO!
HERE USE THIS CANE AND KNOCK HIM OUT!
FUN HOUSE

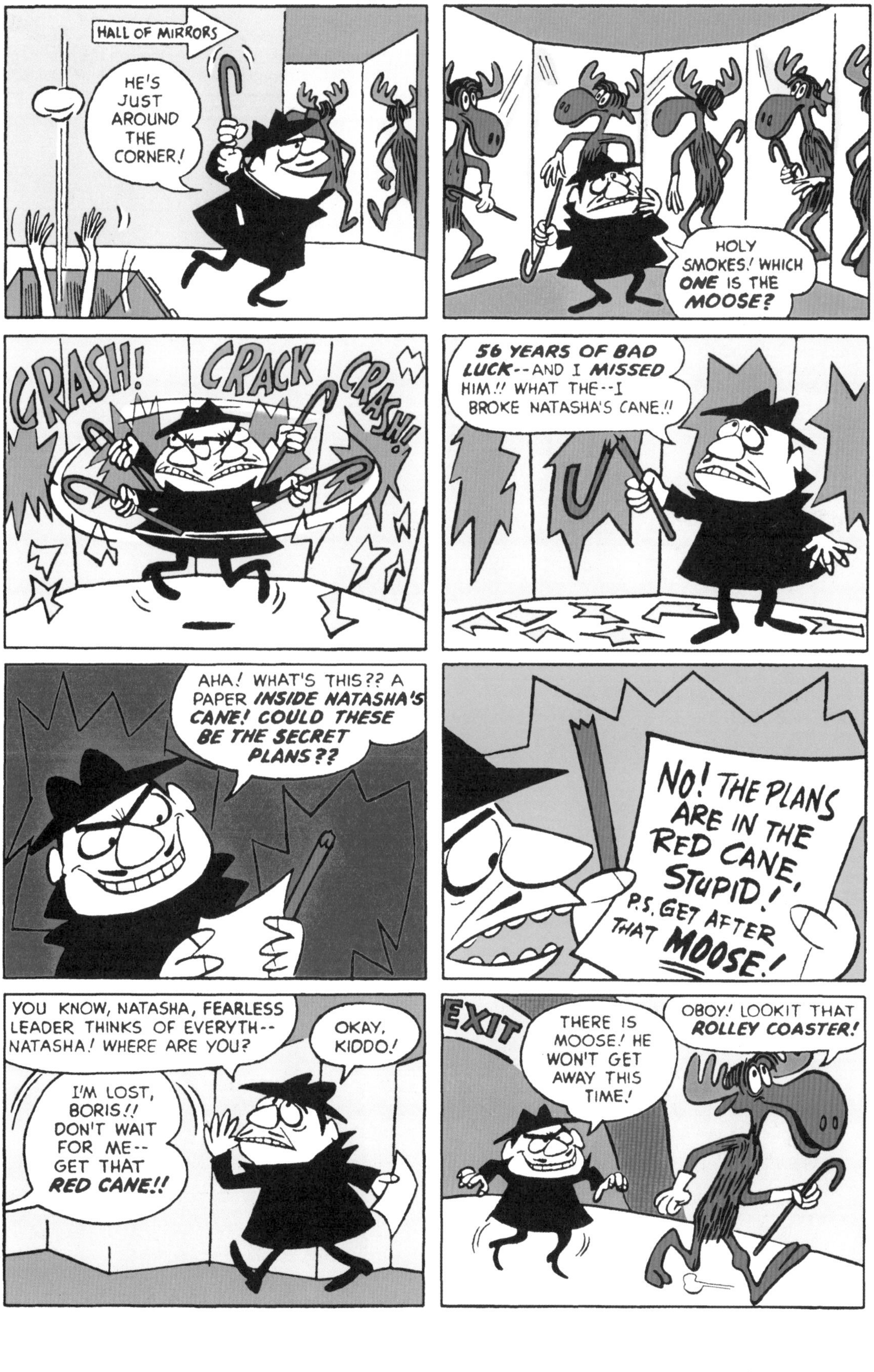
HALL OF MIRRORS
HE'S JUST AROUND THE CORNER!
HOLY SMOKES! WHICH ONE IS THE MOOSE?
CRASH!
CRACK
CRASH!
56 YEARS OF BAD LUCK--AND I MISSED HIM!! WHAT THE--I BROKE NATASHA'S CANE!!
AHA! WHAT'S THIS?? A PAPER INSIDE NATASHA'S CANE! COULD THESE BE THE SECRET PLANS??
NO! THE PLANS ARE IN THE RED CANE, STUPID!
P.S. GET AFTER THAT MOOSE!
YOU KNOW, NATASHA, FEARLESS LEADER THINKS OF EVERYTH-- NATASHA! WHERE ARE YOU?
OKAY, KIDDO!
I'M LOST, BORIS!! DON'T WAIT FOR ME-- GET THAT RED CANE!!
EXIT
THERE IS MOOSE! HE WON'T GET AWAY THIS TIME!
OBOY! LOOKIT THAT ROLLEY COASTER!

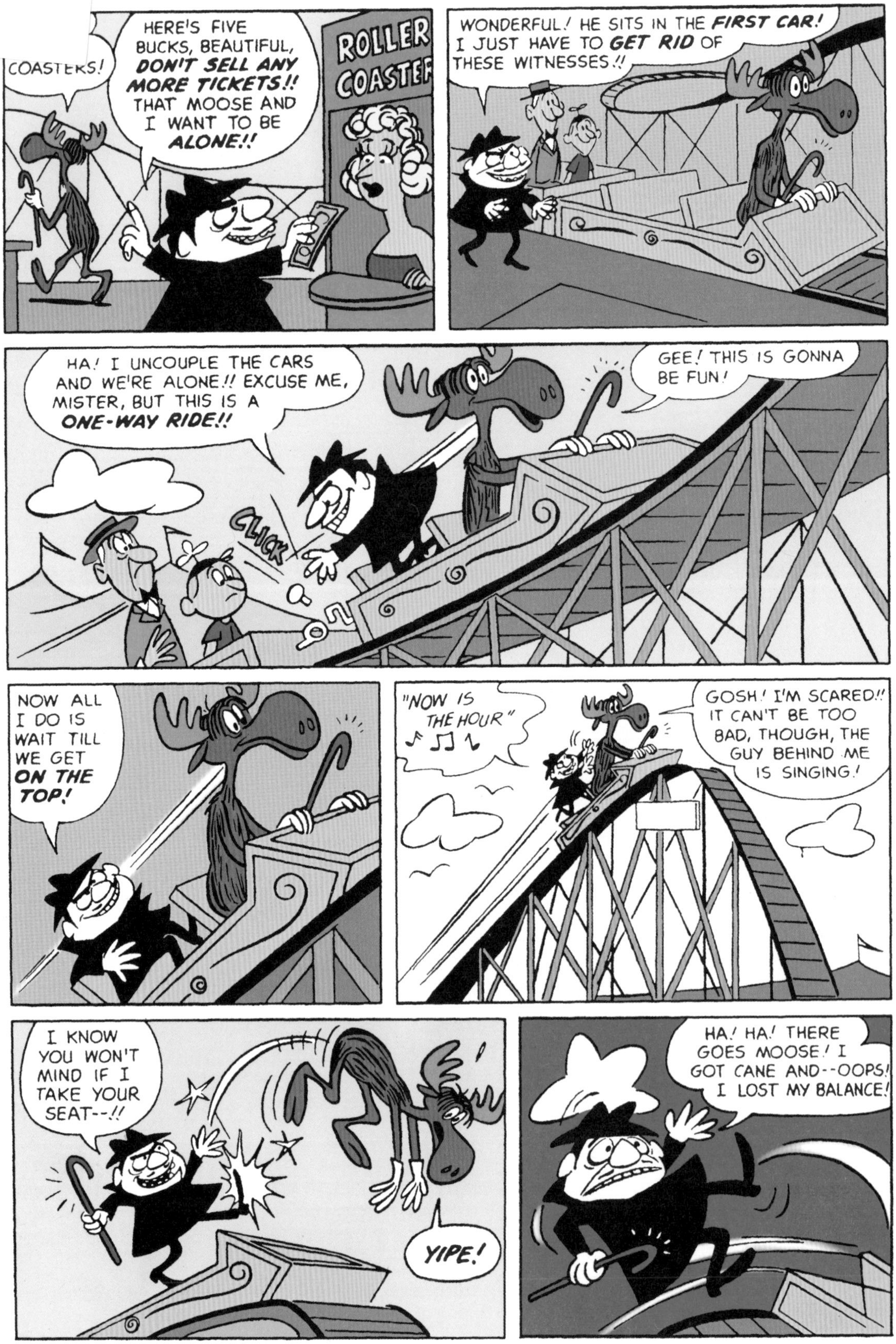
COASTERS!
HERE'S FIVE BUCKS, BEAUTIFUL, DON'T SELL ANY MORE TICKETS!! THAT MOOSE AND I WANT TO BE ALONE!!
ROLLER COASTER
WONDERFUL! HE SITS IN THE FIRST CAR! I JUST HAVE TO GET RID OF THESE WITNESSES!!
HA! I UNCOUPLE THE CARS AND WE'RE ALONE!! EXCUSE ME, MISTER, BUT THIS IS A ONE-WAY RIDE!!
GEE! THIS IS GONNA BE FUN!
CLICK
NOW ALL I DO IS WAIT TILL WE GET ON THE TOP!
"NOW IS THE HOUR"
GOSH! I'M SCARED!! IT CAN'T BE TOO BAD, THOUGH, THE GUY BEHIND ME IS SINGING!
I KNOW YOU WON'T MIND IF I TAKE YOUR SEAT--!!
YIPE!
HA! HA! THERE GOES MOOSE! I GOT CANE AND--OOPS! I LOST MY BALANCE!

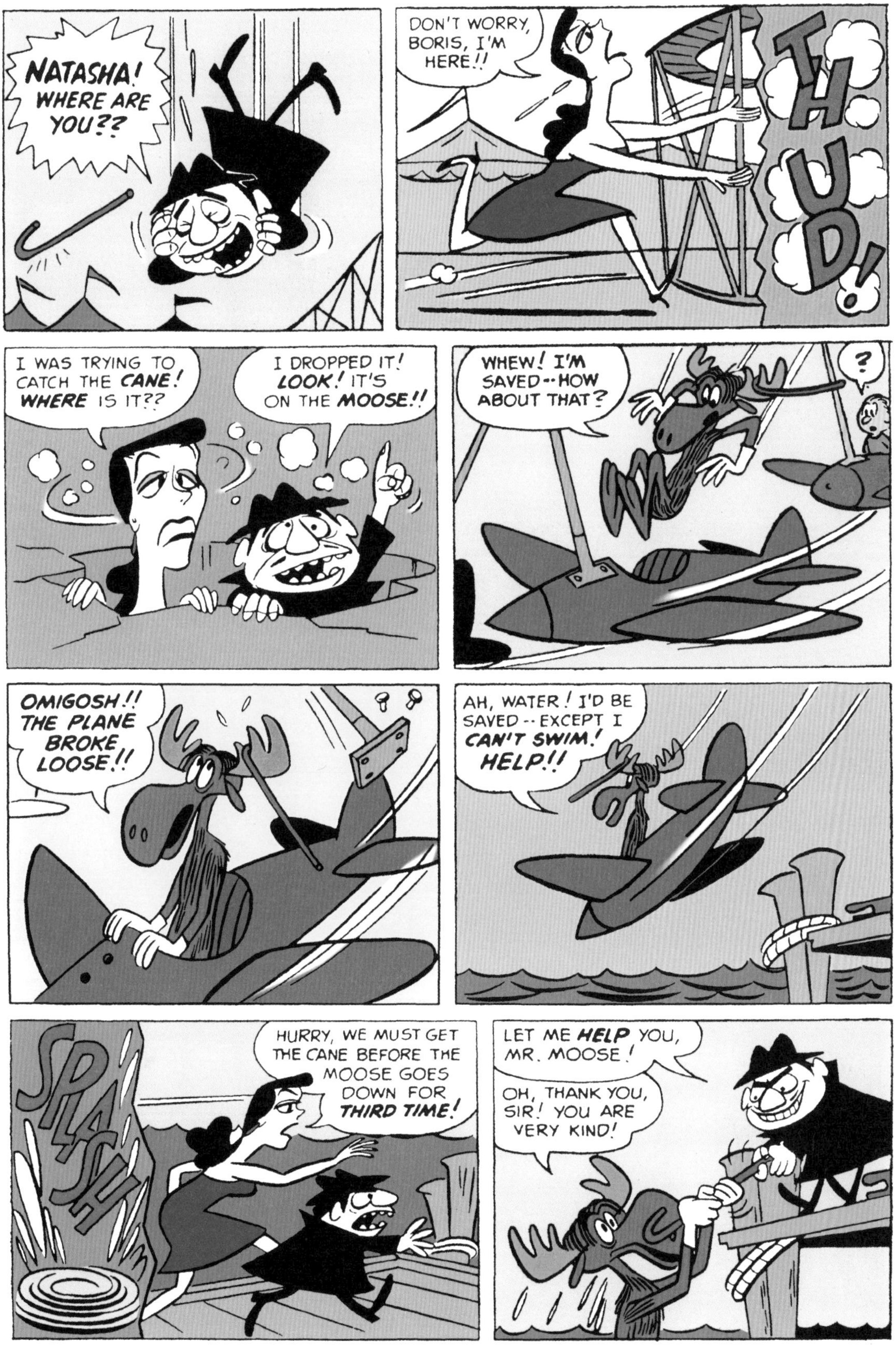
NATASHA! WHERE ARE YOU??
DON'T WORRY, BORIS, I'M HERE!!
THUD!
I WAS TRYING TO CATCH THE CANE! WHERE IS IT??
I DROPPED IT! LOOK! IT'S ON THE MOOSE!!
WHEW! I'M SAVED--HOW ABOUT THAT?
?
OMIGOSH!! THE PLANE BROKE LOOSE!!
AH, WATER! I'D BE SAVED--EXCEPT I CAN'T SWIM! HELP!!
SPLASH
HURRY, WE MUST GET THE CANE BEFORE THE MOOSE GOES DOWN FOR THIRD TIME!
LET ME HELP YOU, MR. MOOSE!
OH, THANK YOU, SIR! YOU ARE VERY KIND!

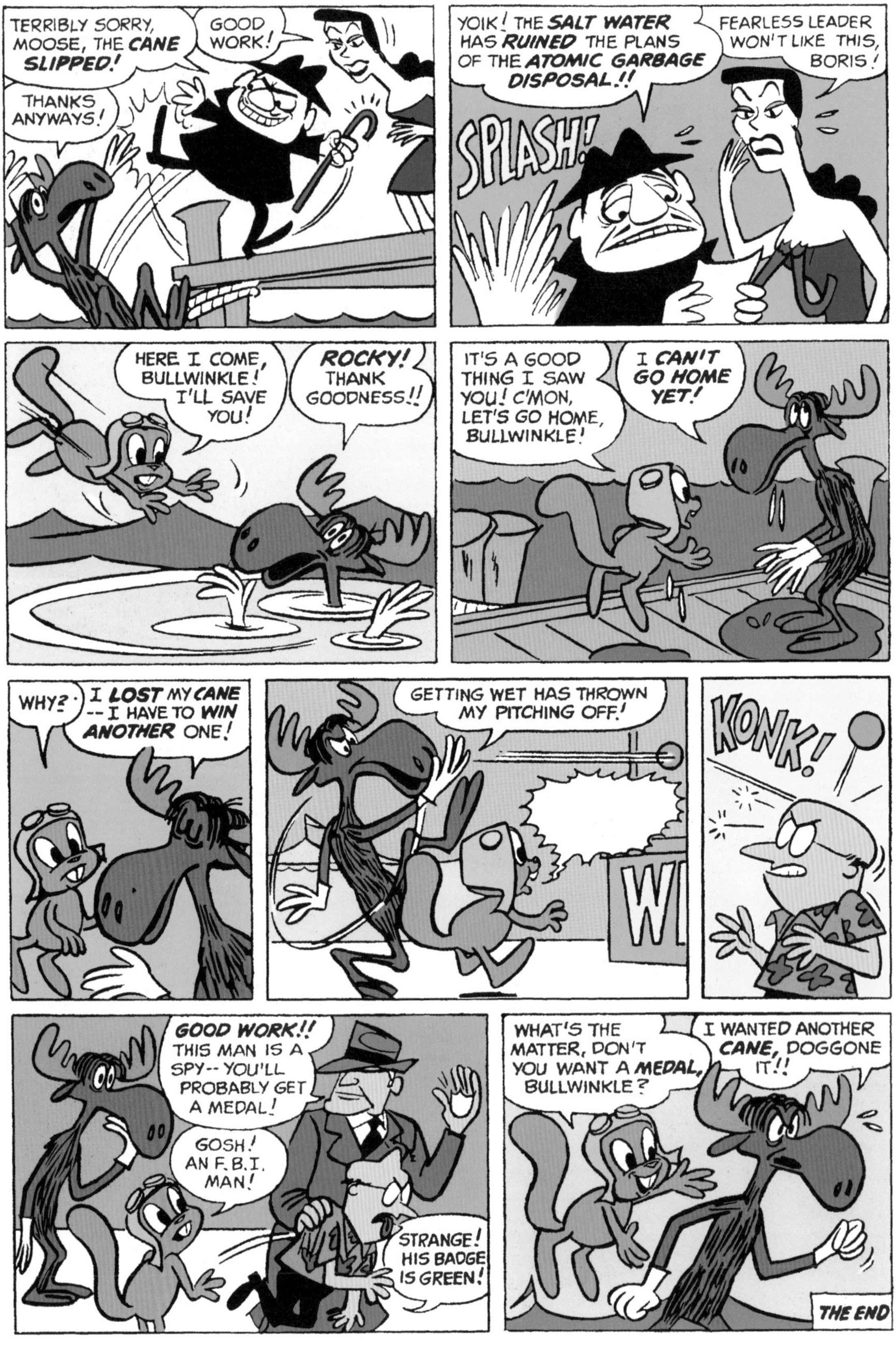
TERRIBLY SORRY, MOOSE, THE CANE SLIPPED!
GOOD WORK!
THANKS ANYWAYS!
YOIK! THE SALT WATER HAS RUINED THE PLANS OF THE ATOMIC GARBAGE DISPOSAL!!
FEARLESS LEADER WON'T LIKE THIS, BORIS!
SPLASH!
HERE I COME, BULLWINKLE! I'LL SAVE YOU!
ROCKY! THANK GOODNESS!!
IT'S A GOOD THING I SAW YOU! C'MON, LET'S GO HOME, BULLWINKLE!
I CAN'T GO HOME YET!
WHY?
I LOST MY CANE -- I HAVE TO WIN ANOTHER ONE!
GETTING WET HAS THROWN MY PITCHING OFF!
KONK!
GOOD WORK!! THIS MAN IS A SPY-- YOU'LL PROBABLY GET A MEDAL!
GOSH! AN F.B.I. MAN!
STRANGE! HIS BADGE IS GREEN!
WHAT'S THE MATTER, DON'T YOU WANT A MEDAL, BULLWINKLE?
I WANTED ANOTHER CANE, DOGGONE IT!!
THE END

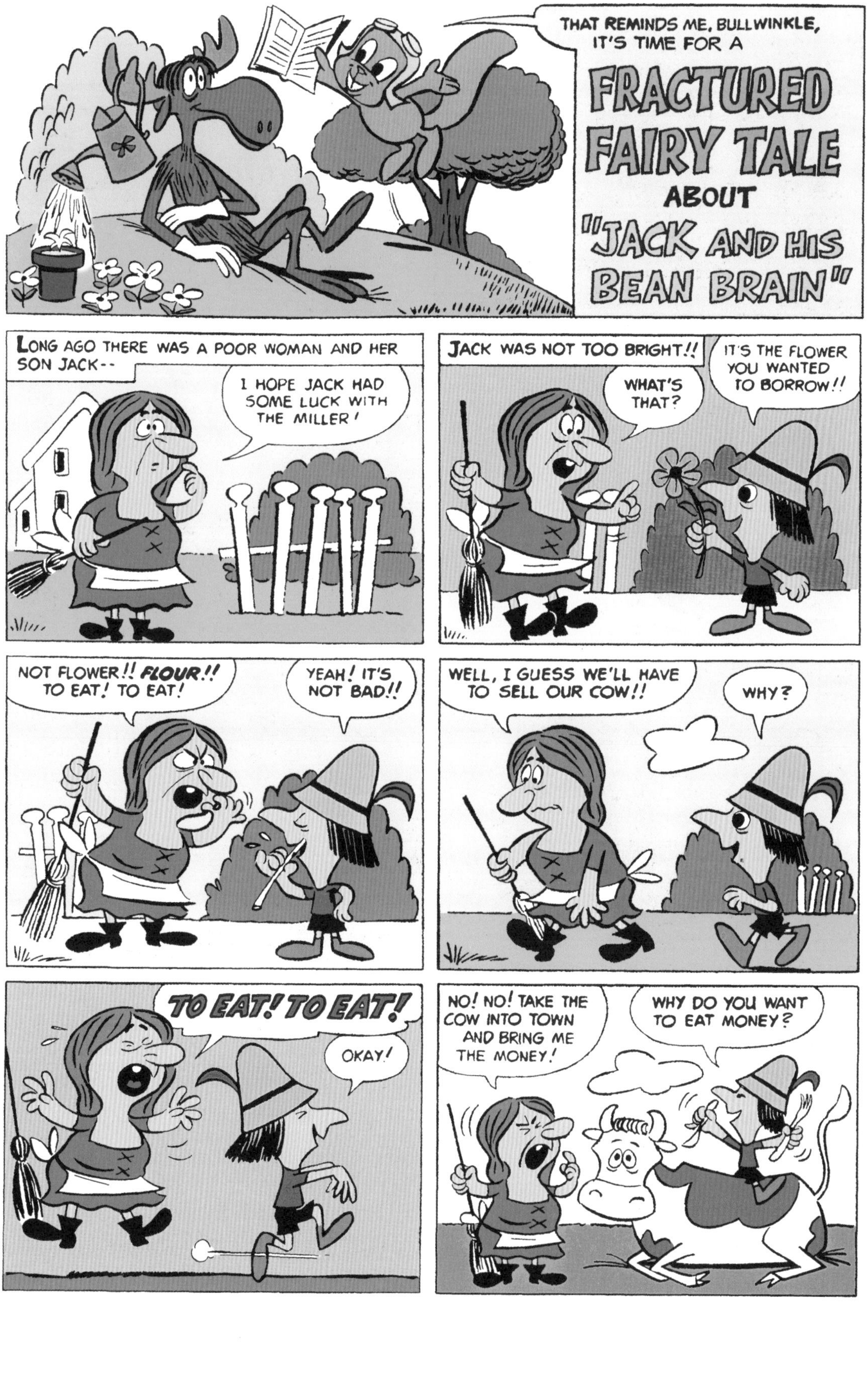

THAT REMINDS ME, BULLWINKLE, IT'S TIME FOR A
FRACTURED FAIRY TALE
ABOUT
"JACK AND HIS BEAN BRAIN"
LONG AGO THERE WAS A POOR WOMAN AND HER SON JACK--
I HOPE JACK HAD SOME LUCK WITH THE MILLER!
JACK WAS NOT TOO BRIGHT!!
WHAT'S THAT?
IT'S THE FLOWER YOU WANTED TO BORROW!!
NOT FLOWER!! FLOUR!! TO EAT! TO EAT!
YEAH! IT'S NOT BAD!!
WELL, I GUESS WE'LL HAVE TO SELL OUR COW!!
WHY?
TO EAT! TO EAT!
OKAY!
NO! NO! TAKE THE COW INTO TOWN AND BRING ME THE MONEY!
WHY DO YOU WANT TO EAT MONEY?

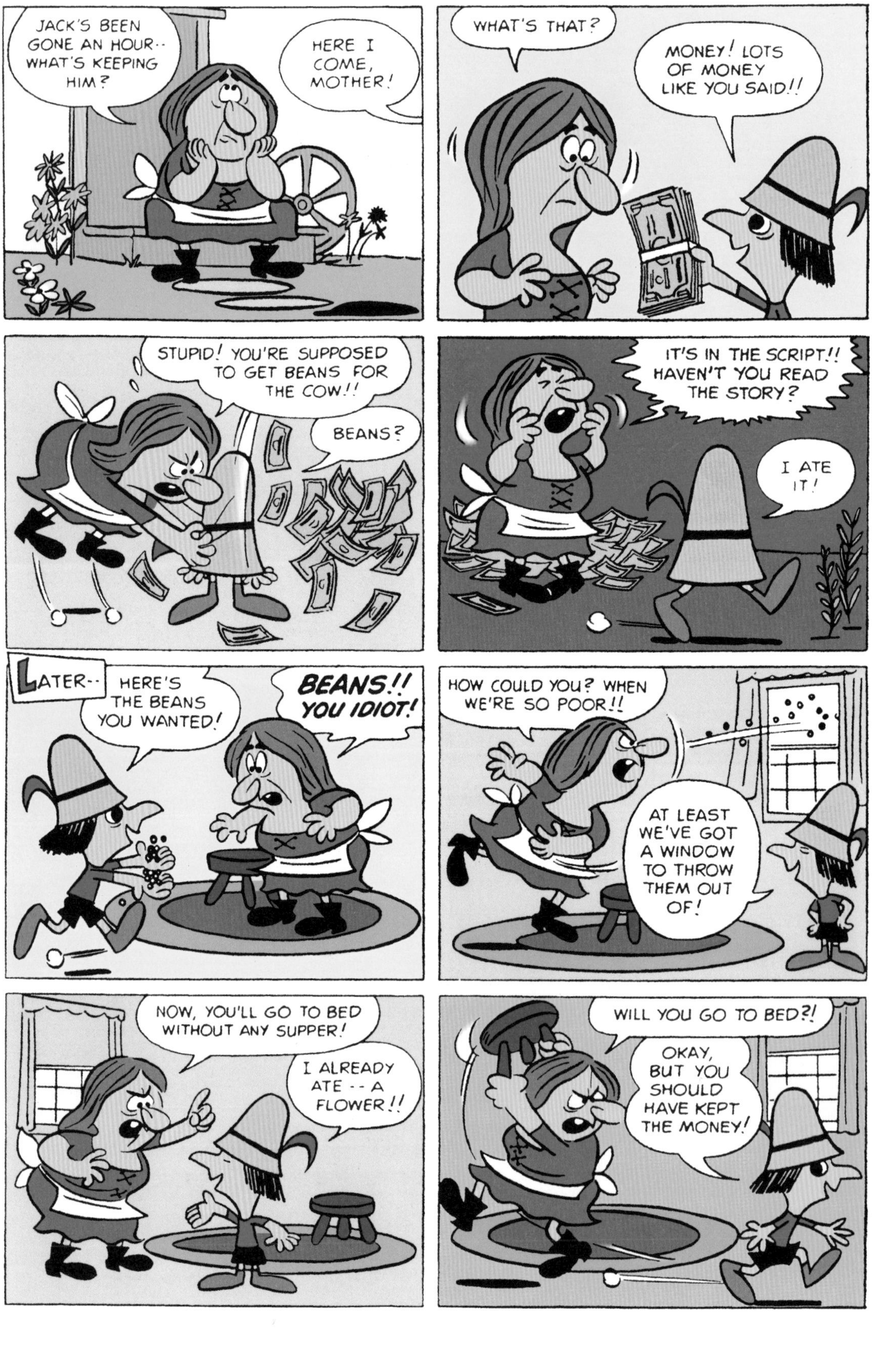
JACK'S BEEN GONE AN HOUR-- WHAT'S KEEPING HIM?
HERE I COME, MOTHER!
WHAT'S THAT?
MONEY! LOTS OF MONEY LIKE YOU SAID!!
STUPID! YOU'RE SUPPOSED TO GET BEANS FOR THE COW!!
BEANS?
IT'S IN THE SCRIPT!! HAVEN'T YOU READ THE STORY?
I ATE IT!
LATER--
HERE'S THE BEANS YOU WANTED!
BEANS!! YOU IDIOT!
HOW COULD YOU? WHEN WE'RE SO POOR!!
AT LEAST WE'VE GOT A WINDOW TO THROW THEM OUT OF!
NOW, YOU'LL GO TO BED WITHOUT ANY SUPPER!
I ALREADY ATE -- A FLOWER!!
WILL YOU GO TO BED?!
OKAY, BUT YOU SHOULD HAVE KEPT THE MONEY!

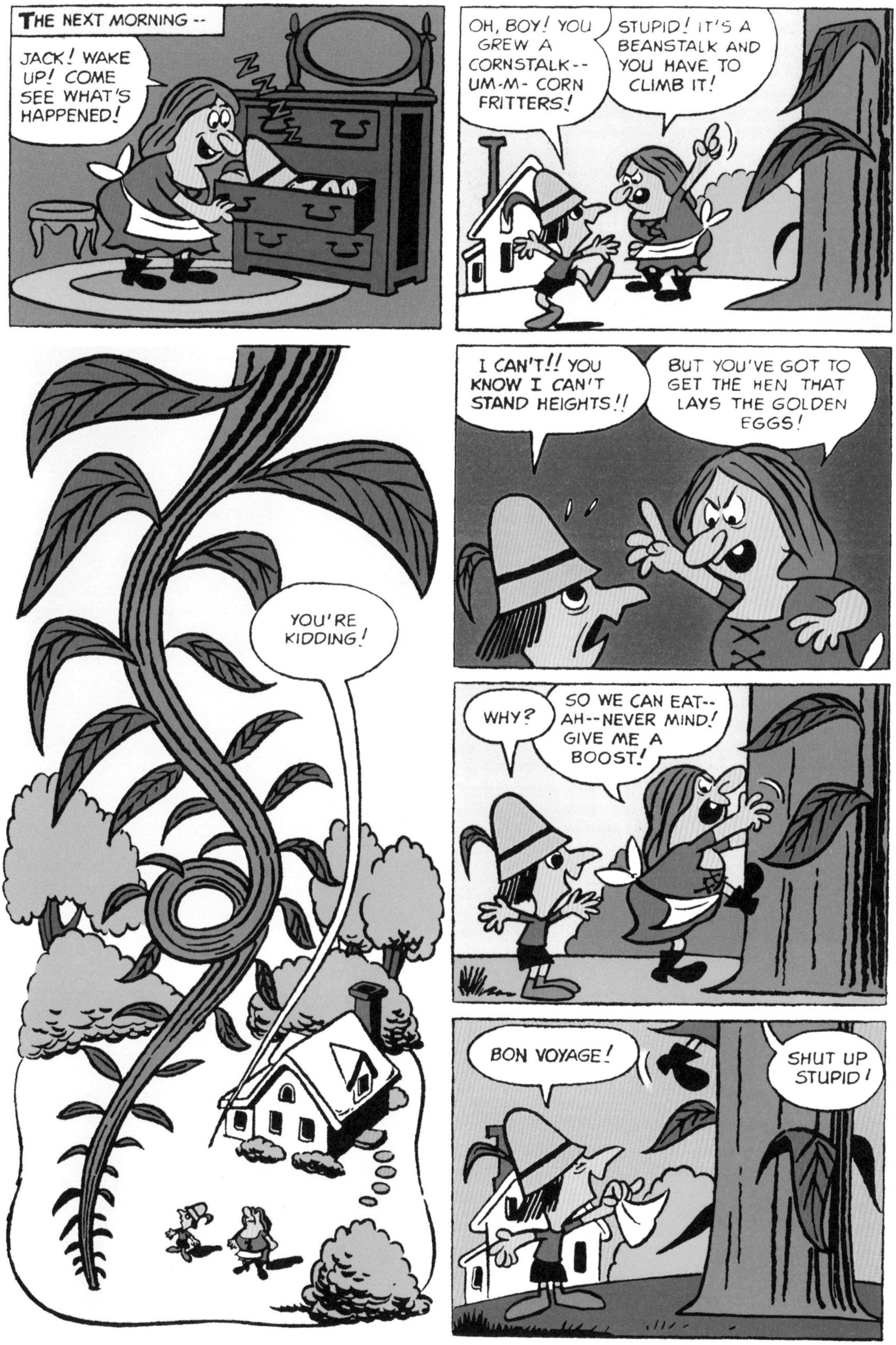
THE NEXT MORNING --
JACK! WAKE UP! COME SEE WHAT'S HAPPENED!
OH, BOY! YOU GREW A CORNSTALK-- UM-M- CORN FRITTERS!
STUPID! IT'S A BEANSTALK AND YOU HAVE TO CLIMB IT!
YOU'RE KIDDING!
I CAN'T!! YOU KNOW I CAN'T STAND HEIGHTS!!
BUT YOU'VE GOT TO GET THE HEN THAT LAYS THE GOLDEN EGGS!
WHY?
SO WE CAN EAT-- AH--NEVER MIND! GIVE ME A BOOST!
BON VOYAGE!
SHUT UP STUPID!

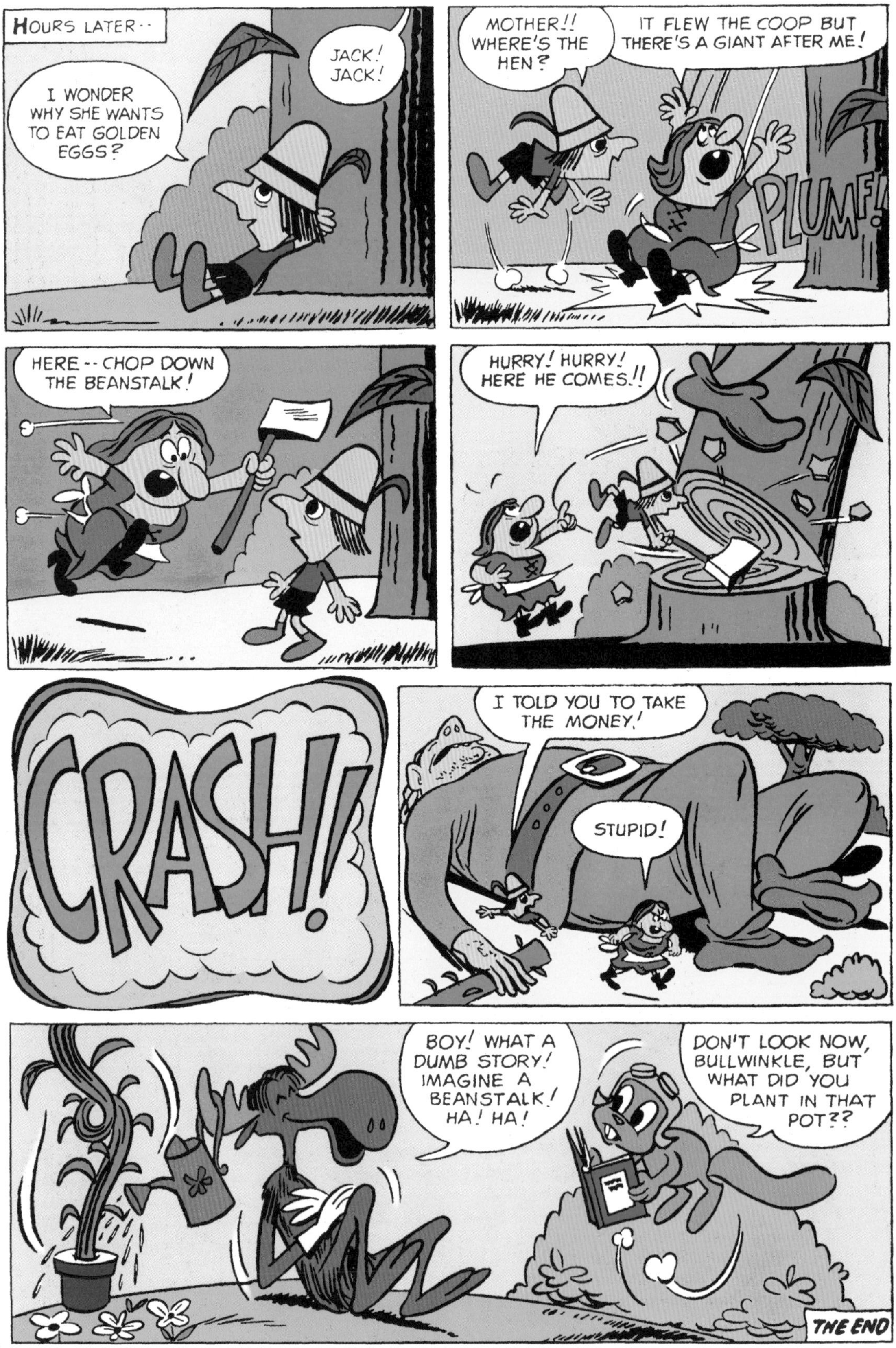
HOURS LATER--
I WONDER WHY SHE WANTS TO EAT GOLDEN EGGS?
JACK! JACK!
MOTHER!! WHERE'S THE HEN?
IT FLEW THE COOP BUT THERE'S A GIANT AFTER ME!
PLUMF!
HERE -- CHOP DOWN THE BEANSTALK!
HURRY! HURRY! HERE HE COMES!!
CRASH!
I TOLD YOU TO TAKE THE MONEY!
STUPID!
BOY! WHAT A DUMB STORY! IMAGINE A BEANSTALK! HA! HA!
DON'T LOOK NOW, BULLWINKLE, BUT WHAT DID YOU PLANT IN THAT POT??
THE END